the whitney guide

THE LOS ANGELES PRIVATE SCHOOL GUIDE

By Fiona Whitney

www.thewhitneyguide.com

6TH EDITION

THE WHITNEY GUIDE

THE LOS ANGELES PRIVATE SCHOOL GUIDE
6th Edition
by
Fiona Whitney

© Copyright Tree House Press - 2009

ISBN 0-9714677-7-3

Published by :
Tree House Press, Los Angeles, California

Cover Design :
Fitch Creative, Pacific Palisades, California

TREE HOUSE PRESS
Los Angeles, California

Email: FionaWhitney@aol.com

www.thewhitneyguide.com

DEDICATION

THIS EDITION IS DEDICATED
WITH LOVE AND THANKS TO THE FOLLOWING PEOPLE:

To Mona Holmes-Nisker for her help in updating both books this year.
I couldn't have done it without her!

To Mars Berman for her help in reviewing new schools.

To my Mum and Dad, who gave me the gift of a wonderful
private school education and who continue to be
my biggest supporters.

To my children, Bevan and Charlotte, who inspire me
with their love of school and learning.

To Marnie and her kids.

TABLE OF CONTENTS

the whitney guide

Dear Parents,

The idea for this Private School Guide began as what seemed like a simple project undertaken by parents every year: the quest for the 'right school' for my child. Like many parents, I was armed with numerous private school directories and brochures and LOTS of opinions from parents who all told me which were the most 'popular schools', but I wanted to make my own informed decisions. So I took the parent tours, went on classroom visits, reviewed the literature provided by each school and spoke to other parents ét voila! "The Los Angeles Private School Guide" was born.

Now in my seventh year at the helm, I have changed the look and format of the book and added a second book to the Whitney Guide series, **"The Whitney Guide: The Los Angeles Preschool Guide."** The more research I did, the more I understood the variety of reasons for parents' private school choices (financial, educational, geographical, religious, etc.), and that all private schools are not created equal. Some of our kids need the challenge of a rigorous, college preparatory curriculum which will admit them into the Ivy League colleges, while others will do just as well in a less-structured, creative environment, which will prepare them for a smaller, artistic school or an Ivy League college as well. When all is said and done, every child should be in the environment where their talents and strengths can be nurtured. As parents we know this all too well. In my case, I had one child in a private school and the other in a public gifted magnet program. Both kids were very happy and I was only paying only one private school tuition!

I wrote this guide in the hope that it would help you focus in on the school which will be the best fit for both you and your child. I have given you an idea of each school's physical setting and philosophy, as well as a more in-depth understanding of its teaching methods and programs, more, I hope, than reading the schools' brochures. Although no two parents will end up with the same short list of schools, I do believe that this guide will save you:

Time – It will help you narrow down the number of places that you visit,

Money – By compiling your own 'short list,' you won't need to apply to eight or more schools at up to a $100 per application, and most importantly,

Frustration – You will find just about everything you've ever wanted to ask someone about a school all in a single book.

Remember, do not feel pressured into selecting the school that others say will 'guarantee' admission to that prestigious university or college. No school can guarantee that. Also, don't be too concerned about getting your child into the most 'popular school' or even the school that is the 'most difficult' one to get into (these can change from year to year). Keep an open mind and select the school that best fits your child's needs.

I thought it important to include information about some different types of public schools. There's one in particular that we will hear a lot more about – the charter school. I wanted to share some of my findings with you because perhaps, like me, there are parents reading this book who cannot afford to send all their children to tuition-charging ones. I hope this is helpful.

Please forgive me if I have left out a school that one of your children went to, or a school that you've heard good things about. I would love to know about it for a future edition. I have tried to keep the information current. Each year I do my best to update information in the body of each review, but this is not always possible, so feel free to e-mail me at: **fionawhitney@aol.com** with any comments, suggestions or information that you feel would make this a more useful guide for you as parents. You can also find information about my **School Guide Consultation Service**, which I offer to parents by visiting **www.thewhitneyguide.com**. or call me at **(323) 309-3521** to make an appointment.

Best of luck in your search!

Fiona Whitney

* The reviews given are based solely on my opinions and the information given to me by the schools.

STARTING FROM SCRATCH

FIRST, ANSWER THESE QUESTIONS:

1. How much are you willing/able to spend on a private school?
2. How far are you willing to drive to and from school?
3. What method of teaching best fits your family philosophy?
4. Are you looking for a school that offers scholarships? Financial aid?
5. How much research are you going to be able to do yourself on each school versus listening to what other parents tell you?
6. How many schools do you feel you need to apply to in order to find the right one?
7. How much homework do you want given to your child?
8. What are your social/academic expectations?
9. Religious beliefs?
10. Co-ed versus single-sex education?
11. Diverse ethnic population?

This should narrow the choices considerably for most families. We saw many schools in our travels that we were crazy about, but when it came down to that 45 minute drive in the morning, neither of us was willing to be on the road an hour and a half per day, not to mention how tedious the drive would be for our children.

Make a list of the schools in your desired area and price range. The next thing to ask yourself is, "What is our family's educational philosophy?"

There are traditional, progressive, and developmental approaches to education, most often you will find a blend. Defining your preferred philosophy is a very important step because when you aren't in sync with the way a school is instructing your child, you will be engaging in a tug of war that can drive both you and the school crazy. Also, when children pick up on your dissatisfaction, it is likely to negatively affect their feelings about the school.

If you're well versed in the different approaches to teaching, you are in luck. You will find most of what you need to know in the school brochure about the philosophy of the school, and you can skip the next section.

If not, read these brief overviews to see how they sound to you. Use the handy worksheet that I've provided for you in the back of the book to keep track of all the schools that fit your child. Then visit as many of the schools on your list as possible. First impressions are usually going to help you make your final decision.

TRADITIONAL

Many parents feel comfortable with traditional schools because it is what they know. Most parents with school age children went to traditional schools because there were no other alternatives at the time. In addition, they are more confident with a no-nonsense approach. The traditional approach is structured and teacher-centered rather than child centered. Children will be expected to sit at desks; there will be times for all activities such as reading, math, art and science; and each week will follow the same schedule.

Academics are stressed in a traditional school, and children are often graded for their work (although there has been a trend recently to hold off grading until fifth or sixth grade). Parents choosing a traditional educational approach will often remark that they feel comfortable knowing their child will have a strong foundation in the three R's: reading, writing and arithmetic. They enjoy seeing a steady flow of papers and homework assignments from which they can chart their child's progress.

Although children from all different approaches go on to college, parents that choose a traditional school feel confident that their child will be as prepared as she can possibly be when making the transition from high school to college.

Progressive and Developmental approach advocates passionately disagree and believe that students from traditional schools are so burned out from years of academic pressure, tests, and deadlines that they can barely face four years of college.

Unfortunately, no one can tell us. We all must judge for ourselves and try to pick the teaching method that we think will best fit our child.

DEVELOPMENTAL

This philosophy of education is based on the work and teachings of (among others) Stanley Hall, Arnold Gesell, and Jean Piaget, who studied the process of human growth and identified its stages and norms for those stages. They gave credence to the "reading readiness" notion that maintained that a child would not learn to read until the appropriate stage in development had been reached. They believed that each child develops at a different rate, and one would no more expect a child to read before he's ready than to try to make a six-month old baby walk when its body is simply not developed enough for the task.

In a development school, the environment is more flexible, and more emphasis is put on developing social skills. Children are often taught in multi-age groups such as:

- Group 1: 5-7 year olds
- Group 2: 7-9 year olds
- Group 3: 9-11 year olds

In this way, a child not quite ready to move to the next group can stay with the same class for an extra year. This allows each child the experience of being both the youngest in a class of older children that he can learn from and also give him the chance to be a leader when he becomes the oldest in the class.

The developmental system makes allowances for the individual. The multi-age structure mirrors the kinds of relationships found in a family where one child is the leader, one the peace maker, another the baby. This structure allows children to move through all these stages and play the various roles as they move from group to group. They learn to get along with others and to work together in a non-competitive way. Things you will hear (and probably see) at a developmental school are that the kids love coming to school, they work out their problems with words and logic, and that they don't burn out. Instead, they develop a great love of learning.

PROGRESSIVE

The Progressive approach is often confused with the Developmental philosophy because they share some of the same beliefs. But the Progressive approach to education is a very specific one, quite different from any other.

It is based on the philosophies of John Dewey, who believed that the educational process must begin with, and build upon, the interests of the child. The child's education must provide an opportunity for the interplay of thinking and doing in the child's classroom experience, and the school should be organized as a "miniature community." In a Progressive education, the teacher should be a guide and co-worker with the pupils, rather than a taskmaster assigning a fixed set of lessons and recitations. The goal of education is the growth of the child in all aspects of his/her being. Dewey has written extensively on the subject of education. If this approach sounds right for your family, it would be advisable to read more of his work on your own.

Children in a progressive school are taught about the world around them in a practical and hands-on way. They study the community. They go out and visit the kinds of places they are learning about such as the county court system, the grocery store oe the Department of Water and Power. They come back to the classroom and discuss what's going on in the world, and they get wood and tools and construct a scaled-down version of what they have seen. Usually the structure will take up the entire room. If it's a grocery store, then one person will be the manager, another the cashier, or the supplier of produce to the store. They will find out through creative discussion and play what possible problems they can run into operating a grocery store and will work together to solve those problems.

In a progressive education, there is a focus on treating children with respect: students are expected to be responsible for themselves. They make their own lunches at home, they are expected to remember to bring items from home for various projects without depending on parents to remind them, and they are encouraged to work on areas where they are weak, rather than areas where they already excel. For example, a student who has a natural talent for math will not be given extra attention and advanced instruction in that subject. Instead the teacher might say, "You seem to have this mastered, so how about working on this painting for our restaurant, or on these buildings for the earthquake preparedness project." The idea is that we should be whole and well rounded people, that we should fit into our environment in a practical way, working together to solve problems rather than focusing on the individual as a separate entity.

Children are divided into multi-age groups and as in developmental schools, often stay with one teacher for several years before moving to the next group. There is a major emphasis on building with blocks. Many skills are learned in constructing block projects by working together, problem solving, and understanding basic math in practical settings (such as a grocery store) where things have to be budgeted, bought, and sold.

Field trips are an important part of the progressive program. Students don't work out of text books. They learn to read when they feel ready, some at six, others at eight years old.

Parents should not expect to see graded papers coming home or a log book of homework assignments. What they will see (hopefully) are self-assured, independent children who ask lots of questions, take responsibility for themselves, are excited about learning, and work well with others.

THE MONTESSORI METHOD

The Montessori Method is a developmental approach to learning devised by Dr. Maria

Montessori. She was Italy's first female physician who developed educational materials and methods based on her belief that children learn best by doing, not passively accepting other people's ideas and pre-existing knowledge.

The main points of the Montessori Method are:

- Learning should occur in a multi-age classroom where children can learn from each other.
- The teacher is a 'guide' to help the student develop into an autonomous individual, competent in all areas of life, not merely someone with the 'correct' answers.
- Children are allowed to work at their own pace. I asked one twelve year old what he thought the biggest difference was between the gifted magnet he had been attending and the Montessori school he was now at and he said, without hesitation, "I don't have to wait for everyone else to finish." If your child tends to work at a slower pace, this way of teaching could be very helpful.
- The class should be set up according to subject areas, and children are always free to move around the room freely.

Personally, I've found the Montessori Method extremely beneficial for many children I know. Although there is a common criticism that some Montessori students 'don't test well,' and might not be prepared for more traditional schools. I haven't found this to be the case at all.

THE WALDORF SCHOOLS

These schools are based on the philosophy of Rudolph Steiner, who believed that "man once participated more fully in spiritual processes of the world through a dreamlike consciousness but had since become restricted by his attachment to material things. The renewed perception of spiritual things required training the human consciousness to rise above attention to matter. The ability to achieve this goal by an exercise of the intellect is theoretically innate in everyone."

At a Waldorf school no textbooks are used. Children 'write' their own books on various subjects through teacher dictation, and thus they learn to write and edit as they go. When a child starts out in kindergarten it is a non-academic program, they will not be learning letters or numbers or anything of the kind. In the first grade, your child will meet the teacher who will 'graduate' with the student from grade to grade. The school that I visited went up to the sixth grade. The teacher spends six years teaching the same group of students, then takes a year off. The following year, the teacher will start with a new group of first graders, and continue with them for six years. The theory believes that it is more comfortable for the child to have the same teacher throughout his primary school training. In September, the class simply picks up where it left off in June with all relationships already established.

Art instruction is offered using a dictation method. The teacher will stand in the front of the room and step by step instruct the children on how and what to draw. Water color is a predominant form of art expression in a Waldorf school. The rooms are filled with the works of the children, all paintings addressing the same subject and looking like the same picture done in slightly different styles.

Math is taught using dance and clapping rhythms. The Waldorf method incorporates art, dance, and music in teaching all subjects.

THE CARDEN METHOD

Mae Carden believed that, "The purpose of education is to teach individuals to think and to develop good judgment. The acquisition of these skills relies on a thorough curriculum that interrelates all subject matter in a sequential manner and is continued from grade-to-grade." Here is an excerpt from a pamphlet handed out during my tour of a Carden School:

> Miss Carden's phonetic approach begins in kindergarten with the alphabet, teaching consonants, vowels, and their sounds. Beginners read by turning letters into sounds and spell by converting sounds into letters. They become sure footed as this method becomes automatic, free, and easy.

> Comprehension, the intellectual character of learning, is emphasized in keyword and outlining training, constant vocabulary study, and grammatical sentence analysis. The Carden system enables the child to read rhythmically, with proper phrasing and to write satisfactory compositions at each grade level.

> The Carden arithmetic workbooks follow the same successful approach: thorough analysis and steady practice.

Even after visiting the school, I was a bit confused. One teacher tried to explain the method to me. She picked up a Carden book and showed me that it had no pictures, explaining that the children must learn to recognize letters and words without using a picture as a crutch.

The teacher tried to be helpful but explained that to understand the Carden method, one really had to experience it. The teachers are trained at a special Carden school. The method is not something you can pick up a book about in a library, it is exclusive to the Carden program. The best advice I can offer is to visit a Carden school, sit in on a class, and ask a lot of questions.

WHICH METHOD SUITS MY CHILD?

This is a question I heard from many puzzled parents. To answer it, simply think about your child and try to imagine him/her in that atmosphere of the school or schools you are considering.

Does your child thrive in a structured environment, and like to be singled out for his/her efforts? If so, he/she would probably do well in a more traditional setting. A child who cannot take confinement (as in sitting at a desk for varying periods of time) and needs more freedom in her/his daily work would probably do well in a more developmental program. Of course, it is impossible to give an exact formula for picking an approach for your child. These suggestions are offered to give you an idea of the kinds of questions to ask yourself.

Picking the right environment for your child takes time and consideration. Don't worry if the right answer does not come to you immediately. Visit a few places, and use your instinct and intuition about whether or not it is a place in which he/she would do well in. Ultimately, most children will thrive in a well-run school with interested, involved, well-trained teachers, no matter what the method.

Last, but not least, decide which teaching approach you as parents are most comfortable with. It is very important for parents to be in sync with the philosophy of the school. If not, you'll spend too much time in the school office asking them to explain why they are teaching in a particular way.

Visiting the School

Once you have narrowed down the choices, make a list of the schools you would like to visit. Most schools start offering parent tours in September for those interested in admission for the following year.

Schools that are smaller or less in demand will often be willing to give you a tour at any time of the school year. A school that doesn't have a line of applicants waiting to get in sometimes makes people wary. If you encounter this situation, please try to keep an open mind. Just because a school is not 'in vogue' does not mean that it won't offer an excellent education.

The best time to call is mid-morning after everyone has had his or her coffee and is ready to get down to business. Try not to call the admissions office from 2:00 pm on because the school staff is usually dealing with dismissal at that time.

Sit down with your calendar in hand and make those calls. Ask to speak with someone in admissions and write down the names of the people you speak to along the way. Take good notes, even the little things that don't seem important enough to write down. You may think you'll remember minor details, but if you forget you don't want to have to call back repeatedly.

The admissions staff will ask if you've received a packet with the school information and admission form. Usually they will have you call back after receiving it to schedule a tour. If you know in advance that you are interested in a particular school, let the admissions office know that you are already familiar with the school and try to schedule your tour at the same time you ask for the brochure. This will save you another set of calls later in the month. This is where visiting a school's website can be very helpful.

Tours usually start between 8:00 and 10:00 am. Some are very simple and straightforward, while others go on for hours as parents stretch the question and answer time with questions like, "What if my six-year-old feels more comfortable sucking on his pacifier in class?"

Tours for the upper schools usually take place on weekends in the afternoon and are well organized and finish promptly on time. Sometimes schools will have open houses on the same day and that's when it's important to find out if there is more than one open house for a particular school so you can see all the ones you are interested in.

Questions for the School Visit

There are many questions here that you may not have thought to ask and many that may or may not be important to you. Many of the questions will be answered in the school literature. Here is a list of often asked questions that we have collected in our travels. It might be helpful to circle the ones that you feel are important and take the list with you to the school open house tour.

School Philosophy
1. How would you describe the school philosophy?
2. Is the school affiliated with any religion or religious institution?
3. Do the children attend church or chapel or temple?
4. What kind of service is it?
5. What holidays does the school observe?
6. Does the school have a community service program?
7. What is the school discipline procedure/policy?

Accreditation

1. Is the school accredited by The California Association of Independent Schools and/or The Western Association of Independent Schools?
2. If not, why?
3. Does the school have any special memberships and/or affiliations?

School Board

1. Is the school run by a Board of Directors?
2. How many of the Board members are parents?
3. What kind of roles do parents play in the running of and decision-making process of the school?
4. How much involvement does the school want?
5. How does one become a board member?

Headmaster/Principal

1. How long has the current headmaster been at the school?
2. Does the school have any plans to change headmaster in the next two years?
3. Questions for the headmaster:
   • Please describe your educational background.
   • Please describe your employment history.
   • What are your hopes/plans for the future of the school?
   • How would you describe the ethnic/socio-economic diversity of the school?
   • If the school is not ethnically diverse, do you have any plans to make it more so?

Teachers

1. What is the teacher to student ratio?
2. What credentials are your teachers required to have?
3. How many of the teachers have been with the school for more than ten years? Five years?
4. What percentage of the teaching staff is male? Female?
5. Does the school require/encourage teachers to take part in ongoing educational seminars/workshops?
6. Are the teachers allowed to create their own curriculum, or do they strictly follow the curriculum set up by the school?
7. Are the teachers trained to work with children who have learning disorders or Attention Deficit Disorder (ADD)?

Physical Environment

1. How long has the school been at its present site?
2. Does the school own or lease the buildings?
3. If leased: how long is the lease, and does the school have a renewal option?
4. Does the school have plans to expand or renovate the campus in the next five years?
5. If so, how much of the financial burden will be on the parents?
6. Does the school have a bus program?
7. Are the rooms air conditioned?
8. Is there a nurse on duty?
9. How many volumes are in the school library? Is it wired to the internet?
10. Does the campus have a: gymnasium, theater, athletic field, computer lab, science lab, kitchen, swimming pool?

Grading/Conferences

1. How are the children graded?
2. How many times per year are reports sent home?
3. How many parent-teacher conferences are scheduled per year?
4. Is it possible to schedule extra conferences with the teacher as needed?

Before and After-School Care

1. Does the school offer before and after-school care?
2. What are the hours?
3. How much does it cost?
4. Are there any after-school programs available, such as gymnastics, dance, karate?
5. Is the library open and staffed before and after school?

The School Day

1. What are the school hours?
2. Is there a hot lunch program?
3. Are school uniforms required?
4. How is the school day structured?
5. Do specialist teachers come to the classroom, or do the children go to them?
6. Are there computers in the classroom?
7. Are foreign languages taught?
8. How many times per week will my child have: art, computer, music, foreign language, library, physical education?
9. At what age is reading taught?
10. Does the school use the phonetic or whole language approach?
11. How much homework will my child have each day?

The Arts

1. Does the classroom have a separate studio for art, or is it done in the classroom?
2. Describe the music program.
3. Does the school have a chorus?
4. What instruments are available/taught?
5. Does the school have an orchestra?
6. Describe the school art program.
7. What portion of the art program is dedicated to art theory?

Gifted Children & Children with Special Needs

1. Is the school equipped to handle children with learning disorders?
2. Is the school open to children with physical handicaps?
3. Does the school have programs for gifted children?
4. If a child is gifted in a particular area such as math or reading, are there accelerated programs to offer him/her?

Sports Programs

1. Describe the physical education program.
2. What sports programs are available at the school?
3. How many times per week?
4. Does the school host team sports that compete with other schools?

Field Trips

1. How often do students take field trips?
2. Where are some of the places that students have gone in the past?
3. If buses are used, are they always equipped with seat belts for each child?
4. What is the average cost per family for an overnight field trip? (Give an example from a prior year).

Yearly Events

1. Please describe the yearly events/festivals hosted by the school, for example: school fair, theatrical productions, student concerts, Halloween parade, Christmas pageant, parents' ball/dinner dance.

Parent Involvement

1. How much parent participation is required?
2. How many parent-run fundraisers take place each year?
3. Are parents welcome in the classroom to assist, i.e., on a daily basis, for special projects?

School History

1. How long has the school been operating?
2. Is the school a for-profit or a non-profit organization?
3. Please give a brief history of the school.

Earthquake/Fire Preparedness

1. Does the school use a phone tree for emergencies?
2. Please describe the school's Earthquake Preparedness Plan.
3. Have the school buildings been bolted?
4. Are the windows upgraded with shatterproof glass?
5. Do the students practice earthquake/fire drills regularly? How often?

Security

1. How does the school maintain campus security?
2. Is there a security guard at the school?
3. If so, during what hours?
4. How do you screen people entering the campus?
5. Describe the drop-off and pick-up procedure.

Application Process

1. What is the deadline to submit an application?
2. What is the age cutoff for kindergarten applicants?
3. Are there any nursery schools that feed into this school?
4. How many applications did you accept last year?
5. How many kindergarten openings were there last year?
6. Of those openings, how many were taken by siblings of children currently attending the school?
7. What is the school policy regarding sibling acceptance?
8. What is a child required to know to be prepared for kindergarten?
9. How does the school decide which children to admit?
10. If a family is wait-listed, what are the odds of acceptance for the fall school year?

11. Are there scholarships or school loans available?

12. Most independent schools require applicants for grades 6-8 to take the ISEE (Independent School Entrance Examination). Does yours?

13. Are teacher recommendations and student transcripts required for my child?

Where Do They Go?

1. What schools do your graduates attend: Junior High School, High School?

2. Last year how many students applied to (pick or fill in your favorite): Harvard Westlake, Brentwood, Marlborough, Oakwood, Crossroads, Campbell Hall, Buckley.

3. Of those applicants, how many were accepted?

4. Do you have a list of colleges that your graduates have attended in the past five years?

Questions Often Asked at Developmental/Progressive Schools

1. Since my child won't be bringing home papers, how will I chart his/her progress?

2. We may have to move in a few years, how will my child make the transition if there is only a traditional school available?

3. Do you ever use textbooks?

4. It sounds like my child will be having a lot of fun here, but will she/he actually be learning reading, writing, arithmetic?

5. How do children get along in a multi-age classroom?

6. Aren't the older kids bored?

7. When do you start giving tests?

8. What secondary schools do your students get into?

9. What high schools do your students go to after they graduate?

10. How do your students do in high school with its strenuous study requirements?

11. Do your students have trouble making the transition?

The question & answer portion at some schools is long and thorough, but it varies from place to place. Make sure you get answers to the questions that are important to you.

Usually administrators are happy to explain all aspects of the school to you, but not always. I have heard them get defensive when asked about things like teachers' salaries, their educational backgrounds (and why huge, school-financed homes are being built for the headmaster). Ask anyway!

How Schools Evaluate Your Child
For Lower Grades

Testing and 'Play Dates'

After an application has been filed and a family member has toured the school, the admissions department must whittle down the number of children applying to fit the number of spaces available. One of the ways they do this is by testing and observing children in small groups.

Traditional schools like John Thomas Dye and Buckley will test the children's academic knowledge. For instance, they may be asked to write their names, recite the alphabet, and to name individual upper and lower case letters on sight. Many schools use the Stanford Binet IQ tests*, even at the Kindergarten level. They may also use Gesell, a kindergarten readiness test.

The admissions staff will often observe the children in a social setting, and this is usually referred to as a 'play date.' A number of children will be invited to the school to play together in a classroom setting. They may then be observed (without parents present) drawing, using manipulative toys like blocks and Legos, and lining up for snack time. Often they are also observed in an open play yard, running and climbing on outside play equipment.

The school staff will take note of the small and large motor skills, the social development of each child, and their particular personality types, (i.e. some are shy, others outgoing, aggressive, comical, etc.). The goal of most schools is to find a good blend of personalities and an equal number of boys and girls. Traditional schools often want everyone at the same learning level, while developmental schools are usually looking for a blend.

Here are some suggestions to keep the 'play date' less nerve racking:
1. Relax. If your child senses that you're uptight, then he will get tense and won't be able to be himself.
2. Dress your child casually. Let him wear his old sneakers and favorite shirt. If you dress your child in brand new duds, he will get the feeling that this is a 'Big Deal,' and it will add to his nervousness.
3. Make sure that your child gets a good night's sleep the night before.
4. Be on time. Allow plenty of extra time to get to the school, especially if it is your first time driving there.
5. Remember, your child is more important than any admissions committee. If your child is clinging or uncomfortable, tend to his needs first and don't worry about who's watching or what they might think.

The play date usually takes place in a kindergarten room filled with toys and activities that will captivate most four and five-year-olds. It can last from one to two hours during which time the children are often served a light snack. After everyone has arrived and the children are acclimated, the parents are directed to a waiting area where they are (sometimes) served coffee and some pastries while an administrator answers their questions.

Meanwhile the children are being observed for the following kinds of behaviors:
- How well they get along with others.
- Do they share?
- Which ones are "leaders?" Which are "followers?"
- Who is the "shy" one? Who is the "friendly" one?
- Do they push to get a seat at the snack table, or do they hang back and wait for an opening?

Your child will usually be asked to draw, cut out, and perhaps write his name while the teachers on hand take note of his small motor development. The play date will often include some outside play activities so that your child's large motor skills can be evaluated, i.e. running, jumping, swinging. There may be a private interview where your child is asked a series of questions to evaluate developmental level.

It is often intimidating and upsetting to know that our small children are being evaluated with an IQ test just to gain acceptance to kindergarten. Often the schools will let you sit quietly in the corner while it's going on. A trained specialist will take out some props such as shapes and pictures and ask your child questions like:

"Which one of the dogs on this page is different?" or
"Can you fit these two triangles together to make a square?"

It can go on for fifteen or twenty minutes during which time you'll have to resist the urge to whisper "You know THAT one!" from your folding chair across the room.

On the following page is an example of a test used to evaluate children at the pre-K and kindergarten level.

SAMPLE INTERVIEW QUESTIONS

Student Evaluation Interview

1. What has wings?

2. What has wheels?

3. Tell me the color of:
    - an apple
    - a banana
    - grass

4. Which is bigger?
    - A dog or a cat?
    - A cow or a pig?
    - A man or a boy?

5. What time of the year do we go swimming?

6. What time of the year does it snow?

7. What is ice when it melts?

8. What makes a cloudy day bright?

9. If today is Monday, what day will tomorrow be?

10. What makes day warmer than night?

11. How do we hear?

12. What are your eyes for?

13. Mother is a woman; father is a _____?

14. A fire is hot, an ice cube is _____?

15. An airplane goes fast, a turtle goes _____?

16. How many feet does a dog have?

17. What are these made of:
    - cars
    - chairs
    - shoes

18. What is a key for?

19. Where does meat come from?

20. How many squares do you see?

21. Repeat: 3725 _____ 4531 _____   8694 _____

22. Define:
    - apple
    - rain
    - to whisper
    - to chase
    - elbow

23. Letter recognition: B   L   Y   D   _ _ _ _
                           d   f   t   e   _ _ _ _

24. Numbers: 5   3   7   4   1   _ _ _ _ _
                8   6   2   9   _ _ _ _

25. Perception: The child will be shown pictures of items and asked to identify them:
    - chair • moon • flower
    - table • doll • box

26. Point to the picture that shows what we use when it rains:
    - umbrella • shovel • bike

27. Point to the picture that shows what we ride in:
    - car • dog • chair

    In addition, the child may be asked:
    - to follow multiple directions
    - to recognize shapes and colors
    - to count objects pictured on a page
    - to write his/her name
    - to recite his/her address and phone number
    - to demonstrate skills with paper and scissors

Each school is different, some are informal and require only general information, while others are specific about what skills they are looking for.

* The Stanford Binet IQ test is used by schools to measure what is generally considered intelligence. The concept of IQ, or "Intelligence Quotient" was first introduced by French psychologist Alfred Binet in 1904. The "quotient" refers to Binet's definition of IQ (Mental Age) divided by (Chronological Age) or M.A./C.A. This quotient is then multiplied by 100 to make it a whole number.

How Schools Evaluate Your Child
For Upper Grades

When applying for grades 6 through 12, most independent schools require that the student take the ISEE (Independent School Entrance Exam). The test is held through February.

For information and to receive a student guide:

Educational Records Bureau
220 E. 42nd St.
New York, NY 10017
(800) 989-3721 x 312 or www.iseetest.org

Tip: Make sure your child is familiar with the format and the scoring card.

If you need some help preparing your child for the ISEE exam I have found a wonderful test prep company right here in California, **Eureka, One-On-One Review**. The company offers individualized courses for the ISEE, preparing students for the grueling three hour admission test for entrance into grades 5 through 12, and follows Eureka's proven one-on-one, in-home tutorial model that they have been using so successfully for their SAT courses.

My daughter took one of their SAT courses and when I asked her what the difference was between this one and one of the others that she's taken, she told me, "Eureka has taught me a logical way of thinking instead of giving me a list of rules to memorize and follow for the test day. I feel really confident about taking the test now." I thoroughly recommend this company. Visit their website at **www.eurekareview.com**, or call them for a consultation at 1-877-463-8735.

For most applications you need teacher and head of school recommendations. Your child may need to complete an essay, or fill out a questionnaire so the admission committee can see if your child fits with the school.

Other schools require a HSPT (High School Placement Test). You can pick up sample tests from many fine bookstores around the city. Others may require a SSAT (Secondary School Aptitude Test).

School Evaluation Worksheet

School	Distance from home/bus available	Tuition & annual fees/ payment plan	Application deadline	Financial aid deadline	Number of students	Teaching Philosophy	Additional parental involvement (fees, time)	Activities Offered	After-school programs/ additional cost

ADAT ARI EL DAY SCHOOL is an excellent school for those considering a Judaic education for their children. The day school is a Solomon Schechter School, affiliated with the Adat Ari El synagogue. Membership in this temple is not required, but families must belong to some local Jewish congregation, temple, or synagogue in order to qualify for admission.

The two-story facility is modern, and its classrooms are bright and airy. The office was bustling the day I visited, but everyone was friendly and eager to answer my questions. There are two enclosed playgrounds: one includes basketball and handball courts for older children. The other, for the kindergarten only, has a playhouse, hollow climbing blocks, and a grassy area. The facility has the feel of an office building (albeit a pleasant one) with a large courtyard in the center which houses the kindergarten play yard.

There is a modern computer lab, large hall for dance and music classes, and a library which includes general as well as Jewish resources.

The kindergarten program, which is developmental rather than traditional, focuses on nurturing social skills first, and placing more academic exercises second. There are two kindergarten classes each with a full-time teacher and an aide. Children are able to choose activities from a variety of learning centers in the classroom.

The curriculum consists of language arts, social studies, mathematics, computer, music, art, library, and physical education. Teaching specialists are employed for music, reading, computers, art, dance, science, and physical education. All teachers are certified by the Bureau of Jewish Education in Los Angeles. Each year the staff is required to spend many hours expanding their professional capabilities through in-service training sessions in order to learn the most recent strategies of curriculum and instruction.

In the upper grades, the curriculum focuses on the traditional subjects which include math, science, social studies, and English, with specialist teachers in Hebrew, library, music, art, computer and physical education.

There is a modern computer lab used by all grades for regularly scheduled instruction, as well as for lunchtime activities such as producing the school newspaper, which is written by the students.

Field trips are a regular part of the program in general and Judaic studies. They are an outgrowth of classroom activities and are coordinated with specific units of study and each grade level participates. For example, the sixth grade students spend a week at an environmental science camp. The fourth grade visits Sacramento and there are also field trips to the Skirball Museum of Judaica, as well as to the County Museum of Art. One of the many activities scheduled for primary students is a visit to a matzah factory.

There are regularly scheduled assemblies, often with guest speakers. The speakers center around the arts, sciences, Jewish and American holidays and celebrations, as well as contemporary issues that affect our children today.

Parent participation in school enrichment activities is encouraged. Many parents lend their expertise to that of the specialists in the after-school program. Private and group lessons are offered in choir, orchestra, drama, cooking, creative arts and sports.

The school takes its role as a community and extended family for the children very seriously. When visiting the campus, I felt the warmth and vibrancy of its community spirit. Adat Ari El is a conservative synagogue and at the day school, traditional Jewish practices such as kashrut (dietary laws), daily prayers, and the celebration of holidays and Shabbat, are included in the program.

While the school reflects conservative Jewish standards, students are taught to respect and understand all forms of Jewish practice.

HISTORY

Established in 1979.

AT A GLANCE

APPLICATION DEADLINE	February
UNIFORMS	Yes
BEFORE AND AFTER SCHOOL CARE	Yes
SEE MAP	A on page 285

THE ARCHER SCHOOL for Girls is located in the heart of Brentwood, a stone's throw from the village and the Brentwood School. You enter from Sunset Boulevard onto a graceful circular driveway which sweeps one up to the entrance of one of the most beautifully restored examples of an old colonial mission-style building. What was once a retirement home is now home to about 480 lucky girls. It is a fairly young school (celebrating its ninth year anniversary and the matriculation of the second graduating class), but their name is on the lips of many parents who are looking for a rigorous athletic and academic curriculum in an all-girl school setting. They moved here about four years ago from a much smaller campus in Pacific Palisades. Their new home is over six acres complete with basketball and tennis courts and a sports field. The seniors have built themselves their own 'secret garden.' In the future they have plans to enclose the outside courts with a dome, creating an indoor gymnasium.

I arrived at one of their several open houses on a beautiful Sunday afternoon in the Fall. We were greeted by so many happy smiling faces that we immediately felt at home. The school went through a lot of trouble to make our visit a pleasant one – tables laden with home-made goodies, and children everywhere making sure that we had everything we needed.

We spilled out into the courtyard garden, a beautifully manicured area with lots of carefully tended flower beds. Once we had all gathered outside and been given a warm welcome by one of the teachers, we were divided into groups. Our children were invited to take a separate tour of the school given by the students. There were approximately 20 to 25 of us in our group, and off we went to experience a day in the life of an Archer girl!

First stop was to meet the athletic coaches who squeezed us into a very small space (I think it was the yoga center). Once we were inside, the coaches gave a very impressive video presentation of their Fitness for Life program. It was shown on three TV screens and included softball, soccer, basketball, flag football, field hockey, volleyball, tennis, badminton, yoga, and something called stuntnastics. I got the feeling they invented this because they don't have a formal gym at present. No matter, it looked fun and unique. Each student, in the Fitness for Life Program receives one full trimester of dance exposure. The type of dance is based on the grade level of the student and could be ballet at grade seven, and jazz at grade eight.

They are especially involved in sports at Archer, and if your daughter plays on a team, she will be expected to practice nearly every day after school. Of course, lots of hands went up by worried parents wondering how the homework was going to get done. Archer has taken care of this by providing a state-of-the-art study center, complete with full-time teachers on hand to help children at any time of the day with their work. There are even cubicles with VCR's and headsets for the girls to watch programs assigned to them by their teachers.

We were then taken upstairs and introduced to the science department teachers, who gave us a comprehensive overview of what a child would be learning with them. The lab was immaculate, well laid out, spacious, and full of up to date equipment. It had me wanting to retake chemistry all over again! As I sat there, I couldn't help remembering my old boarding school's science lab with its rusty bunsen burners, cracked vials and equally 'cracked' professor who made absolutely no sense to me at all. Here I saw teachers that were enthusiastic and smart and knew how to get the information across.

From there we visited a number of other freshly painted classrooms, all of them filled with brand new desks, beautifully laid out, with views out onto the grounds and gardens. The average class size at Archer is 15 students. The teachers were all articulate and informative and welcomed our questions, as did many of the students, who were more than happy to tell us how much they loved the school. I was impressed with their poise and the ease with which they answered a number of fairly difficult questions. They seemed to enjoy the harder ones and would take turns answering them. We also visited several computer labs, the orchestra room, an electronic music studio, and more than one art gallery.

The incoming sixth graders are separated from the rest of the school in a wing all their own. In this wing there are a couple of more homey-looking classrooms, filled with colorful drawings and circular seating, all of which helps them get used to the school. I thought this to be a very, inviting intimate environment. The classrooms for older students were very sophisticated-looking, and I could see a sixth grader feeling a little out of water seeing one for the first time. This way the students spend their first year in more comfortable surroundings which make it a far easier transition into middle school.

The ground floor had more classrooms and a number of faculty offices. There were also a number of delightful library-type rooms where the older students could eat lunch and read. One such room had a collection of china teacups and saucers. As I stood in the room I felt a little like Alice in Wonderland . . . was this really a school? It felt more like a 5-star hotel somewhere in Europe, apparently the food is '5-star' since lunch is catered by a fab local Italian restaurant.

I met up with my daughter who had made friends with one of the students who then offered to take us on our own private tour downstairs to see the theater. This was a wonderful place filled with props, paint, and costumes, and even a beautiful 6,000 square-foot library.

There are a number of art studios (ceramics, drawing, painting, and photography) as well as the fabulous study center and 12th grade common room which looked lived-in and had not been specially cleaned up for our visit, which I liked. I enjoyed this part of the tour the most since it was given by a seventh grader who simply offered; she was not asked by anyone and couldn't have been more charming. I hoped that my daughter would take a little bit of the Archer experience home with her — I could really see her benefiting in so many ways from a school experience like this.

Arrow Week

Every spring, classes are halted for one week and students participate in experimental study, approaching integrated learning beyond the confines of the traditional classroom. Research, hands-on learning, and physical challenge are some of the activities the children experience. All these adventures are designed to incorporate academics, outdoor education, and service learning. Middle school Arrow Week culminates in the traditional eighth grade trip to Washington, D.C.

Service Learning

Archer wants to inspire its students to become more involved, compassionate citizens. They encourage the girls to use their own gifts and abilities to benefit their community. They might travel to a Tijuana orphanage to help celebrate Dia de los Reyes Magos (Three Kings' Day) or deliver lunches to AIDS patients for Project Angel Food.

Community Service

Upper School provides students with the opportunity to challenge themselves in an altruistic way. Students extend themselves beyond their 'comfort zones.' They donate their time and energy to different causes for a specific number of hours to be completed during each year. With the help of the Community Service Board, their families, and the school's resource guide, each individual organizes these hours. Students are required to keep a journal, reflecting on their experiences. Archer School believes that through exploring first-hand the important and difficult issues facing diverse communities, the students will be better prepared to become positive, productive citizens.

The young lady who was showing my daughter and me around told us that they have lockers but there are no locks. Students are expected to respect the property of others, and if a student sees another student with someone else's belongings, it is not considered wrong to tell a teacher. In fact, it is encouraged not only by the teachers, but, more importantly, by the students themselves.

Because the school is in a residential neighborhood, the children use buses to get to and from school unless they are playing sports against another school and arrive back at the campus later in the afternoon — then the parents are allowed to pick them up. The bus fee is included in the tuition fee and none of the girls seem to mind this arrangement. I also think that it's better for parents who work. No more 45 minutes on the freeway at 6:30 in the morning. . . and then 45 minutes back again just to get your first cup of coffee!

If you are looking for an all-girls' education for your child and live on the West Side, or indeed anywhere in Los Angeles, please take a look at this school. They have managed to combine an old-world feel with state-of-the-art facilities to give your girl a very well-rounded, excellent education. The school also offers a variety of scholarships and financial aid packages if your child seems to be the right fit for the school.

HISTORY

In November 1994, Victoria Shorr, Diana Meehan, and Megan Callaway founded The Archer School for Girls in an outdoor coffee shop in Brentwood. All three were alumnae of single sex schools and wanted the same for their daughters. By September of 1995, the school was open thanks to the great enthusiasm of the public and the determination of the founders. Archer immediately benefitted from the support of founding donors, many of whom funded scholarships. In addition, godmothers (leading educators, activists, writers and artists) responded to the school's mission to educate a diverse body of girls who would be the country's future leaders. After a two year search, ending in the spring of the second year, Arlene Hogan became Head of School, after twenty-five years of teaching experience in girls' schools.

AT A GLANCE

APPLICATION DEADLINE	January 19
OPEN HOUSES	October 26, November 9, January 1 from 1-4pm
SCHOOL TOUR	It's required to call school to make a reservation
UNIFORMS	Yes
SUMMER SCHOOL	Yes
SEE MAP	D on page 285

BERKELEY HALL SCHOOL

Tel: (310) 476-6421 • Fax: (310) 476-5748
16000 Mulholland Drive • Los Angeles, CA 90049
www.berkeleyhall.org

HEAD OF SCHOOL	CRAIG BARROWS
DIRECTOR OF ADMISSIONS	NATHALIE MILLER
TYPE OF SCHOOL	CO-EDUCATIONAL
GRADES	PRESCHOOL - 8

- ENROLLMENT: 226
- ACCREDITATION: NAIS/CAIS/WASC
- APPLICATION FEE: $100
- TUITION DEPOSIT: $2,000
- FINANCIAL AID IS AVAILABLE FOR K-8

- NEW FAMILY FEE: $1,500
- TUITION:
  PRE: $7,100-$17,800
  K-6: $19,300
  7-8: $20,700

BERKELEY HALL sits on over sixty acres on a hilltop off Mulholland Drive amid the natural beauty of the Santa Monica mountains, and the campus is spectacular. The modern facilities include eight buildings, among them a 300-seat auditorium and a 2,000 square foot library that is roomy and well-stocked, with plenty of seating. There's a very impressive woodshop full of great looking tools and a special room for art where the children can make ceramics and sculpt, and learn to develop their own photographs. Outside, the children have a full-sized field for football and track, fields for baseball and soccer, and two tennis courts. If your child loves swimming, there is a 75-foot swimming pool, and well-equipped, individual play yards for the preschool children.

Each department (primary, intermediate and junior high) is housed separately in a ranch-style building with its own outdoor lunch and restroom areas. So when students first arrive into the school they have their own area, which gives them a sense of home and identity.

In the primary division (grades K through 3), there is one teacher and a full-time aide for each grade, with a maximum of 22 students per class. The classrooms are large and airy, with reading lofts for those wanting to find a quiet place to read. The classrooms open directly to the outdoors, where they have their own grassy playing field.

Intermediate classrooms (grades 4 through 6) are nestled on a hill above the playing fields, across from the Junior High Building. Each classroom has one core teacher with a part-time aide, and seven specialist teachers in science, art, music, computer, physical education, woodshop and library. There's also a full-time resource teacher who offers enrichment study to help children develop beyond their grade level.

In Junior High, small classes enable teachers to know and address individual interests, abilities, and talents and to help guide the students through the emotional as well as academic transition from junior high to high school. The students have the opportunity to write, produce, direct, and edit their own movies through a digital filmmaking elective. Every year, teachers develop/invent their own elective. It changes from year-to-year from art to technology, to acting or music.

Chapel is a weekly event where students gather and discuss whatever 'quality of the week' is currently being featured in the school's character development program. It could be perseverance, charity, and justice or hope, and is led by the different grade levels, faculty, administrators, parents, or outside role models.

Public speaking holds an important place in the life of the school. Junior high school students compete in regional speech competitions and regularly take home honors. Even kindergarten children are encouraged to develop a sense of ease in front of an audience by leading class assemblies, and participating in all-school chapels.

The students also go on long outdoor trips in the fall. This year, students will go to locations like Catalina, Joshua Tree, Yosemite to study biology or other related subjects in an outdoor and related environment.

The school tells me that this is not a Christian Science school, although it is run by faculty and staff who continue to be Christian Scientists. There is no required minimum proportion of Christian Science families, and they do not teach religion in class. However since it does have a very specific religious philosophy, I think it is important for prospective families to be sure that they have no conflicts with the Christian Science philosophy. Please familiarize yourself with their beliefs before you begin the admissions process.

It is a beautiful school, with a tremendous number of extras to offer its students. The tuition is on a par with all the other private schools, but you'll definitely get your money's worth in terms of facilities and education.

HISTORY

Founded in 1911 by sisters Leila and Mabel Cooper, and Mary E. Steven, Berkeley Hall is one of the oldest independent schools in Los Angeles. It is still run and supported by Christian Scientists who want to establish an educational environment in harmony with the teachings of that religion. Religion is not taught in the classrooms, but a spiritual foundation of fellowship supports all aspects of school life. Berkeley Hall School Foundation is a non-profit corporation governed by a self-perpetuating Board of Trustees.

AT A GLANCE

APPLICATION DEADLINE	January 15
GRADES 2-4 TAKE A PLACEMENT TEST	At Berkeley Hall
ISEE TEST	Required for grades 5-8
UNIFORMS	Yes
BEFORE AND AFTER SCHOOL CARE	Yes
SEE MAP	D on page 285

BRAWERMAN ELEMENTARY SCHOOL OF THE WILSHIRE BOULEVARD TEMPLE

Tel: (310) 445-1280
11661 W. Olympic Blvd. • Los Angeles, CA 90064
www.brawerman.org

HEAD OF SCHOOL	NADINE BREUER
ASSISTANT HEAD OF SCHOOL/ DIR. OF ADMISSIONS	MAXINE KEITH
TYPE OF SCHOOL	REFORM JEWISH ELEMENTARY SCHOOL
GRADES	K-6

- ENROLLMENT: 265
- ACCREDITATION: WASC
- APPLICATION FEE: $150
- NEW STUDENT ADMISSION FEE: $1,850

- TUITION: $18,500 FOR TEMPLE MEMBER
- FINANCIAL AID IS AVAILABLE

It's impossible to miss the campus of BRAWERMAN ELEMENTARY. Located directly on the corner of Olympic and Barrington in West LA, this reform Jewish elementary school is an extraordinarily well run organization, amidst a campus full of clean architectural lines, set amongst grassy and shaded open areas. While this school has extremely high standards, there is a welcoming and warm feel to the place. Maxine Keith's (Assistant Head of School/Admissions) office wall is colorfully decorated with art by her first and third grade students. She's extremely passionate and shares openly about Brawerman, which she describes as an "intimate school community."

Brawerman opened its doors in 1999 with only ten children, and now in its tenth year, the enrollment has grown to 265! Maxine and Head of School Nadine Breuer's strong sense of commitment to education and excellence have made this expansion possible. They have made it their business to forge good relationships with both public and private schools.

The curriculum is designed to prepare students to go on to some of the top private schools in Los Angeles. Students are offered a superb art program housed in a well-stocked art center, math, science, social studies, Judaic studies, a technology lab with brand new Macs along with a specialized technology teacher, and an ever-growing library to study and research in. I was particularly impressed with one of their music programs, where fourth, fifth and sixth graders were asked to become proficient in an instrument of their choice that they had never played before. Mine would have been the trumpet!

Brawerman competes in soccer, volleyball, basketball and track through the Coastal Canyon League. There's also Hebrew immersion and a wonderful exchange program in conjunction with the Jewish Federation of Los Angeles, where Brawerman students visited Israel for two weeks.

Parent-docents lead prospective families throughout the campus after a talk given by Nadine. They look for children from all types of families from various social/economic backgrounds, but most importantly - who are ripe for learning. Their sixth grade graduates are all on their way to the following schools: A.C. Stelle Middle School, Archer, Brentwood, Crossroads, Harvard-Westlake, John Adams, Marlborough, Milken, New Roads, Palms, Paul Revere, Willows and Windward. Acceptance into Brawerman is highly competitive, and I would recommend visiting it right away.

HISTORY

Opened in 1999, the Irmas Campus of Wilshire Boulevard Temple is a Reform Jewish school for grades kindergarten through sixth grade.

AT A GLANCE

APPLICATION DEADLINE	December 15
OPEN HOUSES	9/23, 10/7, 10/29, 11/5, 12/4
ISEE TESTING	Yes
UNIFORMS	Yes
BEFORE AND AFTER SCHOOL CARE	Yes
SUMMER SCHOOL	No
SEE MAP	D on page 285

BRENTWOOD SCHOOL

West Campus K-6

Tel: (310) 471-1041 • Fax: (310) 440-1989
12001 Sunset Blvd. • Los Angeles, CA 90049

East Campus 7-12

Tel: (310) 476-9633 • Fax: (310) 476-4087
100 S. Barrington Ave. • Los Angeles, CA 90049

www.bwscampus.com

HEAD OF SCHOOL	DR. MICHAEL PRATT
DIRECTOR OF WEST CAMPUS	DR. DAWN CUNNION
DIRECTOR OF ADMISSIONS	MARY BETH BARRY K-6
	KEITH SARKISIAN 7-12
TYPE OF SCHOOL	CO-EDUCATIONAL DAY SCHOOL
GRADES	K - 12

- ENROLLMENT: K-6: 300, 7-12: 690
- ACCREDITATION: WASC
- MEMBERSHIPS: ABC/ISAMA
- APPLICATION FEES: $75-$100
- YEARLY REGISTRATION/DEP. FEE: $2,500
- TUITION:
    K-6 $23,850
    7-12 $27,650
- NEW FAMILY FEE: $1,750
- 7-12 BOOK FEE: $600
- FINANCIAL AID IS AVAILABLE: (OVER 3 MILLION IS AWARDED EACH YEAR).

BRENTWOOD SCHOOL expanded from a seventh through twelfth grade, one-campus school to a kindergarten through twelfth grade, two-campus school in the fall of 1995. The West Campus enrolls 300 students from kindergarten through grade 6. The East Campus currently accommodates 690 students.

Brentwood's elementary campus is a beautifully landscaped 3.5 acre site located between Saltair and Bundy on Sunset Blvd. The facilities include a three-story main building with 14 classrooms, a small library, a common meeting area with stage, and a soccer/football field and basketball court. There are also freestanding science and art facilities with their own restrooms and outdoor flagstone patios. Brentwood just opened a state of the art aquatics center in Spring, 2008.

The kindergarten has a separate, secured outside area with tables, a grassy play area with swings, and climbing equipment. The entire campus is fenced, and an updated security system is in place.

The campus is large and open, but there is noise from Sunset Blvd. The main building is built into a hillside, thus the lower floors facing the slope have a closed-in feeling. All the walls are bright white, and there are drop-ceilings which even made me (I'm 5'4") feel like I was in munchkin-land.

There are 28 teachers, two classes at each grade level, and approximately 21 students per class. Children receive instruction from their core teachers in language arts, social studies, and math. They travel to other classrooms for specialist teachers in art, music, computer and physical education. Health classes begin in first grade, and Spanish is taught starting in kindergarten. In 5th grade Japanese and French are added as a language option, and in 6th grade, Latin is offered as well.

Kindergarten
The kindergarten program has a traditional, teacher-centered format for a large part of the day, but also allows time for children to work alone or in small groups. Brentwood has a full-day program beginning at 8:15 a.m. and ending at 3:15 p.m. The emphasis in kindergarten is on language arts and mathematics, with a special focus on communication skills: reading, writing, speaking and listening. Both phonics and whole-language recognition are used to teach reading skills. Mathematics is taught using manipulatives and workbooks with skill-building exercises.

Each kindergarten class has one master teacher and a full-time assistant. There is an average of 44 new students that enter Kindergarten each year. The class also utilizes staff and faculty from other areas of the West Campus for art, music, drama, library skills, and physical education. A reading specialist is available for those children who need extra help.

Grades 1-6
The curriculum is made up of language arts, mathematics, science, social studies, computer, health, physical education, music, art, and drama. Also included is a library and study skills program. There is an emphasis on using the communication skills: reading, writing, speaking and listening, with the goal of teaching students to exchange ideas effectively. The social studies program links history, geography, economics, and the study of modern cultures with other areas of the curriculum (literature, writing, math, and science etc.).

The mathematics program teaches students basic facts and skills and tries to guide students to use that foundation to develop mathematical reasoning. Life, physical, and earth sciences are presented in lessons that relate to the students' life experiences. The science program also introduces the use of scientific tools and equipment.

There are computers in each classroom, which are used in conjunction with every subject to enhance and extend the ongoing classroom instruction. The (voluntary) extracurricular program of the West Campus includes leadership organizations and interscholastic athletic teams.

Grades 7-12
The East Campus of Brentwood is easily one of the most aesthetically pleasing schools I've had the pleasure of visiting. Palm trees, ivy, and colorful bougainvillaea surround the attractive Mediterranean-style main structure that sits, literally, in the shadow of the new Getty Center. New additions to the campus include an athletic complex and tennis courts.

Brentwood School's academic program is extensive for it offers more than 100 courses.

The year long 'Senior Seminar' was of particular interest. In this course, seniors wrestle with age-old social, political, and philosophical questions about human life. They explore issues such as truth and knowledge, freedom and responsibility, and the nature of ethics and happiness. In addition to lectures and discussions, students must complete a thesis on a topic of their choice. Each year a selected theses are bound and placed permanently in the library.

One was entitled, "I Want My MTV: The Contradictions Behind the Cultural Arbiter of Today's Youth."

Admission to Brentwood (7-12) is very competitive. In any given year, Brentwood receives up to 450 applications for the 70 openings in the seventh grade. Technically, there are 105 openings, but the West Campus school students automatically fill 35 to 40 of the openings.

HISTORY

Founded in 1972, the Brentwood School took over the Brentwood Military Academy, which had existed since 1902. The Academy was founded by Miss Mary McDonnell in a remodeled residence at 9th and Beacon in Los Angeles. During the period from 1902 to 1972, the Academy was operated as a for-profit institution. It was primarily a boarding school, enrolling students of all ages and grade levels. The goals and objectives were those of the founder and her family members. The property was sold to a non-profit corporation, which opened in 1972 as the Brentwood School, a coeducational day school serving students in grades 7 to 10. Grade 11 was added in 1973. Brentwood graduated its first Senior Class in June, 1975.

AT A GLANCE

APPLICATION DEADLINES	K-6 by October, and 7-12 by January
MAJOR OPENINGS ARE IN	K and seventh grade, with sporadic openings in other grades. For the three kindergarten classes of 15 students, they anticipate 250 applicants.
UNIFORMS	Yes
BEFORE AND AFTER-SCHOOL CARE	Yes
SEE MAP	D on page 285

I heard about BRIDGES ACADEMY for the first time while touring another school out in the Valley. Doug Lenzimi, Bridges' Director of Admissions, a very affable chap was on the same school tour and over a cup of coffee we started talking. I very quickly realized that his school needed to be in my book and you'll see why. Bridges is located in Studio City on Laurel Canyon Blvd. It leases space from Osaka Sangyo University of Los Angeles (OSULA). OSULA offers Japanese and English language classes to the community and to international students who come over for a couple of weeks to learn the language. Sometimes a small number of international students sign up for a more intense 1-4 month program. In both cases these students stay in dorms. It reminded me of a (very) small college campus with young people of all ages outside throwing Frisbees and relaxing on the lawns.

Bridges has become one of the nation's educational leaders in helping bright, complex students overcome educational and emotional challenges that meet both academic and social goals. Or as Doug likes to put it "to help our "twice-exceptional" (both gifted and challenged) kids." Some of the learning issues they accommodate, are nonverbal learning differences, organizational challenges, attention deficit disorder, audio and visual processing problems, and dysgraphia. Have any of these terms been used to describe your child? Yes? Well read on.

Unlike many other private schools, they can meet the needs of such a diverse student body because they offer a structured learning environment that simultaneously allows for individualized instruction and an awareness of different learning styles within the same classroom. Note, "awareness of different learning styles", which brings me to a story that I'd like to share with you.

In my work as a school consultant I am often asked to help find the right school for a child. One such family asked me for help. Their son had been struggling at a very prestigious private school and no matter what they did to help him it just wasn't working. He was a very smart child so that wasn't the problem. After spending some time with the family and learning more about the child, I suggested that they look at Bridges. They did and it felt like a "fit". They loved it. More importantly their son loved it and is now thriving there. I saw him recently and without any prompting from his mother, he turned to me and thanked me for finding him the school! Sometimes a kid just needs to be understood by a school and given a different way of learning. Bridges does that.

It's difficult sometimes to understand the "jargon" that schools' use in their brochures so I asked Doug to explain in his own words what they are looking for in a student and why that child might do better at Bridges. Here's what he said:

The intellectual profile

> "Bridges offers a stimulating/challenging program for students who have been identified as gifted or highly gifted (we even have a few profoundly gifted students) so we want to feel comfortable that the program is a good match. Our students may not be gifted across the board but are gifted in one or more academic disciplines and usually gifted in other areas such as technology, visual and performing arts, etc."

The learning profile

> "We need to understand the learning style; visual, auditory sequential, kinesthetic and the student's learning challenges. The vast majority of Bridges students are struggling with Non Verbal Learning Disabilities -ADD or ADHD, processing issues, mild dyslexia, and weak executive function skills. Some have not been successful in other settings simply because they are quirky and don't fit in or their social skills are delayed".

The social/emotional/behavioral profile

> "Bridges students are inherently good kids. They don't present behavioral problems nor do they possess deeper emotional or psychological issues that require a therapeutic environment. However, Bridges students do possess the normal range of challenges that go with adolescence and the teenage years. Some may also exhibit anxiety or depression and frustration, much of it due to not being in the right environment".

Their class size is very small — an average of eight and no more than twelve for the high school core classes. The kids are required to have laptops and bring them to school just like you would a text book. Every classroom has both wireless and hard-wire internet access so the kids can learn how to search for information, but also critically examine quality and relevance. They've found that seminar-style seating, which they have in some of the classrooms helps to promote discussion and the exchange of ideas – sounds like a mini-college experience to me! There are 16 classrooms, 8 administrative offices, two faculty rooms and three office/technology work stations. They occupy the entire second floor of the classroom building and have offices and classrooms in a second building, as well as a gymnasium and large cafeteria.

In the Middle School
Bridges employs a 6th/7th grade "House" for the core classes of social studies. Math, science, art, fitness, drama and computer classes are taught by separate teachers. Parents are provided with progress reports on a regular basis. Since the 6th grade is the transition year for students entering Bridges, extra special attention is given to each student's social and emotional needs.

In the High School

Their program meets or exceeds the University of California A-G requirements for high school graduation. They offer honors courses in Biology, Chemistry, Geometry, English and History. Prep for AP exams are available in select subjects. Technology classes include web design, 3D animation, computer programming and audio/video editing. Could they be educating our next big movie makers and web designers? Sure they could! In addition, visual and performing arts electives are offered. Spanish and Japanese are their foreign language offerings and I'm sure students have been known to practice their Japanese on those poor international students!

The kids compete in the California Interscholastic Federation (CIF) in basketball and cross-country. Other school activities include Outdoor Education and other off-campus field trips, Yearbook, Prom, various school clubs and their Service Learning program. All students must complete a minimum of 30 hours of community service in order to graduate.

Now here's what I like - Parents receive school information through email discussion lists. For High School students and parents, homework assignments, tutoring sessions, grades, attendance, and teacher comments can be monitored through their web-based program, Power School. Now that's brilliant! How many times have you pulled out your hair trying to find out what homework has been assigned and when it's due by? Or wished you could ask a teacher how your kid did at school that day? Fret no more.

The school offers good solid college counseling and since their first graduating senior in 1996, graduates have been accepted at virtually all Cal State and UC schools, as well as universities and four-year colleges all over the country. So if anything you've read in this review is striking close to home, do give Doug Lenzini a call and take a closer look at this very special school.

HISTORY

Bridges Academy opened in 1994 when the lives of three young international tennis competitors collided with the career of an enterprising educator named Carolyn McWilliams. With their sights set on college as well as tennis, the young men were looking for a study program that would afford them time to play while still preparing them for college. McWilliams developed and oversaw such an independent study program for the aspiring athletes. McWilliams also was busy helping gifted students with organizational deficits. These were students who struggled to achieve in the traditional college preparatory school or other settings. Within a year, Bridges expanded to serve nearly 30 students.

AT A GLANCE

APPLICATION DEADLINE	3/1. If space available, rolling admissions
OPEN HOUSES	In the fall and January
ENRICHMENT CLASSES	Yes
UNIFORMS	Yes
ISEE TESTING	No
SEE MAP	C on page 285

BUCKLEY is nestled in a valley surrounded by mountains. The 32-acre campus is so lush that you almost forget that you're in Los Angeles. The buildings are modern, tastefully designed one story structures set up like a small village with walkways throughout.

There are 51 air-conditioned classrooms, an outside picnic area with aviary, an indoor pool, two libraries, three computer centers, a gymnasium, orchestra and choral rehearsal areas, science labs, sports stadium, field house, green house, health care, and transportation services. All facilities are designed for the appropriate age level. For example, the lower school has a scaled-down 'child-size' library and a theater designed for the young children.

Buckley is fully accredited, and included in its admission packet is a list of Buckley staff and teachers giving their very impressive educational history and degree levels. Even at the kindergarten level, in addition to their regular teacher, children see specialists for art, music, physical education and library.

Buckley is nestled in a valley surrounded by mountains. The 32-acre campus is so lush that you almost forget that you're in Los Angeles. The buildings are modern, tastefully designed one story structures set up like a small village with walkways throughout.

There are 51 air-conditioned classrooms, an outside picnic area with aviary, an indoor pool, two libraries, three computer centers, a gymnasium, orchestra and choral rehearsal areas, science labs, sports stadium, field house, green house, health care, and transportation services. All facilities are designed for the appropriate age level. For example, the lower school has a scaled-down 'child-size' library and a theater designed for the young children.

Buckley is fully accredited, and included in its admission packet is a list of Buckley staff and teachers giving their (very impressive) educational history and degree levels. Even at the kindergarten level, in addition to their regular teacher, children see specialists for art, music, physical education and library.

Buckley's educational philosophy encompasses four principles: academic training, creative self-expression through the arts, physical development, and moral education. Dr. Buckley's approach addresses the development of the whole student, enabling each child to become well-rounded, knowledgeable, and independent.

The purpose of an education at Buckley is to develop critical reading and thinking skills an age-appropriate manner including the ability to observe, analyze, synthesize, deduce and make inferences. The school aims to foster a love of learning and develop an appreciation of and proficiency in the visual and performing arts. Students' development should include an awareness of their own abilities, the value of teamwork and sportsmanship allied to a character based on integrity, compassion, and honesty. A sense of responsibility to the community, respect for diversity, and belief in the value of living a life based on principle are traits fostered at this school. It is intended that Buckley students will view themselves as citizens of the world with attendant responsibilities, and develop intellectual, emotional and ethical attributes needed to live in a world of diversity and change.

There are approximately 40 students admitted to kindergarten each year, 10 to 12 students for grade 6 and 25 to 30 students in grade 7. Typically there are 12 to 20 spaces available for grade 9. This is a traditional, academically oriented school geared for students who plan to go on to a four-year college or university. Ninety-nine percent do just that. Founder Dr. Buckley believed, "College begins at two." The preschool accepts children at three years of age and if you are seriously considering Buckley, then you should try to enroll your child at this time. There are typically only two to three openings at the kindergarten level, since most are reserved for siblings. Many Buckley students are from wealthy families. This concerned several of the parents on the tour who wanted their children's school experience to be made up of a more integrated socio-economic blend of students. However, I also heard from several of the applicants that they were happy to find a good private school that had no religious affiliation.

To get a good idea of what the students are like, I strongly suggest reading a copy of the current yearbook. All graduating students get a full page to express themselves, some have used artwork, some poetry, some letters to parents and step-parents, and monologues written to the world in general. You will find the yearbook very illuminating.

In addition to a foreign exchange program, there is a department set up solely for college counseling. A full sports program, includes football, basketball, tennis, field hockey and horse-back-riding. The boys varsity basketball team came in first place in the Liberty League last year and made it to the CIF quarter-finals. In addition, the 6th grade boys basketball team ended their season undefeated, and they were the San Fernando Valley Private School League champions.

At the annual Scholastic Art Awards, Buckley's middle and upper school students competed against nearly 900 entrants from more than 60 public, private, parochial and home schooled applicants. The 14 selected works, seven gold and seven silver award winners, were exhibited at Otis College Bolsky Gallery in Los Angeles. In 1999, Buckley was awarded the prestigious BRAVO award for outstanding educational programs in visual and performing arts. It is the only time in the seventeen-year history of the award that a private school has been selected.

If art or sports is not your child's strength, then Buckley's twenty clubs are a great way for your child to get involved in the Buckley community. The clubs include Junior Statesmen of

America, Varsity Club, Social Action Team (SAT), International Thespian Society, Pre-Med Club, Ecology Club, and The Buckley Jazz Ensemble. The school puts on two major theatrical productions each year as well as several smaller ones. Recently, Buckley's Junior Statesmen of America delegation (JSA) won nine Best Speaker gavels.

In order to graduate from The Buckley School, a student in grades 9 through 12 must fulfill the following requirements:

- History, English, math: 4 years
- Computer science: 1 year
- Foreign language, science, physical education: 3 years
- Health: 1/2 year
- Visual or performing arts: 2 years

Buckley is one of the most expensive private schools in Los Angeles, but if it fits your budget and philosophy, consider it money well spent. This school delivers all the extras you could want for your child.

HISTORY

Buckley was founded in 1933 by Dr. Isabelle Buckley, based on the schools she observed in Europe and Australia. She believed that young people needed greater structure, more guidance, values training and more discipline in their lives . . . and that it was the school's responsibility to give it to them.

AT A GLANCE

APPLICATION DEADLINES – ONLINE	K-5: December 1, 6-12: December 15
OPEN HOUSE	K-6: Oct-Nov, Mid/Upper: Oct-Dec
UNIFORMS	Yes
BUSING	Yes
SUMMER PROGRAMS	Yes
AFTER-SCHOOL PROGRAMS	Yes
24-HOUR CAMPUS SECURITY	Yes
EMERGENCY PREPAREDNESS PLAN	Yes
SEE MAP	A on page 285

CALMONT SCHOOL

Tel: (310) 455-3725 • Fax: (310) 455-7209
1717 Old Topanga Cyn. Road • Topanga, CA 90290
www.calmontschool.org

HEAD OF SCHOOL	JUDITH CHAMBERLAIN
TYPE OF SCHOOL	CO-EDUCATIONAL DAY SCHOOL
GRADES	PRESCHOOL - 9

- ENROLLMENT: 150
- ACCREDITATION: CAIS
- NEW FAMILY FEE: $1,000
- FINANCIAL AID IS AVAILABLE
- YEARLY REGISTRATION FEE: $500-$1,500
- APPLICATION FEE: $75
- TUITION:
  PRE: $10,800-12,800
  K-5: $19,000
  6-9: $19,500
- ACTIVITY FEE: $400
- MEMBERSHIP: CAIS

CALMONT SCHOOL is located in Topanga Canyon on 20 acres, a very impressive piece of land. When you first enter the campus, you may think that you've stumbled upon a Huck Finn/Tom Sawyer adventure park with a western accent. This may be because the grounds are also used as a summer camp for kids. "Cali Camp" and the school are totally separate, and unrelated organizations.

The School has tennis courts, a swimming pool, athletic field, new basketball and handball courts, an amphitheater, and a running stream – all nestled under a canopy of huge, old oak trees. The rustic buildings, are fairly modern, and set among grounds, not meticulously manicured which is a welcome relief to parents who prefer, a more relaxed atmosphere for their children.

The school's philosophy emphasizes development of social and academic skills, the following being taken from their website:

> "Calmont school offers an enriched education. The teachers engage the students by helping them to develop their own unique strengths and set personal goals to explore other areas of potential interest, The supportive and professional staff provides the children with a safe environment is which they can grow intellectually, emotionally socially, physically, and creatively.

> Calmont cultivates a close, caring, personable campus where children feel secure, appreciated, and successful. The learning environment is one where challenge, support and risk-taking converge. In the early years, that includes creating a series of controlled risks by which students explore and test their ideas and abilities. Older students are encouraged to meet the same challenges in more open-ended areas."

So similar are the different schools' philosophies, parents must be careful in deciding which approach is most beneficial for their family (i.e. academic, progressive, developmental).

Observing at the school will give you a more exact idea of the school's philosophy and enable you to arrive at a decision.

The instructional groups in reading and math are fluid, and children may move along at different paces according to their abilities and motivation. The program recognizes children's developmental differences, and student works at his/her own level.

The students have specialists in physical education, music, science, art, environmental studies and computers. Twice a week, Spanish and science are taught in grades K through 5, and five days a week in grades 6 through 8. Spanish is even offered twice a week in preschool! The Middle School offers electives in Flash computer programming, robotics, study skills, art, stained glass and kick-boxing. The reading program is literature-based and includes oral reading, critical thinking, and problem-solving. Homework is given daily.

HISTORY

The school was founded in 1977. Calmont school promotes academic excellence in a magnificent natural setting. The nuturing faculty and small class sizes present a personalized and challenging education.

AT A GLANCE

APPLICATION DEADLINE	January 31
OPEN HOUSE	Nov-April. Call for open house dates.
AFTER SCHOOL CARE	Yes
ISEE TESING	Yes
BUSING	Yes
SEE MAP	D on page 285

CAMPBELL HALL

Tel: (818) 980-7280 • Fax: (818) 762-3269
4533 Laurel Canyon Blvd. • North Hollywood, CA 91607
Mail: P.O. Box 4036 • North Hollywood, CA 91617-0036
www.campbellhall.org

HEAD OF SCHOOL	REV. JULIAN BULL
DIRECTOR OF ADMISSIONS	ALICE FLEMING
TYPE OF SCHOOL	CO-ED EPISCOPAL DAY SCHOOL
GRADES	K - 12

- ENROLLMENT: 1,087
- ACCREDITATION: CAIS/WASC/NAIS
- NEW FAMILY FEE: $1,500
- APPLICATION FEE: $100
- REGISTRATION FEE: $1,000
- FINANCIAL AID IS AVAILABLE
- MEMBERSHIPS: CEEB/CLS/NAES/NAEYC/NAIS

- TUITION:
  K-6: $19,890
  7-12: $24,910
- BOOKS & SUPPLIES:
  K-6: $550
  7-12: $750

CAMPBELL HALL is the place to go to enjoy all the advantages of a private school education. The lush campus setting provides 14 acres of open space, modern buildings, sports fields, and grassy play areas surrounded by huge, old eucalyptus groves.

Construction has been completed on Campbell Hall's three-story academic center which was designed by architect Louis Liets (formerly of the firm Laffen-Liets). Its architectural beauty reflects Mr. Liets' own style as well as the influence of Frank Lloyd Wright. This extraordinary building uses well-placed windows and skylights to make the outside foliage and open spaces part of the atmosphere within.

Touring the school gave one the feeling of what one would experience in a grade school of the fifties. Many of the parents with whom I toured were warmed by the sight and feeling of a place that reminded them of their own school experiences.

One of the first things that impressed me about the school was that everything was incredibly well-organized. The parent tour was scheduled to begin at 10 a.m., and it did! By the time I visited Campbell Hall, I had been on many (large group) tours where starting anywhere from 30 to 45 minutes late was the norm. This, punctuality as well as the thorough presentation that was to follow, gave me the impression that Campbell Hall was a well-run organization, an area in which it excels. Indeed, this is the area where it excels most.

The campus has two playgrounds, two gyms, four computer labs, five science labs, a theater, dance studio, weight room, basketball and handball courts, a football field, soccer field, baseball diamond and a running track. The 35,000 volume library serves the entire school. Elementary classes visit the library every other week. There is a nurse on duty from 8:30 a.m. to 4 p.m.

The high point in the building tour is the beautiful Ahmanson Library. It features 35 computer terminals, a special story time room for younger students, and huge windows (all with window seats) letting in the light, with greenery of the lush campus as a backdrop.

On the first floor there are three computer application labs (25 computers in each), an elementary science lab, three seminar rooms, a kitchen, an archive studio, and offices for admissions and administration.

The top floor of the building houses the executive offices of the headmaster, the development staff, an executive kitchen, and many conference facilities for administrative use.

Campbell Hall has a unique Scholar-in-Residence Program that brings a highly respected educator to campus for several days each year, for the faculty professional education and development.

The teaching approach is traditional, but children are allowed to work at their own developmental pace with an emphasis on creating a nurturing rather than competitive environment. Language arts, mathematics, science, social studies and Spanish (beginning in the third grade) provide the core of classroom work. Specialized study in music, art, and computer skills enriches the academic curriculum. There are two classes at each grade level for Kindergarten thru sixth grade, with 23 students in a class and 46 students per grade.

The teachers weave the subjects together in a way that allows one section of the curriculum to relate to another. For example, first-graders exploring a unit on apples spend their English lesson reading "Johnny Appleseed," and their math lesson estimates the number of seeds in an apple. Meanwhile, fifth-graders learn to make paper and ink as part of their discussions about the United States during the 1800s.

The Kindergarten Day consists of reading readiness, story time, mathematics readiness, "Show and Tell, "computer skills, music, lunch, snack and playtime, calendar activities, science, drawing and painting, language arts, printing, physical education, building block play, chapel and listening skills.

The upper school offers a challenging, college preparatory curriculum in the traditional disciplines: English, mathematics, science, foreign language, social science, the arts, and physical education. Supporting this core curriculum is a variety of studies and experiences in athletics, visual arts, music, drama, computer science, and environmental education.

The school orchestra gives spring and fall concerts, and children may study violin in kindergarten with more choices added each year. Campbell Hall also offers a ballet program with two performances each year.

The school brochure lists all the teachers and gives their educational backgrounds. Most hold advanced degrees, either in education or in their subject discipline. All are encouraged to continue their education while at Campbell Hall through additional graduate courses, and through attendance at professional conferences and workshops. The school also has a strong professional development program funded in part by gifts to the school's growing endowment.

The school's goal is to provide an environment where students learn the value of working together as a community, and are taught to have respect for themselves and others. These are themes that are regularly addressed during chapel, which takes place Monday through Thursday from 8:40 a.m. to 9 a.m. in the lower gym. Campbell Hall is committed to encouraging both the intellectual and the spiritual growth of its students. An emphasis on moral and ethical behavior is woven throughout all aspects of school life.

At chapel, the children sing hymns and listen to Chaplain Richards talk about various themes relating to spiritual and moral growth. All religions are welcome, and many holidays are celebrated such as Christmas, Hanukkah, and holy days of other religions from around the world.

A full 98 percent of Campbell Hall graduates go on to four-year colleges, and a list of those institutions is included in the school literature.

There are many fundraising events at Campbell Hall such as the Hot Lunch Program, Ad-Book, PTC Picnic, and the annual Bagpipe Ball. The 21st Century Fund raised huge amounts of money over the years to make construction of the new three story building possible. Many donations have been received from the school's families, although much of the funding came from grants from large corporations and charitable donations. One-in-six Campbell Hall students receives financial aid. Parents are encouraged to give to the school but are never pressured.

Involvement is strongly encouraged and provides the backbone of the school's activities. Parent volunteers play an important role in the daily life of all Campbell Hall students, and enrich the school by sharing their time, energy, and talents.

Here is a list of parent-run and parent-volunteered school activities/functions:

Parent-Run: P.T.C. Picnic, the Bagpipe Ball, Faculty/Staff Appreciation, class coordinators, Student Store, Hospitality, Parent Resources Register, Events Boards, Pizza and Pasta Lunches, Hot Dog/Hamburger Lunch,

Parent-Involved: Library, Emergency Preparedness, Fine Arts Guild, Chapel Program, Homecoming, Ad-Book campaign, College Counseling, Developmental Office, High School Athletic Booster Club, Studio Art Class

Campbell Hall supports many different opportunities for students to serve their communities through the chapel program as well as the student council. Elementary student aides assist in the classroom, the office, the chapel, and in the primary grades.

In addition, the Alternative Gift Fair (held during November) teaches children about the needs of people around the world and provides them with ways to help. Each student in the high school is required to complete 50 hours of community service. Three ongoing projects provide support for Hillsides Home in Pasadena an Episcopal home for abused and neglected children, for the Church of the Advent in South Central Los Angeles, and for Holy Innocents, a partner Episcopal school in Port-du-Paix, Haiti. Outreach projects have included work with organizations like Heal the Bay, and The Tree People.

Campbell Hall has thrived under the dedicated leadership of the Rev. Canon Thomas G. Clarke. He is an alumnus of the school and has devoted twenty-six years of his professional life to making it the outstanding institution of higher learning that it is today. He is passionate about the school, the quality of education and its progression into the 21st century.

HISTORY

The school was founded by theReverend Alexander Campbell on February 7, 1944, with a group of 74 students. Incorporated as a non-profit organization since its founding, the school is guided by a Board of Directors. Under its charge the school grew steadily and by 1964 included kindergarten through twelfth grade. In 1971, Dr. Campbell's familiar mandate, "Carry on friends" was taken up by the Reverend Thomas G. Clarke. This former student's appointment as headmaster provided the school with the continuity it needed to flourish and grow to its present student body of 1,000.

AT A GLANCE

APPLICATION DEADLINE	Ongoing, but no later than February 1
OPEN HOUSE	Call school for fall open house dates
BEFORE/AFTER SCHOOL CARE	Yes
UNIFORMS	Yes
ISEE	Required after 5th grade
SUMMER CAMP	Yes
SEE MAP	A on page 285

CARLTHORP SCHOOL

Tel: (310) 451-1332 • Fax: (310) 451-8559
438 San Vicente Blvd. • Santa Monica, CA 90402
www.carlthorp.org

HEAD OF SCHOOL	DOROTHY F. MENZIES
TYPE OF SCHOOL	COED DAY SCHOOL
GRADES	K - 6

- ENROLLMENT: 280
- ACCREDITATION: CAIS/WASC/NAIS
- NEW FAMILY FEE: $1,000

- TUITION: $18,690
- APPLICATION FEE: $100
- FINANCIAL AID IS AVAILABLE

CARLTHORP SCHOOL is located in a residential neighborhood in Santa Monica. In the last couple of years it has undergone extensive remodeling and added a new school building on the recently purchased lot next door. The main building is an attractive, modern, Spanish-style structure, and sits discreetly among the surrounding homes. In Santa Monica, where zoning and codes are very strict, the new building blends nicely into the neighborhood.

The school office is comfortable with plush carpeting, draperies, and upholstered chairs. During my visit the school receptionist was attentive and helpful. Then my student tour guide arrived, a very nice sixth grade boy with an unmistakably famous last name. He gave me the tour in record time, and I found myself hustling after him with raised finger saying ". . . but wait a minute, what about the . . ."

The campus is small and compact although the last remodeling has helped solve the school's space problem. In 1998 an additional class per grade was added, in addition to a larger library and a new science lab. There is a playground behind the school, and another building at the back of the lot that houses the lower elementary grades. I found the rooms to be modern, pleasant, bright, and well stocked with resources. The credentialed teachers are enthusiastic, passionate about their work, and willing to stop and talk when you drop in.

This is a very academically-oriented school with advanced programs set up for accelerated learners. The boy who showed me around took a certain pride in showing me the 'advanced' classes in math, English and reading.

The majority of students entering kindergarten have attended preschool and are ready to begin the academic studies of reading, phonics, arithmetic, and printing. There are 40 students in kindergarten, 20 boys and 20 girls. Fifty percent are new students and the rest are siblings. So unless you have a child already in the school, it might be difficult to get in.

Math, reading, phonics, spelling, English, written composition, geography, history, science, and penmanship are introduced at the appropriate grade levels. There are specialists in art, music, and library science weekly. Computer and typing classes are scheduled in grades 4 to

6, while an introductory course in computer graphics is offered to children in grades K to 3. Spanish is taught in grades 4 to 6, and all students participate in physical education.

I liked the idea of the Great Books Program. Children in grades 2 through 5 can meet one day before school and discuss selected reading material. To avoid homework battles your child can go to the after-school homework club, where teachers provide support Monday through Thursday from 3:30-5:15 p.m.

In 2006, Carlthorp School received the National Blue Ribbon Award for Excellence by earning standardized test scores that ranked in the top ten percent of all independent schools in the nation. They were one of two secular independent schools in the nation to relieve this award.

Carlthorp provides an academic education in the purest sense and it is well run and serious. Although there are many wealthy and celebrated families here, Carlthorp puts the focus on providing a high-quality academic education, and it does not feel like a 'celebrity kids school, ten percent of families relieve financial aide. There is little diversity. But if your philosophy is in accordance with a strong academic education, then this is your school.

HISTORY

Founded in 1939 by Mercedes Thorp and Ann Carlson Granstrom, Carlthorp School is Santa Monica's oldest independent nonsectarian elementary day school.

AT A GLANCE

APPLICATION DEADLINE	Ongoing, but the kindergarten deadline for is 11/1
REPORT CARDS	Issued each trimester, honor rolls for grades 4-6
BEFORE AND AFTER SCHOOL CARE	Yes
UNIFORMS	Yes
BUSING	Mandatory fee
SEE MAP	D on page 285
OPEN HOUSE	Call school for an appointment

Surrounded by hills in a private and stunning property, CAVALRY CHRISTIAN is nestled in the Pacific Palisades. Though traditional in approach, the school is exceedingly warm and welcoming to children and their families. The school is run by a board of parents from the non-denominational Calvary Church.

With a total of 430 students, and 20 students per classroom, each with its' own teacher and an aide, this school has everything needed for a first-class education of your child. There's a good balance of male and female teachers, lovely classrooms, massive playing fields, gym and music rooms. I was impressed by their reading lists and their technical savvy – all the kids know Excel and PowerPoint by fifth grade!! The school develops the whole child by balancing the academic, the physical (athletics) and the spiritual nature of the child. This spiritual nature is developed by bible classes and a strong desire for everyone to have a personal relationship with Jesus. In the admission process, their goal is to accept students and families best served by their mission. Nearly half of the student body does not belong to this church and the school is committed to a policy of non-discrimination on all levels.

Cavalry has another clear vision for their students: they are being prepared for service and leadership. As taken from the school's brochure:

> "Students are encouraged to be responsible, creative leaders and to use their academic skills and Christian values to better our world. We achieve this by developing and encouraging our students' faith, critical thinking skills, core academic skill base, and service-oriented leadership."

To help achieve this vision, they work with six separate organizations to provide community service opportunities for the children. On any given day, a Cavalry student might gather supplies and send them to one of these organizations or someone in need, visit a retirement home, send letters to soldiers serving in the military, help the Los Angeles homeless, and many other "good works." They are a committed bunch!

The School has a state-of-the-art Technology Center, which is surprisingly bright and airy for a computer/media lab! One-third of its' technology equipment is updated each year to keep the software and services current, providing students with up-to-date tools to work with. All students enjoy weekly classes in a well-stocked art-room where they're exposed to 3-D design, print-making, art history, multi-media art and ceramics to name a few.

The layout of the Elementary school (K-5) makes for an intimate and interactive environment, with desks that face the center of the room, like a half circle. The Elementary school has an excellent group of teachers who are well versed in their subjects with advanced degrees. Their middle school is chock full of subjects: science, math, social studies, language arts, bible study, physical education and annual field trips. Cavalry's curriculum is very strong and far exceeds the state standards.

A very active Parent Association keeps families involved in their child's education. They provide a link between the parents, faculty and administration by hosting meetings, promoting Cavalry in the local community and fundraising. Through their annual Holiday Boutique, Book Fair and weekly Pizza Day, the PA raised over $130,000 in 2008. Most impressive!

For athletics, the school competes in the Delphic League, along with many other private schools throughout Los Angeles. Here are some of the sports that Cavalry offers: flag football, volleyball, basketball, soccer, track and golf. The Cougar is Cavalry's mascot, and there's loads of school pride!

Even more impressive is that the students all move into the top high schools throughout Los Angeles including: Archer School for Girls, Brentwood School, Crespi, Harvard Westlake, Loyola, Marlborough, Marymount, Oaks Christian, Pacifica Christian High, Notre Dame, Viewpoint and Windward.

HISTORY

Calvary Christian School began as a small preschool in 1963 in the heart of the town of Pacific Palisades with approximately 20 children. Today, Calvary Christian School is in its' nineteenth year of providing a high quality education for children in preschool through eighth grade on the Westside of Los Angeles. Calvary Christian School has grown to become the second largest private school on the Westside with two classes per grade.

AT A GLANCE

APPLICATION DEADLINE	December 5
PRESCHOOL OPEN HOUSE	October 1
K AND TK OPEN HOUSE	October 15
ALL SCHOOL OPEN HOUSE	October 29
AFTER SCHOOL PROGRAM	Yes
UNIFORMS	Yes
SEE MAP	D on page 285

CENTER FOR EARLY EDUCATION

Tel: (323) 651-0707 • Fax: (323) 651-0860
563 N. Alfred St. • West Hollywood, CA 90048
www.centerforearlyeducation.org

HEAD OF SCHOOL	REVETA BOWERS
DIRECTOR OF ADMISSIONS	DEEDIE HUDNUT
TYPE OF SCHOOL	COED DAY SCHOOL
GRADES	PRESCHOOL - 6

- ENROLLMENT: 535
- ACCREDITATION: CAIS/WASC
- FINANCIAL AID IS AVAILABLE
- TUITION: $13,750-$20,215
- NEW FAMILY FEE: $1,200
- APPLICATION FEE: $85

THE CENTER FOR EARLY EDUCATION offers a developmental education with all the extras. The building is a glorious architectural achievement with clean, simple lines, and well-planned exterior spaces. The classrooms are large, bright and full of all the modern educational tools money can buy. Since last year, the Center's campus has been totally remodeled adding a separate science lab and provided teachers for K through 3, as well as 4 through 6.

The school is located on three-quarters of an acre in West Hollywood, not far from the Beverly Center Mall and across the street from a Los Angeles Public School. There is a rooftop playground.

This preschool is a showcase for preschools. It is wonderful. In fact, I wanted to go there myself. The rooms are full of toys and musical instruments, and the play structures outside are state-of-the-art. If you detect any bitterness in this accounting, it is no doubt because I was unable (like so many of us with our noses pressed against the double-thick tinted glass) to get my child enrolled.

Each class has an average of 24 to 28 students and two credentialed master teachers. There are specialists in art, music, science, computer/library skills, and physical education. The teaching philosophy there is decidedly developmental. Each child works at his/her own pace, and emphasis is placed on building social skills, self-esteem, and developing an enthusiasm for learning rather than focusing solely on academic achievement.

The style of teaching at the Center is non-traditional, with emphasis on the 'whole-child' philosophy. Classrooms are organized in continuums rather than traditional grade levels. Team-teaching is employed with two teachers giving lessons to different groups in the same physical space. The focus is on whole-child education, allowing each child to progress at his/her own pace and level.

The Art Program is spectacular, and the school has spared no expense. All teachers have a great deal of training, experience, and enthusiasm. The art room is large and airy, well-stocked with materials, and the students' work can be seen gracing the walls of the entire school. Art History is taught in conjunction with watercolors, oils, pastels, sculpture, pen and ink, and cut and paste shapes a la Monet. Some of the work the children displayed was breathtaking. If art is important to you, this is a school you will definitely want to check out.

This is one of the few private schools where there is a provision for mainstreaming minimally to moderately disabled children.

Now for the bad news...getting in.

In the first page of the brochure, the Director of Admissions, Deedie Hudnut (a charming, gracious lady with a very tough job), starts right off warning prospective applicants about the low rate of attrition, and the growing number of siblings applying each year.

Perhaps in response to the increased demand, the school has increased its enrollment by 100 students over the past three years. Yes, there are many wealthy families here and quite a few celebrity children, but The Center does try to create some ethnic and social diversity among its student population.

The following criteria are used in the selection of new children entering the school:

1. A balance of boys and girls,
2. Families from different racial, ethnic, and socio-economic groups,
3. Integration of children with different personalities, learning styles, and individual needs.
4. Children's birthdays are equally represented.
5. A mix of first, second, and third children.
6. Families from different geographical areas.
7. Special circumstances are: single-parent families, adopted children students on financial aid, families needing daycare.
8. Siblings are not automatically accepted. Sibling families are expected to have demonstrated a level of support, commitment, involvement and participation within our community.

You are further informed in the application that the $85 fee does not guarantee an interview for your child. You are invited to the Open House (attendance is a mandatory part of the application process), but unless you fit one of the special circumstances listed above, or your last name is Nicholson, Puck, or Getty, I wouldn't wait by the phone. When Reveta Bowers, Head of School, addresses prospective parents she is forthright about the scarcity of available spaces, so have a second and third choice lined up.

HISTORY

The Center For Early Education is a private, nonprofit educational institution. It was founded in 1939 by a group of psychoanalysts and parents who believed a child's emotional and social development was as important as his or her educational growth, and that the early years were critical to both. It started first as a nursery school, then as a college to train teachers and administrators, and in 1971 it became an elementary school.

AT A GLANCE

APPLICATION DEADLINE	December 15
BEFORE AND AFTER SCHOOL CARE	Yes
UNIFORMS	No
COMMUNITY OUTREACH PROGRAMS	Yes
SEE MAP	C on page 285

CHADWICK SCHOOL

Tel: (310) 377-1543 • Fax: (310) 377-0380
26800 S.Academy Drive • Palos Verdes Peninsula, CA 90274
www.chadwickschool.org

HEAD OF SCHOOL	TED HILL
DIRECTOR OF ADMISSIONS	RITA MILLS
TYPE OF SCHOOL	INDEPENDENT CO-ED DAY SCHOOL
GRADES	K - 12

- ENROLLMENT: 822
- ACCREDITATION: WASC
- NEW STUDENT FEE: $1200
- MEMBERSHIPS: CAIS/ERB/CEEB/ CLS/ERB/ISAMA/NAIS
- TUITION: $19,650 - $24,205
- APPLICATION FEE: $125
- FINANCIAL AID IS AVAILABLE

CHADWICK'S SCHOOL, founded in 1935 by visionary educator Margaret Lee Chadwick, sits atop a peaceful, verdant hilltop on the Palos Verdes Peninsula with sweeping views of the Los Angeles basin. The only K-12 independent, college preparatory day school in the greater South Bay area, Chadwick currently enrolls approximately 815 students. Their 55-acre campus (yes 55 acres) provides a beautiful and safe setting for all those lucky children attending this school.

Here is part of the Chadwick's Mission Statement as taken from the brochure:

"Chadwick, a K-12 school founded in 1935, is dedicated to academic excellence and to the development of self-confident individuals of exemplary character. Students are prepared through experience and self-discovery to accept the responsibilities inherent in personal freedom and to contribute positively to contemporary society. The Chadwick Community is committed to living in accordance with its core values of respect, responsibility, honesty, fairness and compassion."

The academic facilities include science classrooms, labs and preparation rooms, foreign language rooms, Chadwick also has a new middle school science building, a science laboratory and a botanical garden! The Village School Complex has art rooms, music facilities and playgrounds for younger students.

The arts facilities are impressive, with a performing arts facility with indoor theaters, classroom space and studios, an art gallery, a fine arts studio and digital photography studio, a technical theater and an ampitheater.

Leavenworth Library Learning Center includes 28,000 volumes, four classrooms, audio-visual room, reading and periodical lounges, three study rooms and lounge, technology area with desktop computers and wireless connections for students. There is also a separate library for grades K through 6 including a research area and a story corner.

There are eight fully-equipped computer labs in the Technology Center, as well as computers in all Village School classrooms, with athletic facilities closeby.

Chadwick is composed of three educational divisions: the Village School, kindergarten through Grade 6; the Middle School, Grades 7 and 8; and the Upper School, Grades 9 through 12. While each division has its own director and distinct area on the campus, the curriculum is coordinated for smooth transitions between the divisions.

Chadwick's faculty is recruited from across the nation and more than half of them have advanced degrees. The Admission Office conducts extensive outreach to identify and admit "the best and the brightest" students. In doing so, the student body reflects the school's commitment to both socio-economic and cultural diversity. The school provides more than $1 million annually in student financial aid.

This is a fabulous school and well worth the commute if you are one of those families who don't live on that wild and far away peninsula and are always aghast whenever someone says they are going there! Go on, fill up the car, turn on your navigation device and take a closer look. And remember when you hear the words, "Location, location, location...think, "Car pool, car pool, car pool!"

HISTORY

In 1935 Margaret Lee Chadwick founds Chadwick Open-air School in her San Pedro home with four students, two of them her own children. In 1938 the Palos Verdes, Calif., campus of "Chadwick Seaside School" opens. Seventy-five day and boarding students attend. In 1963 Commander and Margaret Lee Chadwick retire after 28 years of service to the school. The Roessler-Chadwick Foundation is created and appoints its first Board of Trustees. In 1968 The boarding program is discontinued. The school's endowment fund is established, today valued at nearly $20 million. This fund ensures Chadwick's long-term financial stability. In 1981: Chadwick's first community service program is established. It was recognized by "U.S. News and World Report" as one of the finest in the United States. Today, more than 90 percent of Upper School students participate in the program.

AT A GLANCE

APPLICATION DEADLINE	January 26
OPEN HOUSES	October-December, call school for dates
UNIFORMS	No
ISEE	Required for students grade 5 and above
SUMMER SCHOOL	Yes
AFTER SCHOOL CARE	Yes
SEE MAP	E on page 285

CHAMINADE MIDDLE & HIGH SCHOOL

Middle School:
19800 Devonshire Street • Chatsworth, CA 91311
Tel: (818) 363 8127 • Fax (818) 363 1219
High School:
7500 Chaminade Avenue • West Hills, CA 91304
Tel: (818) 347 8300 • Fax: (818) 348 8374
www.chaminade.org

HEAD OF SCHOOL	BROTHER TOM FAHY
DIRECTOR OF ADMISSIONS (LOWER):	BARBARA WILLICK
DIRECTOR OF ADMISSIONS:	ESTHER BONINO-BENNETT
TYPE OF SCHOOL	COLLEGE PREP DAY SCHOOL
GRADES	6 - 12

- ENROLLMENT:
    MIDDLE: 640, UPPER: 1,100
- NEW FAMILY FEE: $500
- REGISTRATION FEE: $700
- ACCREDITATION: WASC
- FINANCIAL AID IS AVAILABLE
- TUITION: $10,500
- INSURANCE FEE: $125
- BOOKS: $300-$600
- APPLICATION FEE $100
- PTA/YEARBOOK: $25/$75

Driving to Chatsworth seemed as if I were leaving L.A. behind as I drove out along the 118 freeway to the Tampa exit. THE CHAMINADE MIDDLE SCHOOL campus is separate from the high school and it is georgous. The grounds are enormous with sprawling playing fields that seem to go on for as far as the eye can see. It was such a pleasure to drive into the ample parking area. Everything is spread out and easily accessIble. I strolled around the campus and was given an impromptu tour by Ms Stacey Phillips (who was then the Director of Admissions), is an engaging woman, whose enthusiasm for the school clearly showed. She was like the Pied Piper of Hamlin-for-everywhere we went more kids joined us, all jostling to get my attention and tell me how great their school was, and all the cool things it has to offer. They showed me their baseball, hockey and soccer fields, the Assembly hall, music rooms, science labs, and classrooms that seemed to go on forever. As we walked around the campus, I was struck by the warmth and genuine pleasure that the kids exuded when I talked to them about their school life. They were very confident and introduced me to some of their teachers along the way. We were all quite out of breath by the time we returned to the main office!

Chaminade works closely with the families enrolled to provide a challenging, coeducational education in the Marianist tradition. This tradition, grounded in the values of Jesus, educates the whole person while emphasizing family spirit in a nurturing, caring environment, attentive to the moral, spiritual and religious development of students. As Ms. Phillips explained, "The school prepares college-bound students throughout their middle and high school years in a rigorous program of academic excellence. Students from a diversity of cultural, religious and economic backgrounds come together for an active and varied curricular and extra-curricular program. The mission of Chaminade College Preparatory is to form morally aware and academically capable people to be outstanding contributors to the future."

The following is the course of studies that is offered to the students. It is a reflection of California state standards, university requirements, and individualized programs of study. The curriculum is designed to develop academic skills and to foster inquiry, creativity, and a love of learning and to prepare young people for high school and college.

Advanced or honors classes are offered in mathematics, Spanish, band, and computer science in the eighth grade, and in mathematics and band for sixth and seventh grade. Students qualify to be in each advanced class separately. That is, students may be in one or more of these classes for each year. Evaluation is an ongoing process for admitting or releasing students from the program.

Remedial classes are held each year for those students who are in academic difficulty. Students may be required to attend remedial classes held either concurrently during the school year or during the summer. Required attendance is determined by the classroom teacher, and is indicated through report card comments.

Chaminade believes that athletics play a very important role in the holistic education of their students. In their brochure they point out that their program "encompasses the areas of spiritual, social, emotional, intellectual, creative, and physical growth for the student-athlete, and emphasizes the principles of good sportsmanship." I noticed that after my daughter's school having played hockey against many different schools, I found the girls at Chaminade to be excellent "sportsmen." If your child is athletic, then take a look at this list of sports this school offers:

Cross Country, Golf, Football, Tennis, Volleyball, Basketball, Wrestling, Lacrosse, Softball, Track, Swimming and don't forget Cheerleading (considered a sport of sorts!) Plus fencing and sailing.

All students are required to take the religious education classes and attend the liturgical celebrations and retreats. The school expects your child to show up for test dates and to turn in homework without fail. A friend of mine, whose daughter attends Chamindale, told me that the school really is tough about not turning in homework assignments. I then spoke to the school and students told me that it's not that bad and there's plenty of wiggle room if you miss a day of school. The homework is posted on the school's website. There is tutoring and after-school make up time if a child is absent. Should you be looking for a school that offers your child a well-rounded school experience do take a closer look. The school expects a lot from your child, but in return gives a lot.

HISTORY

Founded 1956 by Marianist Order of Priests and Brothers. Chaminade is an independent school guided by a Board of Directors.

AT A GLANCE

APPLICATION DEADLINE	Call school
OPEN HOUSES	Wednesdays at 9am, call (818) 363-6907
ENTRANCE EXAM	January
UNIFORMS	Yes
SUMMER SCHOOL	Yes
AFTER SCHOOL PROGRAM	Yes
SEE MAP	A on page 285

CHANDLER SCHOOL

Tel: (626) 795-9314 • Fax: (626) 795-6508
1005 Armada Drive • Pasadena, CA 91103-2802
www.chandlerschool.org

HEAD OF SCHOOL	JOHN FINCH
ASSISTANT HEAD OF SCHOOL	DAN GREENWOOD
DIRECTOR OF ADMISSIONS	GRETCHEN LURIE
TYPE OF SCHOOL	CO-EDUCATIONAL DAY SCHOOL
GRADES	K - 8

- ENROLLMENT: 411
- ACCREDITATION: CAIS/WASC
- MEMBERSHIPS: CAIS/NAIS
- APPLICATION FEE: $75
- NEW STUDENT FEE: $1,500
- YEARLY REGISTRATION FEE: $500

- TUITION:
  - K-5: $15,255
  - 6-8: $17,680
- SUMMER SCHOOL: $400
- FINANCIAL AID IS AVAILABLE

CHANDLER SCHOOL is located in a residential neighborhood in northwest Pasadena. The four and one-half acre campus overlooks the Arroyo Seco (at the Rosebowl), and the view is spectacular. There are beautiful old pine trees outside the older campus buildings, which houses grades K-5. The school has a great athletic field which sits between the upper and lower school buildings.

The mission of Chandler School: to provide each student with the highest quality and most academically challenging education in a nurturing, balanced and diverse environment. We strive to have our students gain a love of learning, a means of thinking independently and an ability to work collaboratively. A Chandler education seeks to develop character, self-reliance and a commitment to community in students as a foundation for academic and personal success.

The entire lower school was renovated with new classrooms in 1999, and in 2008 they are renovating the middle school. There remains a hexagon-shaped kindergarten room, and all the other rooms are a generous size with lots of light. The two kindergarten classrooms share a patio where the children have juice at recess time, and a dedicated play space for them that includes a dramatic plays area. Classrooms have reading libraries and centers appropriate to the age of the children. All classrooms have computers with each class also visiting the lower school computer lab once a week.

This is a traditional, academic school starting right off in kindergarten. There is paperwork on display. Parents choosing this educational approach usually feel comfortable when they are given a concrete way to track their children's progress.

Chandler has a Resource Center office with a full-time educational associate on staff to help children with scholastic tutoring. They also have a part-time school counselor. The art studio which the lower school students visit once a week for 45 minutes, is located in the middle school.

Lower School Curriculum

The Chandler Lower School Curriculum fosters intellectual curiosity and achievement in its students while nurturing their emotional and social development. The lower school program emphasizes basic skill development, and encourages children to become confident learners. The academic programs are challenging, but age appropriate. Composition, mathematics, science, social studies and foreign language are all taught within a structured classroom environment.

The language arts program includes a phonics-based reading program in K through 2. Beginning in 3rd grade, the reading program is literature based with students reading and analyzing novels, poetry, and short stories. Frequent field trips and visiting speakers enhance the academic programs. "Character Counts" is used as a framework for the children to learn and practice the six pillars of character: respect, fairness, citizenship, responsibility, caring, and trustworthiness.

The math curriculum in the lower school sets out to ensure that children have a firm understanding of a variety of basic math concepts. In Kindergarten, there is an emphasis on patterning, sorting, classifying, counting and sequencing numbers. In grades 1 to 4, children work on whole number computation, geometry, measurement, whole number operations, fractions, and decimals. In 5th grade, students review the basics and explore number systems, estimation, computation, probability, and two and three dimensional geometry.

Chandler offers a science program starting in Kindergarten. Their new science lab allows them to provide students with solid science training. K through fifth grade visit the lower school science lab weekly in small groups for a hands-on introduction to basic science concepts and techniques. The students in the lower school cover the basics of science investigation with an emphasis on the physical, Earth and biological sciences.

Physical education classes and athletic activities form a regular part of the daily schedule for all lower school students. The purpose is to develop self-esteem, pride, and an appreciation of teamwork through physical and motor development. More formal activities begin in third grade.

All Lower school children participate in the Foreign Language Program. Students meet with their instructors twice weekly for half hour lessons. Children study both French and Spanish in any given year.

Starting in Kindergarten, children begin their exploration of the world through a social studies curriculum that serves to expose children to new ideas, and to widen their knowledge about their community and beyond. They learn geographical locations and concepts throughout the grades.

In weekly computer lessons held in the lab, lower school students learn how to search for information and practice basic skills using software appropriate to their grade level. Each classroom is equipped with computers, where students can work on writing and research skills.

Beginning in Kindergarten, children visit the library once a week. The Chandler lower school library is a warm and inviting place for children to hear stories, read aloud, and develop skills on how to choose appropriate literature for one's reading level. The library is well equipped with computer terminals for searching the internet.

Art classes are held in a separate art studio equipped to provide students with experiences in a variety of media and techniques including: painting, weaving, sculpture and ceramics. Each spring the students present an art exhibit for the entire school community.

In music, kindergarten students develop basic rhythm and movement through the Orff-Schulwerk method. They continue this study through their fifth grade year. Choral instruction, learning basic notation and exposure to diverse music are also components of the music curriculum. There is an after school program that introduces children to string and wind instruments.

Chandler's community projects are often done in tandem with the Middle school students, which encourages students to look beyond the classroom as a learning opportunity, and help them understand how they can impact someone's life and learn from their community. Past partnerships include Friends-In-Deed, Children's Hospital, Pasadena Senior Center, and The Tree People.

Communicating student progress to parents is a high priority at Chandler. Parent/teacher conferences are held twice a year while written reports are sent home at least three times a year. Both parents and faculty are encouraged to communicate with each other whenever they believe there is a need.

Middle School Curriculum
The curriculum is departmentalized and includes English, history, mathematics, science, and foreign language. Class size is small (from 12 to 20 students) and the student-to-teacher ratio is 9:1.

Advanced classes of math and foreign languages are offered in grades seven and eight. The focus of the upper school level is on developing strong writing, speaking, critical thinking, and problem solving skills. Homework? Expect one to two hours per night.

The English program includes writing, vocabulary, spelling, grammar, and literature. Writing skills are taught with an emphasis on organization of thoughts and ideas first, and later focus on correct writing technique.

The history curriculum offers ancient and medieval history to grade six, world history in grade seven, and US history and government in grade eight. There is a focus on learning research techniques, oral presentations, note-taking, and an awareness of current events.

Mathematics in sixth grade offers pre-algebra and teaches computation and conceptual skills. In seventh grade the students have an advanced algebra program.

The three year science program covers general science, biology, and introduction to physical science. There is also a three-year French and Spanish program which offers grammar, vocabulary, conversation, and an appreciation of the cultures.

The upper school computer lab has 18 computers served by a high-speed dedicated direct link to the internet. The three-year program develops skills in word processing, spreadsheets, and databases.

Art classes are offered in drawing, printmaking, ceramics, and watercolor. Grades six and seven study the principles of design and color theory.

Music for upper school students focuses on creating, composing, improvising, and interpreting. Theater works are created by the students who write the text and music and choreograph the dances.

Mini courses are offered (as electives) in art, music, drama, human development, community service, and drug prevention. Advisor-advisee groups consisting of a faculty member and a small group of students meet twice a week to discuss values, teenage issues, and moral and ethical decision-making.

Boys' interscholastic sports teams compete (after school) in flag football, basketball, soccer, track, and baseball. Girls' teams compete in volleyball, basketball, soccer, and track and field. Co-ed competition is offered (off campus) in tennis, swimming, bowling, golf, and cross-country.

The Tower, Chandler's school yearbook, is published each year by upper school students who are responsible for creating, designing, writing, and editing it. The school's newspaper, Charger Express, is issued six times each year by upper school students who oversee its publication.

Parent participation is strongly encouraged. Volunteers serve as class representatives, work in the hot lunch program, staff the school's Shamrock Shoppe, and instruct the Art Docent Program.

Community service programs are conducted through organizations such as Friend-In-Deed, Union Station, and Pasadena Head Start.

One of the missions at Chandler is to prepare the students for success at a competitive college preparatory school. There is an Advisory Program for Middle School students. Chandler students have been accepted into Campbell Hall, Flintridge Preparatory School, Harvard Westlake, Polytechnic, and Westridge School for Girls.

HISTORY

In 1950, Katherine and Thomas Chandler founded Chandler School with a vision to provide students with innovative, inspired academic programs taught by a caring, dedicated faculty. There were fourteen students attending grades four through eight on opening day at the Altadena campus.

With the help of forty parents, a down payment was raised to purchase the school's present site in September of 1958. The school began with only two buildings and an athletic field, but steadily added classrooms and multi-purpose facilities during the next two decades.

By 1979, 366 students were being instructed in grades kindergarten through eight, and most classroom buildings were completed. Current enrollment is 411 students with a faculty of 48.

AT A GLANCE

APPLICATION DEADLINE	Kindergarten: Dec. 12, Grades 1-7: Jan. 30
OPEN HOUSE	Nov. 4, from 9-11:30 a.m.
5-DAY AFTERSCHOOL PROGRAM	2:00-6:00
CUB SCOUT AND BROWNIE	Yes
SUMMER SCHOOL	Required for all new students entering grades 6-7
CANDIDATES FOR GRADES 1 THROUGH 4	Given achievement tests and brief interviews
CANDIDATES GRADE 5 AND MIDDLE SCHOOL	Must take the ISEE
UNIFORMS	Yes
SEE MAP	B on page 285

CHILDREN'S COMMUNITY SCHOOL

Tel: (818) 780-6226 • Fax: (818) 780-5834
14702 Sylvan Street • Van Nuys, CA 91411
www.ccsteaches.com

HEAD OF SCHOOL	NEAL WRIGHTSON
TYPE OF SCHOOL	CO-EDUCATIONAL PROGRESSIVE
GRADES	K - 6

- ENROLLMENT: 100+
- ACCREDITATION: NONE
- FINANCIAL AID IS AVAILABLE

- TUITION: $16,700
- APPLICATION FEE: $75

THE CHILDREN'S COMMUNITY SCHOOL is a gem, a truly authentic example of Progressive education in Los Angeles. There is no other place like it. It is located in a modest residential neighborhood near Victory and Van Nuys Boulevards.

The main building, formerly a church, has been converted to house the school offices, library, music room, printing press, and various work spaces. Outside is a warren of modern classrooms, all sharing a common courtyard. The rustic quality throughout reminds one of summer camp, and the students seem to enjoy it as if it were. This is not a chi-chi, manicured place, and it doesn't want to be. The school is not about appearances, but method and philosophy. So if you're looking for a classroom with spanking clean desks all lined up in a row, move on!

If you are looking for a genuine Progressive education for your child, then your search is over. The approach at CCS is based on the philosophies of John Dewey, the preeminent educator/philosopher of the 1900's, whose educational ideas earned him the title of Father of American Education. Dewey believed the following:

"The educational process must begin with and build upon the interests of the child; that it must provide opportunity for the interplay of thinking and doing in the child's classroom experience; that the school should be organized as a 'miniature community,' that the teacher should be a guide and co-worker with the pupils, rather than a taskmaster assigning a fixed set of lessons and recitations; and the goal of education is the growth of the child in all aspects of its being."

As a classroom observer, I sensed in the students an openness and mutual respect for one another. There was a feeling of equality and a lack of competition among the group, despite the varying ages. During a group discussion, each student waited for his/her turn, listened attentively and asked thoughtful, specific questions. I never got the feeling that anyone was putting on airs and graces simply because there was a visitor in the room. Compliance with the rules seems to come from a knowledge and respect for them, rather than from fear of what will happen if they don't follow them.

CCS has a social studies core curriculum, with an emphasis on field trips. For example, a second grade study of Southern California might lead to an exploration of who lived here first. So in this case, the Chumash Indian lifestyle would then be delved into and questions would be asked about what they ate, wore, lived in, and valued. Students would also explore the kind of music, dances and games of the Chumash Indians.

Students go on field trips to places like the Southwest and Natural History Museums, Missions, and the Arboretum. Children enriched with new information would then begin to write, paint, dramatize, build with blocks, sculpt with clay, and cook, solidifying for themselves and illustrating for others, what they have learned.

The curriculum places an emphasis on block building. After a field trip, the children will have a chance to reconstruct the place that they visited with blocks. For example, if the trip were to a market, they would work together to figure out how the market was planned and would discuss what jobs would be needed to run the business in the market might even use the site for dramatic play, which would in turn call upon their math and organizational skills. Through situations like these they learn not only math, history, and critical thinking skills, but how to work together, to problem solve, and to see the world beyond the sandbox.

Kindergartners, because of their social and academic needs, are grouped separately, while children in grades 1 to 6 are divided into four multi-age groups. 'Traditional academics' are introduced in a non-traditional, age-appropriate manner. Children are expected to take responsibility for making their own lunches to bring to school and to remember their homework. The emphasis is on making the child more self-reliant and less dependent on parents.

There are specialists in dance, art, and music, and for the oldest group a print-shop teacher is available. The average class size is 20 with one full-time, credentialed teacher and a shared assistant. There is homework, which for kindergarten could be to remember an ingredient for cooking, in the first grade to count the number of rooms in their house, while in fifth grade, it might be to go to the library and do research on Greek mythology. There are no report cards. Standardized tests are given at the fifth and sixth grade level, but solely for practice, not to submit for admissions to seventh grade.

HISTORY

The Children's Community School was founded in 1981 by Leni Jacksen, a native of Berlin, who fled Germany in the Thirties and returned in 1971 as principal of the city's German-American school. She is an advocate of the educational ideas of philosopher/educator John Dewey. In 1995 at age of 75, Jacksen returned to Berlin to revise the communist school system. There she drew up a core curriculum in sync with the inspirations of a democratic society where the educational focus is on thinking and interaction rather than on simply being obedient citizens.

AT A GLANCE

APPLICATION DEADLINE	February 1
OPEN HOUSES	November 15
SCHOOL TOURS	Each week by appointment
UNIFORMS	No
AFTER SCHOOL CARE	Yes
CCS will go to your child's present school to observe your child for possible admission	
SEE MAP	A on page 285

CHRIST THE KING SCHOOL

Tel: (323) 462-4753 • Fax: (323) 462-8475
617 N. Arden Blvd. • Los Angeles, CA 90004

HEAD OF SCHOOL	MARY A. KURBAN, ED. D.
TYPE OF SCHOOL	CO-ED CATHOLIC DAY SCHOOL
GRADES	K - 8

- ENROLLMENT: 250
- ACCREDITATION: WASC/WCEA
- FAMILY DISCOUNT OFFERED

- TUITION: $3,200-$3,700
- APPLICATION FEE: $150
- NEW FAMILY FEE: 325/PER CHILD

CHRIST THE KING SCHOOL is located in Hancock Park on the corner of Arden about a block down from Melrose. For those who live or work in the neighborhood, this school is certainly an option for those considering a Catholic education for their children who have been unable to get into St. Brenden. St. Brendan suggests the Kindergarten program at Christ the King to parents if their child is under the prescribed entrance age.

I visited the school during the summer break, and I was buzzed into the courtyard where I was met by the school secretary, who gave me a brochure and invited me to walk around. I was a little disappointed by the size of the playground, which seemed rather small and had almost no greenery. But there were shaded areas where the children could eat under, and I am sure that once the playground was full of children it would look a lot more inviting.

The philosophy of Christ the King school is to educate the whole child, including on-going academic excellence, personal growth, as well as moral, social and spiritual development.

They offer a full physical education program and have many extra-curricular activities. Their sports program features football, volleyball, basketball, and track.

I had a long discussion with one of the teachers who told me that their school attracted a large percentage of non-English speaking parents, and that perhaps their curriculum was not quite as aggressive as St. Brendan's. This teacher was a delight, very warm and welcoming. She introduced me to her daughter who had recently graduated and been accepted to U.C. Berkley. She told me that she had loved her time at the school and had made long-lasting friendships.

The school offers an academic curriculum comprised of religion, reading, language arts, math, science, social studies, family life, art, music, and computer education. An important part of its religious program is sacramental preparation, which is implemented with the help and guidance of the parish priests. They also have the Instructional Television Program in all the classrooms and integrate it into the whole curriculum.

The two-story facility is clean and compact. As they point out in their brochure, and I quote:

> "One characteristic which exemplifies Christ the King School is the small school atmosphere built on family spirit and closeness of the school community. Parents are encouraged to become active in the Parent Organization and to participate in all our fundraisers."

I did look into several classrooms which appeared to be well-stocked and nicely laid out. Conveniently next to the auditorium is a large dining room and kitchen next door.

If you are looking for a Catholic private school education that is far more reasonable than most other private schools, then I would recommend that you visit the campus of Christ The King School.

HISTORY

Christ the King Parish was founded in 1926, and the elementary school was opened in 1959 by the Sisters of the Sacred Heart.

AT A GLANCE

APPLICATION DEADLINE	Ongoing
UNIFORMS	Yes
AFTER SCHOOL CARE	Yes
SEE MAP	C on page 285

CLAIRBOURN SCHOOL

Tel: (626) 286-3108 • Fax: (626) 286-1528
8400 Huntington Drive • San Gabriel, CA 91775
www.clairbourn.org

HEAD OF SCHOOL	ROBERT W. NAFIE PH.D.
TYPE OF SCHOOL	CO-EDUCATIONAL DAY SCHOOL
DIRECTOR OF ADMISSIONS	MS. JANNA WINDSOR
GRADES	PRESCHOOL - 8

- ENROLLMENT 418
- ACCREDITATIONNAEYC/CAIS/WASC
- MEMBERSHIPS NAIS
- YEARLY REGISTRATION FEE $600
- APPLICATION FEE $75

- TUITION $14,850-$16,600
- OTHER FEES APPLY DEPENDING ON GRADE
- NEW FAMILY FEE NONE
- FINANCIAL AID IS AVAILABLE

CLAIRBOURN has a beautiful campus: eleven acres of rolling lawns, a swimming pool, handball court, all landscaped, manicured and spread out like a college campus. The jewel in the crown of this setting is an old Georgian-style 23 room manor house built in 1915, situated at the center of the property. The manor came from a gentleman's mansion with functional orange groves, to the thriving educational business that it is today. Originally used as the headmaster's residence, it now serves as a meeting place for the Board of Trustees, the Clairbourn Families Associates, and the Student Council.

There is a feeling of orderliness throughout – everything in its proper place. The school was strictly for Christian Science families from its inception in 1926 until in 1967 the board of directors voted to open the enrollment to people of other religions. Today, while the school considers students of different religions and ethnic backgrounds for admission, the staff, faculty, and administration remain active Christian Scientists. Please note: there is NO religion taught.

The curriculum is a strong academic one with an emphasis on math, science and the development of higher-level thinking skills, such as analysis, synthesis and evaluation, original observation. There are specialists in physical education, music, art, and computer skills. The music teacher really impressed me, she was very passionate about her work with the students and answered all the parents' questions with enthusiasm and wit.

The following Purpose and Premise Statements are taken from the Clairbourn brochure, and are included here to give prospective parents a clear understanding of the school's approach:

"Purpose: To demonstrate practically the unlimited nature of all true instruction through educational opportunities which are harmonious with the teachings of Christian Science and in accordance with accepted professional standards of educational excellence.

Premise: The achievement of this purpose is formulated on the following collective premise:

1. That any student who is receptive to instruction can experience success in proportion to his/her receptivity and application.

2. That the best education is one that assists the student in acquiring basic study habits including active listening, critical thinking, disciplined effort, and obedience to principle.

3. That the joy of learning is enhanced and enriched through the use of variety, creativity, and self-expression in developing essential physical, mental, and social skills.

4. That the gift of understanding carries with it certain moral and spiritual obligations to mankind for its constructive use in a way that fosters noble ambition, unselfish service, and world brotherhood.

5. That a deep respect and reverence for God as an active power in human affairs provides the foundation for strength, courage, integrity, humility, and compassion, and leads to an establishment of sound Christian character and a respect for the conviction of others.

6. That the education of children is a shared responsibility between the school and the family, requiring the school to carry forward its instructional program in a way that preserves, supports, and enriches the basic family unit of which the student is a member.

7. That the protection and preservation of our democratic form of government requires an alert, informed, and active citizenry, anchored in a love of country, appreciation of heritage, and a deep respect for law."

In 2008, Clairbourn began it's final phase of construction for the west campus. The center includes a multimillion dollar preschool with three new classrooms, an age-appropriate play yard that will feature areas to bike, climb, swing and slide, sections for digging and planting, and an outdoor theatre area for dramatic play.

HISTORY

Clairbourn school started in the music room of Mr. and Mrs. Arthur K. Bourne's home in San Marino, California in 1926. The idea of a kindergarten for children of parents interested in Christian Science grew from four students to a full elementary school, and high school. by 1931 the school had acquired 3.5 acres of the present property for that purpose.

In 1938 the school returned to the original idea of educating younger students and discontinued the high school grades. During the early 40s Clairbourn struggled along with thirty-five students, half of whom comprised the Nursery school. With increased enrollment through the late forties, money was raised to buy more property at the present site and to add buildings. In 1953 the kindergarten building was added, while in 1958 the Manor house and its properties (including orange groves and swimming pool) were acquired. 1967 saw the school open its doors to students of other faiths and establish three sister schools in San Gabriel, Redwood City, and San Rafael.

During the late 1980s and through the early 90s, a library was added as well as an art studio, music room, multi-purpose building, a facility to house the second, fourth, and fifth grades, and a faculty lounge.

AT A GLANCE

APPLICATION DEADLINE	July 1
OPEN HOUSE DATES	See website for latest information
UNIFORMS	Yes, starting in Kindergarten
BEFORE AND AFTER SCHOOL CARE	Yes
SUMMER SCHOOL	Yes
SEE MAP	B on page 285

THE COUNTRY SCHOOL

Tel: (818) 769-2473 • Fax: (818) 761-9509
5243 Laurel Canyon Blvd. • North Hollywood CA 91607
www.country-school.org

HEAD OF SCHOOL	JOSEPH PEREZ
DIRECTOR OF ADMISSIONS	MARIA GERRARD
TYPE OF SCHOOL	CO-ED DAY SCHOOL
GRADES	PRESCHOOL - 8

- ENROLLMENT: 200
- ACCREDITATION: CAIS
- MEMBERSHIPS ERB/ISAMA
- FINANCIAL AID IS AVAILABLE

- TUITION: $3,050-$23,375
- APPLICATION FEE: $125-$150
- OTHER FEES DEPENDING ON GRADE

THE COUNTRY SCHOOL has a warm and cozy feeling starting with its small-but-efficient campus setting, pleasant classrooms, and kind, friendly staff. The Country School site has been expanded to over two acres. It is located on busy Laurel Canyon, but once inside the compound, you leave the traffic and dust behind and step into a protected little community of offices and classrooms.

The preschool and elementary school classrooms are wrapped around a common courtyard, which houses a well-equipped playground. There is a new grass playing field, and a large paved area for basketball and other group sports located at the back of the property, which houses the after school athletics program there is also a playground area (with sand) for the older children.

The campus expansion includes a new library and Art Studio. The kindergarten room is large, bright, and modern, with high ceilings, which gives it a lovely open-air feeling.

During my visit, Headmaster Paul M. Singer, is very popular with several of the Country School parents with whom I spoke. After serving as Headmaster for quite some time. Joseph Perez is now Headmaster.

It is well to keep in mind that these kinds of changes can take place at any time at the school of your choice and may affect the way you feel about sending your child there.

Here is the Country School's description of their approach for grades kindergarten through sixth grade:

"At the elementary level, the school continues to provide a strong, nurturing environment where students' academic needs are met. During elementary years, development varies from child to child. Our school makes every effort to serve each child's readiness and potential, by creating a smaller student-teacher-ratio, insuring that the learning process takes place within an environment that is attentive and supportive for the individual child."

Each class has two full time teachers. With specialists in music, physical education, art, science and computer skills. Portfolios of the children's work are kept and reviewed during the year to show change and progress.

Note: The Kindergarten hold 25 children, and priority is given to those already enrolled in preschool.

The feeling here is warm and nurturing, an atmosphere which is created by the staff and by the small size of the school and a surprisingly diverse student body. Many of the parents that I spoke with loved the school but worried that it was not academic enough for their children. They were mainly concerned with the transition from sixth grade to another, perhaps more academically challenging school, although Country school has an excellent matriculation record to secondary schools and universities. The "word" on the Country School is that it gets its highest marks for the preschool school rather than the elementary school program.

The best way to know if this school is right for your family is to see it. Be sure to take along a list of questions to ask the staff and parent volunteers who will be at the open house.

HISTORY

The Country School was founded in 1948 by Rafe and Laura Ellis to offer children a chance to reach their own individual potential within the atmosphere of balanced freedom and structure. For twenty-four years it operated as a preschool, then in 1972 was expanded to include grades K-6. It is a non-profit, private institution run by a Board of Trustees.

AT A GLANCE

APPLICATION DEADLINE	Call school
OPEN HOUSES	October through January
	Check websites/call for dates and times
SCHOOL TOURS	Call school to make reservation
UNIFORMS	Yes
SEE MAP	A on page 285

CRESPI CARMELITE
SCHOOL FOR BOYS

Tel (818) 345-1672 Fax: (818) 705-0209
5031 Alonzo Ave.● Encino, CA 91316
www.crespi.org

PRINCIPAL	FR. PAUL HENSON, O. CARM.
DIRECTOR OF ADMISSIONS	ROBERT KODAMA
TYPE OF SCHOOL	CATHOLIC, ALL BOYS DAY SCHOOL
GRADES	9-12

- ENROLLMENT: 600
- ACCREDITATION: WASC
- MEMBERSHIPS: NCEA/WCEA
- FINANCIAL AID AVAILABLE
- FAMILIES MAY ANTICIPATE ADDITIONAL COSTS FOR BOOKS AND FEES
- TUITION: $10,950
- APPLICATION FEE: $90
- REGISTRATION FEE: $700

CRESPI CARMELITE SCHOOL for boys is a small school in Encino, just off the 101 and Ventura Blvd. The walls here are white, with very little to distract a young man from his studies. In fact, discipline and character development is what Crespi is all about. The Dean of students who conducted my impromptu tour said, "The Campus itself is not a large footprint, but more important is what we do in the buildings, not the building itself."

Crespi is a Catholic school. It is, however, open to students of other faiths. All students, however, must take the religion courses required for graduation. Crespi cherishes three fundamental values: Lifelong learning, productive and mature behavior, along with a moral and spiritual life. Is your son a "Crespi Man"? Here's what a Crespi man is according to the school's brochure:

"Life-long learner uses logical, analytical creative thinking skills; uses appropriate methodologies, strategies, and current technologies to solve problems and extend his knowledge. He acquires, interprets, organizes, synthesizes, applies and evaluates knowledge; and speaks, writes and uses other forms of expression accurately, effectively, and creatively.

As a productive and mature person, a Crespi man strives to improve community, takes risks in order to grow and claims responsibility for his actions. He understands and participates in the democratic process, and strives to enhance and maintain physical, mental, and emotional well-being.

And lastly, as a moral and spiritual person, he models Christ by learning and practicing Gospel values; is committed to living an ethical life, is involved in service to others and social justice. He also recognizes and respects the uniqueness, dignity, and personal gifts of all people."

Most students enter in the ninth or tenth grade, and admission is based on four considerations:

1. Academic and testing records from previous school
2. Recommendations from previous school
3. Entrance exam taken at Crespi
4. Personal Interview

Of these four, the personal interview with prospective students and parents is perhaps the most important. They want to be sure that Crespi Carmelite High School is the right place for you and your son. Not a lot of boys want to go to a same gender school, but it delineates activities, school time is school time, and social time is social time.

One of the most impressive and unique elements at Crespi is that they work very closely with the Gurion Institute, which is developing a program for educating young boys. This research includes how genders think and learn, which allows them to teach specifically to the way boys learn and behave. Their teaching is geared specifically to the way boys learn best, and this also works for each boy's character development and discipline.

So, for example, in the art room, and in an all male environment students prefer to building architectural structures, carving from rocks, or sculpting in clay. Of course, students still get in a fair amount of painting and drawing, a more female oriented art. Art at Crespi is about exploring imagination in a fun way and being surprised and rewarded for your creativity. Although the Dean of students added, " I don't know how many students come here for Art". If you are seeking a more art-oriented school for your son, this probably isn't the best choice for you.

Crespi has recently created more classrooms, which allows them to have smaller class sizes, and a better teacher/student ratio. The past few years has seen new construction for a commons area, a new chapel, audio/visual, counseling and music departments. There are also new locker rooms, and a relatively new gymnasium.

Academics and athletics are stressed at Crespi. They recognize the important role that science plays in the world and have invested in technology, and are constantly upgrading their equipment to give students every opportunity to become cognisant of progressive developments. There are two computer labs, and up-to-date science and biology labs.

Crespi has a strong tradition of athletic excellence. Students are encouraged to try one or more sports during their high school years. Many young men find they do better in the classroom when they play sports. They emphasize sportsmanship, teamwork, hard conditioning, and skills. Crespi teams have won State Championships, CIF championships and 80 league championships at all levels. Crespi fields teams in 12 sports: baseball, basketball, cross country, football, golf, soccer, tennis, track, volleyball, water polo and wrestling.

There are also many extra curricular activities, and two or more students can even create a new club based on their interests for that particular year. Besides excellent academics, with the majority of students going to major universities and Ivy League Schools, the school has a very strong Alumni Association. Many students come back to teach, volunteer, and coach. Alumni can often be seen in the stands during football season and other sporting events, for there is a fraternal bond that is created in an all-boy school, a brotherhood, that Crespi men carry with them for life.

HISTORY

Established in Encino, California in 1959, Crespi Carmelite is a non-profit, Catholic, four-year, college preparatory school for young men, owned and operated by the Carmelite Order. Dedicated to excellence and responding to the challenges of education in our time, Crespi offers a holistic model of education emphasizing the spiritual, intellectual, moral, physical, and social development of their students.

AT A GLANCE

APPLICATION DEADLINE	February 6
OPEN HOUSES	November 9, from 1-4pm
ENTRANCE EXAM	January and February
SEE MAP	A on page 285

CRESTVIEW PREPARATORY SCHOOL

Tel: (818) 952-0925 • Fax: (818) 952-8470
140 Foothill Blvd. • La Cañada, CA 91011
www.crestviewprep.org

HEAD OF SCHOOL	MARIE KIDD
TYPE OF SCHOOL	CO-EDUCATIONAL DAY SCHOOL
GRADES	K - 6

- ENROLLMENT: 230
- ACCREDITATION: CAIS
- MEMBERSHIPS: ERB/NAIS
- APPLICATION FEE: $90
  ($250 OF ABOVE FEE APPLICABLE TO LAST PAYMENT)
- YEARLY REGISTRATION FEE: $750

- TUITION:
  K: $11,370
  1-6: $12,195
- FINANCIAL AID IS AVAILABLE

CRESTVIEW has a wholesome, old-fashioned feeling of a small school from 50 years ago. The children play in a large, grassy play yard equipped with swings and climbing structures, among them a wonderful rocket ship that even I wanted to climb into! The school has a soccer/baseball field.

What appeals to many of the parents considering Crestview is:

1. It's not high-pressure.
2. The property has a large, grassy play-yard.
3. It has a small-town feel to it.
4. It's less expensive than many of the other area-schools.

While visiting the school, I found all of these things to be true. Extended daycare is available from 7:00 a.m. to 6 p.m. The library is large and is entirely computerized. They have also added a second 4th grade class, and each classroom is equipped with several computers with flat screen monitors and digital projectors.

Kindergarten hours are 8:30 a.m. through 2:30 p.m. Monday through Friday, with before and afterschool care available. First thru sixth grade hours are from 8:30 a.m. to 3:15 p.m.

Marjorie Hanna, Head of School, is a bright, affable woman with a commanding presence that lets you know right away that she is in charge. During the Open House, she addressed questions from parents with the ease of one who knows the school inside-out. (She has been at Crestview since 1982).

Crestview follows the 'whole child' philosophy of teaching. The core curriculum includes reading, creative writing, spelling, mathematics, science, handwriting, social studies, and language arts. There are specialists in physical education, music, computer, art, library, and Spanish.

The teachers are described in the brochure as holding Bachelor's degrees and appropriate teaching credentials. Fifty percent of the faculty at Crestview have, or are in the process of obtaining, advanced degrees.

Crestview suggests that new students should attend their summer school, unless family situations prevent attendance. This is probably a great idea to help the children acclimate themselves into the school for the beginning of a new school year.

As guideline for parents they also suggest that homework should be about 15 minutes per grade level per night. So first graders have 15 minutes, all the way up to grade 6 who have approximately one and a half hours – yes, that's 1 1/2 hours, not the 2 1/2 to 3 hours in some of the schools we visited.

If you are interested in applying, go for the tour. They are very open to answering all questions and will take the time to explain anything you might want to know about the school. So give them a call!

HISTORY

Crestview Preparatory School was moved to La Cañada and incorporated as a non-profit corporation in 1986. It has been located on its present site since 1988. Originally, there were 100 students in the school and currently there are 220 students in kindergarten through sixth grade.

AT A GLANCE

APPLICATION DEADLINE	February 1
OPEN HOUSES	January
SCHOOL TOURS	September through January
UNIFORMS	No
BEFORE AND AFTER SCHOOL CARE	Yes
SUMMER SCHOOL	Yes
ENRICHMENT CLASSES	Yes
SEE MAP	B on page 285

CROSSROADS SCHOOL FOR ARTS & SCIENCES

Elementary Campus: K – 5
Tel: (310) 828-1196 • Fax: (310) 392-9611
1715 Olympic Blvd. • Santa Monica, CA 90404

Middle/Upper Campus: 6 - 12
Tel: (310) 829-7391 • Fax: (310) 828-5636
1714 Twenty-first St. • Santa Monica, CA 90404

www.xrds.org

HEADMASTER	ROGER H. WEAVER
DIRECTOR OF ADMISSIONS	CECILIA LEE
TYPE OF SCHOOL	CO-EDUCATIONAL DAY SCHOOL
GRADES	K – 12

- ENROLLMENT: 1,141
- APPLICATION FEE: $125
- ACCREDITATION CAIS/WASC
- MEMBERSHIPS: ABC/ASCD/CAIS/CEEB CLS/ISAMA/NACAC/NAIS/NPAS
- TUITION:
  - K–5 $22,800
  - 6–12 $27,210
- NEW FAMILY FEE: $2,000
- FINANCIAL AID IS AVAILABLE

CROSSROADS LOWER SCHOOL (K-5), the admissions office, and the K through 12 athletic facility are located two blocks away from the middle and upper schools. The school buildings are in a variety of styles ranging from aesthetically distinguished to urban industrial. There are fully equipped laboratories, multi-disciplinary classrooms, a 25,000 volume library, theater, music performance space, computer centers and a photography lab. Then there is the magnificent Peter Boxenbaum Arts Education Center, with two dance studios, art studios and a screening room. There is also their own gallery, The Sam Francis Gallery, which I visit from time to time and always see interesting exhibitions.

The teachers are the heart of Crossroads Elementary. They are focused, passionate, lively, dedicated and have (if you'll excuse the pun) done their homework. Usually every school has at least one truly outstanding educator on staff, but at Crossroads they all stood out as exceptional in one way or another.

If I had to use one word to describe Crossroads School it would be 'balance.' There seems to be a respect for people and nature as well as an equal mixture of academics, the arts, and science. Crossroads was founded upon five basic commitments: academics, the arts, the greater community, student development, and the attainment of social, economic and racial diversity in its stud population.

The curriculum in the lower school (K-5) is social studies based, which becomes the unifying content for the learning of reading, writing, and math skills. For example, children may apply math skills by making scale maps of a country they are studying by developing 'businesses' like operating a store, or by calculating the amounts of food needed for a camping trip.

In language arts children are encouraged to work at their own pace sharing both works-in-progress and finished compositions, thus providing each other with questions and feedback.

Each child receives instruction in art, drama, music, and dance movement – all taught by specialists. (Crossroads was the only place where drama and dance were offered during the school day and not as part of an after-school program). The general music program is based on the principles of Orff Schulwerk. There are also specialists in science, computers, physical education, and library science.

By the sixth grade, students have been taught writing, literature, math, social studies, and science in self-contained classrooms. The overall theme is immigration and multi-culturalism. Note taking, vocabulary development, writing skills, discussion techniques, and literary analysis are emphasized. Students are grouped by skill level in math. There are specialists in visual arts, drama, chorus, instrumental music, life skills, and physical education. Again, this inclusion of chorus and drama in the school-day is unusual.

In the seventh and eighth grades, Latin is required along with English, history, math, science, physical education, arts and electives. A two-year Spanish course is optional for sixth and seventh-grade students.

The upper school (or high school as it was formerly known) is described by Director, Ann Colburn, as demanding and rigorous, and designed to prepare its students for college.

In order to graduate, students must meet the departmental graduation requirements, as well as take a minimum of four academic classes every semester of enrollment. Advanced placement courses are available to qualified students in English, U.S. history, mathematics, biology, physics, chemistry, music theory, French, Spanish, Latin, visual arts, and art history.

At the upper school level students with long-standing, focused talents, interests and skills in a particular discipline may apply to the Specialized Majors Program in one of the following areas: languages, computer science, dance, film and video, music and visual arts.

The school has a great curriculum guide, take a look at it if you time.

HISTORY

Crossroads Elementary School was founded in the mid-fifties as a day school for the Parish of St. Augustine By-the-Sea Episcopal Church. In 1970, Paul E. Cummins became Headmaster and one year later simultaneously started Crossroads upper school with a group comprised of sixth-grade parents and educators. After separating the elementary school from the church affiliation in 1982, Dr. Cummins merged it with his Crossroads School (Grades 7-12), and in the spring of 1982 the Crossroads School for Arts and Sciences (K-12) was born.

AT A GLANCE

APPLICATION DEADLINE	K due October. Grades 1-12 due December
OPEN HOUSES	Call school for dates
BEFORE & AFTER SCHOOL CARE	Yes
UNIFORMS	No
SEE MAP	D on page 285

CURTIS SCHOOL

Tel: (310) 476-1251 • Fax: (310) 476-1542
15871 Mulholland Drive • Los Angeles, CA 90049
www.curtisschool.org

HEAD OF SCHOOL	STEPHEN E. SWITZER
DIRECTOR OF ADMISSIONS	MIMI W. PETRIE
TYPE OF SCHOOL	CO-EDUCATIONAL DAY SCHOOL
GRADES	DK* - 6

- ENROLLMENT: 520
- ACCREDITATIONS: CAIS/NAIS
- APPLICATION FEE: $100
- OTHER FEES APPLY DEPENDING ON GRADE
- FINANCIAL AID IS AVAILABLE

- TUITION:
  DK-6 $17,850
  7-8 $21,090

CURTIS SCHOOL is located on Mullholland Drive's 'restaurant row' of schools which includes: Berkeley Hall, Westland, Mirman and Steven Wise.

In describing the physical setting, one word that comes to mind is: deluxe. The school's 27 hilltop acres make it both beautiful and very private. The new administration building houses the 14,000 volume library and provides 10,000 square feet of space. There are fields for football, soccer, and track. Other athletic facilities include: an outdoor gymnastic pavilion, a 25-yard heated swimming pool, a volleyball court, three tennis courts, a handball/racquetball court, and three basketball courts. The staff is proud to tell you that the facility is valued at over $20 million. At the Open House, a full auditorium of parents listened to a description of the school and the admission process. The Headmaster was encouraging, but did not hide the fact that it was very difficult to gain acceptance to the school. He told of application files containing letters from senators and foreign dignitaries all recommending a child for kindergarten. Who do you know? But seriously, take advantage of the fact that this school accepts letters of recommendation. The goal of Curtis is to provide a college-preparatory academic program. The school also places a major emphasis on physical education and athletics.

In the early grades the focus is on teaching children to read. Curtis has a *Developmental Kindergarten (DK) that feeds into the kindergarten class. DK is not preschool, and accepts children who are either slightly younger or not developmentally ready for reading instruction.

Mathematics instruction moves through basic skills to familiarity with fractions, decimals, positive and negative numbers, probabilities, and elementary algebra. Computers are introduced early, and the computer lab is state-of-the-art and equipped with many games too!

Science instruction is incorporated into language arts in first grade and deals with plants, animals, and environment. In fifth grade, children go to a science lab with a specialist teacher.

The music program is primarily a vocal one, but also incorporates listening, writing, reading, conducting, and playing instruments. There is an orchestra that meets weekly where children have the opportunity to learn an instrument beginning in grade 3. The art program is based on a study of art appreciation and applied skills: drawing, painting, graphics, sculpture and ceramics projects. Latin is required in grades 5 and 6.

The yearbook was filled with large, bright photos of all the teachers and children, and beautiful photographic layouts of all the year's events. Included were many pages of the children's poetry, and eight pages in full color called the 'the art gallery' showing beautiful reproductions of the children's art work during the past year. It was a magnificent piece of work, and it put my own high-school yearbook to shame. When I got up to leave, I handed the book to Ms. Trahey who waved me off and said, "Oh that's all right, you may keep it."

HISTORY

Curtis School was founded in 1925 by Carl Curtis who operated the school with his family for forty years. In 1964, Willard E. Badham assumed the role of Headmaster and enlarged and developed the school over the next three decades. He retired in 1992 and was succeeded by Clay V. Stites, former Headmaster of Friends Academy in Massachusetts. In 1997 Stephen E. Switzer was appointed the Headmaster. Curtis moved to its current location in 1983 where 532 children attend its 25 acre campus.

AT A GLANCE

APPLICATION DEADLINE	December 15
OPEN HOUSES	9/23 and 10/14 at 7p.m.
UNIFORMS	Yes
BEFORE AND AFTER SCHOOL CARE	Yes
SEE MAP	D on page 285

JOHN THOMAS DYE

Tel: (310) 476-2811 • Fax: (310) 476-9176
11414 Chalon Road • Los Angeles, CA 90049
www.jtdschool.com

HEAD OF SCHOOL	RAYMOND R. MICHAUD JR.
DIRECTOR OF ADMISSIONS	JUDY HIRSCH
TYPE OF SCHOOL	CO-EDUCATIONAL DAY SCHOOL
GRADES	K - 6

- ENROLLMENT: 320
- ACCREDITATION: CAIS/WASC/NAIS
- MEMBERSHIPS: NAIS
- FINANCIAL AID IS AVAILABLE

- TUITION: $20,850
- APPLICATION FEE: $125
- NEW FAMILY FEE $2,000

JOHN THOMAS DYE occupies eleven beautiful acres in Bel Air and feels very exclusive from the moment you drive up to the campus until the time the tour is over. Included in the application packet is an exquisitely detailed little map – don't lose it – because the school is quite difficult to find.

At first I thought I had taken a wrong turn and stumbled upon an Arabian Horse farm enclosed by impeccably kept white split-rail fences. But, of course, I still had that little map clenched in my hand so eventually I made my way to the parking lot.

The whole facility is gorgeous and generously laid out on the property with spectacular views. It is so removed from the chaos and smog of the city that it feels more like a vacation resort.

The school began on the estate of the Dye family in 1949, so the buildings have a warm, homey feeling about them. The John Thomas Dye Hall contains administrative offices, an assembly hall, computer and science labs, and a music room. Two identical wings extend east and west from the main building housing classrooms. Three Kindergarten classrooms are housed in a separate adjoining facility. They accept 70 boys and 70 girls into Kindergarten, on a first-come, first-served basis, although siblings do get a first chance. A multi-purpose facility located on the lower field houses an art studio, a large gymnasium, and a 13,000+ volume library. The younger children enjoy two large play areas. Physical education and after-school sports programs take place on the athletic field.

Dye is a traditional academic school using an integrated curriculum. Students learn specific subjects and also how these subjects relate to each other. Emphasis is placed on the development of problem-solving abilities, effective written and oral communication skills, good study skills, and work habits.

Courses taught by classroom teachers include language arts, mathematics, science, and social studies. Grades five and six are taught by separate departments of English, math, science, and social studies. All students receive instruction from specialists in art, computer science, library, music, and physical education.

Students are given homework assignments, which become more challenging at each grade level. Written reports are issued quarterly, and parent-teacher conferences are held twice a year. Educational Records Bureau Tests are administered each spring.

The first grade class that I observed was working in independent groups spread out among all the different 'centers' in the room (i.e. the reading area, the science area, etc.). The teacher was assisting students as they came up to her with questions, but she was fully aware of what was going on. The children were aware of my presence, but always stayed focused on the tasks at hand. The classroom was impeccably organized with every scholastic aid one could imagine. There were two sets of encyclopedia, a miniature library, a large fish tank, and lots of state-of-the-art audio/visual equipment. I got the feeling that this group of children got many things accomplished in a day, and that the teacher kept them interested in what they were learning.

One couple I spoke with told me that they were all set to send their preschooler to Dye, but withdrew when their child was asked to sign a contract agreeing to do the assignments to the best of his ability and to follow all the school rules. They were just appalled. It is interesting to note that I met them on a tour of Westland, a school that has the absolute opposite approach to education from that of Dye. So you see, it all depends on your philosophy and style; what was appalling to this couple might have sounded great to another.

Traditional Dye events include Grandparents Day, Christmas Carols Program, Open House, the Athletic Awards Program, the Sixth Grade Musicale and the County Fair. If you have a chance, go to the Open House and the Country Fair because these events will give you a clear picture of what the school is all about.

This school seems to prepare the students well for their next step; a full one hundred percent of the 2003 graduating class went onto leading independent secondary schools. In case you haven't already guessed, to enroll in Dye School is difficult.

HISTORY

Cathryn Robberts Dye and her husband, John Thomas Dye II, founded the school in 1929. It was originally called Brentwood Town and Country School and was started in their home for their only son, John Thomas Dye III, and his friends. By 1949 the school had outgrown its original home. It moved to its present site and was renamed The Bel Air Town and Country School. In 1959 the name was changed to the Thomas Dye School in honor of John Thomas Dye III who was killed in action in WWII. Today the vision of the founders is being carried into the 21st century by the present headmaster, Raymond R. Michaud, Jr, and his elected 18-member Board of Trustees.

AT A GLANCE

APPLICATION DEADLINE	Applications availabe in August
SCHOOL TOURS	October through January
UNIFORMS	Yes
BEFORE/AFTER SCHOOL CARE	Yes
PARENTING CLASSES	Are conducted by the Headmaster at each grade level
SUMMER SCHOOL PROGRAM	Yes
SEE MAP	D on page 285

ECHO HORIZON SCHOOL

Tel: (310) 838-2442 • Fax: (310) 838-0479
3430 McManus Avenue • Culver City, CA 90232
www.echohorizon.org

HEAD OF SCHOOL	PAULA R. DASHIELL
DIRECTOR OF ADMISSIONS	JENNY BOONE
TYPE OF SCHOOL	CO-EDUCATIONAL DAY SCHOOL
GRADES	PK - 6

- ENROLLMENT: 285
- ACCREDITATION: CAIS/WASC
- MEMBERSHIPS: ERB/ISAMA/NAIS
- (LIMITED) FINANCIAL AID IS AVAILABLE
- THERE ARE ADDITIONAL FEES DUE FOR FIELD TRIPS, HOT LUNCHES, PTA, ETC.

- TUITION: $18,500
- APPLICATION FEE: $75
- NEW FAMILY FEE: $1,000

ECHO HORIZON SCHOOL's Paula Dashiell is an outstanding educator with a passion for the work she is doing. She speaks to parents at the Open House concisely, with humor and wit, giving a very thorough description of all aspects of the school.

The main building was formerly an elementary school in the Culver City Unified School District and was renovated in 1995. It is a beautiful, old-fashioned, two-story structure with wide hallways and huge sash windows throughout.

Echo Horizon just added space for a pre-kindergarten, math center, science center, and performing arts classroom. It has a new 15,000 volume library, technology center, art studio, and two beautiful, exciting playgrounds.

Some parents may ask, "Who is paying for all this?" And there is indeed a Capital Campaign instituted to raise funds for the project, in which every family will be asked to participate. This is separate from the Annual Giving Fund, which is earmarked for general operating expenses, and bridges the gap between the cost of education and tuition.

The Echo Horizon School is operated by the ECHO Foundation which is dedicated to providing educational opportunities for hearing and hearing-impaired children in grades pre-Kindergarten to sixth. In addition to Echo Horizon, the ECHO Foundation operates the ECHO Center for hearing-impaired children. The ECHO Center provides unique mainstreaming opportunities into regular classes, and strong verbal and auditory support services. Children with impaired hearing comprise ten percent of the Echo Horizon School population.

The school bases much of its educational philosophy on the work of Dr. Madeline Hunter (from Corinne E. Seeds University School at UCLA). Principal Paula Dashiell spent seven years at UES working with Dr. Hunter before coming to Echo Horizon.

The following is the school philosophy:

> "That children learn at varying paces with spurts, jumps, and lulls at different points. Although children are grouped by grades, this is more in terms of social-emotional growth than academic skill or readiness. An individualized approach to instruction is utilized. The strengths and needs of each child are continually assessed by the teachers. Expectations are always clearly stated. Horizon emphasizes developing independence in the child."

Paula Dashiell believes that it is critical for a child's self-esteem that he/she is successful. Children must be presented with challenges that they can face, overcome, and succeed. This fosters an excitement for the love of learning.

The kindergarten curriculum provides experiences and activities that help students learn basic skills in reading, mathematics, science, and social studies. Students learn to function effectively in a group and to become self-directed learners. This means that they will have more of an experiential instruction rather than doing paperwork at a desk.

In grades 1 and 2, students who are intellectually, socially, and physically ready for a more structured and formal learning program undertake basic activities such as reading from books appropriate to their ability level, performing mathematical computations, and writing their own stories.

In grades 3 through 6 these activities are extended to include the study and analysis of children's literature and specific forms and styles of writing. There is also an emphasis on math concepts and applications. Instruction in art, music, computer, and physical education is part of every child's weekly schedule. They also have a wide variety of extracurricular classes.

Most of the graduating students go on to independent schools such as Brentwood, Campbell Hall, Crossroads, Oakwood, Harvard-Westlake, Marlborough, Winwood and Wildwood. A few students choose to go on to local public schools.

HISTORY

The ECHO Foundation was created by parents, educators, and interested community leaders in 1970 with the goal of integrating hearing impaired children into the hearing world by teaching them to listen and to speak. In 1983 the ECHO Foundation established ECHO Horizon School, a main-stream environment in which hearing-impaired children can work and learn alongside hearing peers. The ECHO Board of Trustees oversees the educational, administrative, and financial operation of the school.

AT A GLANCE

APPLICATION DEADLINE	The first 100 applications are accepted by Dec.
UNIFORMS	No
BEFORE/AFTER SCHOOL CARE	Yes
SIX-WEEK SUMMER SCHOOL	Yes
SEE MAP	D on page 285

FLINTRIDGE PREP is situated at the base of the San Gabriel Mountains in the community of La Cañada–Flintridge. It's a wonderful area, the sort of place where you don't have to lock your doors at night. The kind of place where your kids can hop on the 'free' bus and get around on their own without your having to be the chauffeur 24/7. The school is made up of 1950s bungalows and pleasant vine-covered walkways that lead you around the campus with grassy areas and lots of shade. The newer additions resemble a combination of Frank Lloyd-Wright architecture and buildings you would find on the South Bank in London built in the late 70s.

Mission Statement (as taken from school brochure):

> "Flintridge Preparatory School offers a rigorous, moral, and intimate learning environment, nurturing in its students the skills, knowledge, values, and inspiration essential to a rewarding college experience, a lifelong embrace of education, a devotion to community, and a full and responsible life."

In the center of the campus is the Jorgensen Memorial Library equipped with books, periodicals, reference materials, audiovisual equipment, computers, internet access and a complete technology media center. The art studios offer ceramics, painting and drawing. Flintridge Prep's fully equipped photography studio includes professional camera and developing equipment and a darkroom.

The School's cultural/science center includes the Norris Auditorium, the Keck Biology Lab, the Braun Computer Lab and the Murfey Chemistry Lab.

The Randall Performing Arts Center includes classrooms for dance, drama and music, as well as a state-of-the-art performance venue in the Miller Black Box Theatre.

Athletic facilities include: the Olympic size Lowery Swimming Pool, the James Wood Memorial Field, a gymnasium for basketball and volleyball, the Swift Tennis Courts and a well-equipped weight room. The list of the names of benefactors in the generous parent body reads little as, a statement taken from the school brochure: "We strongly hope that parents will contribute to the school. This contribution may take several forms. Parents can support Flintridge Prep by giving to the Annual Fund, or by participating in activities associated with the Mothers' Club or the Fathers' Club."

I must make one observation about the noise from the freeway that passes directly above the swimming pool. It is quite loud. The school could have better thought out the placement of the pool in relation to the freeway overpass. On a positive note, the parking lot has been cleverly built directly underneath the freeway, which provides great shade and protection from the rain.

There's no doubt about it, this is a wonderful school, and one that is going to equip your child for entry into a college or university. Your money will be well spent here. Just look at the curriculum for English and Foreign Language Programs.

English:

    Literature/Composition, 7th grade
    English, 8th Grade
    English I
    English II: composition/American Literature
    English III: Advanced Composition/British Literature (Regular & Honors)
    English IV:

        American Identity
        The Beat Generation
        The City in Literature
        Contemporary Fiction
        Contemporary Latin American Literature
        Imitations of Genius
        Language, Style and Sounds in Modern American Literature
        Language, Style and Sounds in Modern American Poetry
        Literature in Translation (H)
        Literature of Dissent
        Shakespeare (Regular & Honors)
        Short Story
        Writing Fiction in a Modern World

Foreign Language:

    Latin I, II, III/IV, V (AP Lyric Poetry)
    French I, II, III, IV, IV/V (AP Literature & Language †)
    Spanish I, II, III, IV, IV/V (AP Literature & Language †), VI
    (Latin-American Women Writers)

The academic curriculum at Flintridge Prep includes a full complement of regular, honors, and Advanced Placement classes which prepare students for attendance at the most selective colleges in the nation. Prep's graduation requirements exceed the subject requirements for the University of California. A yearly appraisal of each student's composite performance determines if that student will be recommended for placement in honors and Advanced Placement classes.

In grades 10 to 12, there are honors and regular sections in all subject areas. Honors Courses (H) cover extended content and require more work than do standard courses. Advanced

Placement Courses (AP) are available in French, Spanish, Latin, calculus and computer science. All students enrolled in AP classes take the AP exam, the majority of students enrolled in honors classes also sit for AP exams.

HISTORY

Founded in 1933, Flintridge Prep is a nonprofit, independent, co-ed college preparatory day school.

AT A GLANCE

APPLICATION DEADLINE	End of January
OPEN HOUSES	Call school for details
ISEE	Required
UNIFORMS	No
SUMMER SCHOOL	Yes
%AGE OF STUDENTS ADMITTED TO 4-YEAR COLLEGES	100%
SEE MAP	B on page 285

FLINTRIDGE SACRED HEART ACADEMY

Tel: (626) 685-8500 • Fax: (626) 685-8555
440 St. Katherine Dr. • La Cañada-Flintridge, CA 91011
www.fsha.org

PRESIDENT	SISTER CAROLYN MCCORMACK
PRINCIPAL	SISTER CELESTE MARIE BOTELLO
DIRECTOR OF ADMISSIONS	LUANA CASTELLANO
TYPE OF SCHOOL	ALL GIRLS CATHOLIC DAY & BOARDING SCHOOL
GRADES	9 - 12

- ENROLLMENT: 403
- APPLICATION FEES: $125
- REGISTRATION FEE: $1,000
- ACCREDITATIONS: CAIS/WASC/WCEA
- MEMBERSHIPS: ACSA/CAIS/CAPR/CASE/CSEE/NAIS/ NASBP/NASC/ NCEA/NCGS
- TUITION: $17,950-$21,325
- NEW FAMILY FEE: $1,000
- FINANCIAL AID IS AVAILABLE
- MISC. FEES: (APPROX) $1,000

FLINTRIDGE SACRED HEART ACADEMY occupies 41 acres on a hilltop in the city of La Cañada-Flintridge. The views are spectacular overlooking the San Gabriel Valley and the Pasadena Rose Bowl from the crest of the San Rafael hills. Follow the directions carefully as there are many turns and a long steep climb up the hill.   Arriving at the main building and walking up the steps and into the lobby one couldn't help but wonder if it is not in fact a fabulous hotel – well it once was! (See History).

Today the main building provides housing for boarding students and staff, a convent area for the Dominican Sisters, a dining room and administrative offices. My friend Sue and I were given an impromptu tour by the bookkeeper who was more than happy to show us around, even inside one of the girls' dorms. Having once been a hotel, the rooms hardly looked like the ones I slept in as a child, each one with a bathroom en suite! Two or three boarders share a dorm, and there's plenty of room. The dining room is a beautiful hall with high ceilings and wonderful furniture. The menu looked delicious – plenty of choice and variety. On our way out, we were shown a model of the school and its grounds, and it was only then one really got a feeling for just how big the campus was. Our guide pointed out the site where there are plans to build new tennis courts, and talked about how much she loved working for the school. It was obvious she adored it.

Between the main building and the swimming pool lies Senior Lawn, home of the FSHA's graduation ceremony for most of the school's history. It was there we were introduced to two girls who were on their way to their next class. They stopped and chatted with us and gave us an overview of 'a day in the life' . . . it sounded great. They were articulate and extremely amusing, and told us that they were treated with the utmost respect and loved everything about the school. They couldn't think of one negative thing to say about anything. They were especially proud of their math teacher, and boasted about the recent award she had been given and wanted to take us into class with them so we could see what they were talking about. Unfortunately we had to decline. As we walked over to the admissions office to pick up a brochure, we noticed a landmark of the school, the bridge connecting the old campus to the new.

A high school classroom building and an auditorium for the performing arts were built in the 1950s. The Visual and Performing Arts Department produces two theater shows each year, and the fall production usually takes places in November, and the spring production (often a musical) is generally in March. Music students give recitals throughout the year and FSHA's dance students produce a dance concert in late spring. Both perform at Flintridge assemblies, liturgies, and various other functions throughout the year. Art students also have the opportunity to display their work. Through courses and co-curricular activities students are allowed to express abilities different from those found in traditional academic courses. Particular emphasis is placed on the experimental, the interpretive, and the creative in order to enrich students' lives through self-expression, self-awareness or through response to the expression of others.

In 1998, a $9 million science and athletic complex was added to the campus which is quite outstanding – over 26,000 square feet. In addition to the gymnasium and multi-purpose athletic field, the complex includes a sizeable aerobics room and a weight room. There's also a training room with massage tables and whirlpools for the students to use. Flintridge athletes compete in CIF (California Interscholastic Federation) as members of the Mission League. Their teams often reach league and state finals and have achieved numerous championships over the years. Their basketball team is known all over Los Angeles as one of the best. The state-of-the-art science wing, including biology, chemistry, and physics classroom/laboratories, as well as a computer research lab, is located on the second level. This site also provided a space for the Byrnes Amphitheater. The new area, named for an alumnus from the class of 1935, has provided a new location for student gatherings and annual events.

The Academy was recently honored by the United States Department of Education as a Blue Ribbon School of Excellence for its success in meeting National Education Goals through the conditions of effective schooling. These include leadership, teaching environment, curriculum and instruction, student environment, parent and community support, and organizational vitality.

The curriculum includes 70 University of California-approved college-preparatory courses. Following the Academy's mission, their curriculum is intended to prepare students for the next level of education. The program is designed to provide students with effective oral and written communication skills, to teach students to think conceptually, to encourage students to share their artistic skills, to be effective problems solvers, and to help students explore moral, political, social, and economic issues.

The school offers 15 honors and advanced placement courses for more capable students. In addition, it administers a comprehensive English as a Second Language (ESL) program in order to mainstream the international students into the college preparatory curriculum. Here are some of the courses offered:

Advanced Computer Applications; honors English II, AP English IV; Spanish I-IV; Latin I-IV; French I-IV; AP Spanish IV; AP French IV; algebra I; geometry; Honors calculus; advanced algebra I; honors geometry; AP calculus-AB; algebra II; pre-calculus; honors algebra II/trig.; honors pre-calculus; physical education.

The student-teacher ratio is 10:1. Almost 100 percent of the students go on to attend four-year colleges and universities all over the country.

The students have the opportunity to pursue interests, and test and expand their leadership skills in a variety of clubs and organizations such as:

> Alpha Sigma Mu (science club); Ambassadors; Amnesty International; Art Club, California Scholarship Federation, C'est la Vie (French club), Christian Action Movement (CAM), ComedySportz, Junior Statesmen of American, La Vanguardia (Spanish club), Multi-cultural Club, National Honor Society, Students Against Driving Drunk (SADD), Student Alumnae Relations Council (SARC), Saltatrix Dance Company, Theatre Club, Thespian Troupe, Varsity Club and the Young Writers Society.

In addition to curricular demands, students must complete 15 hours of Christian service each year. The Academy's Christian service program seeks to expose students to the responsibility of service as Christians, while helping them discover their own individual gifts and talents.

Approximately 20 percent of the students receive financial aid. Endowment funds and foundation grants support annual need-based tuition aid. Merit-based scholarships are awarded to qualifying incoming freshmen.

From the school brochure:

> "From its opening days, the Academy's college preparatory curriculum has attracted to its resident program international boarding students seeking an education in the United States. Today, approximately two-thirds of the Academy's 90 resident students are international. Now with nearly 400 students, the Academy continues to enroll vibrant, gifted young women who mirror the diversity of cultures, ethnicities, religious affiliations, and socio-economic backgrounds found in southern California. Over the years, this mosaic of students and their families has built a truly global community essential to the 'Flintridge experience.'"

HISTORY

Southern California architect Myron Hunt designed the main buildings of the school as a luxury resort hotel in the 1920s. The resort opened in 1927 as the Flintridge Hotel. It was soon sold to the Biltmore Hotel chain and renamed the Flintridge Biltmore. Unfortunately, the hilltop retreat was deemed too expensive, especially after the onset of the Great Depression in 1929 and was unable to attract more than eight to ten paying guests at one time.

When the resort failed, Archbishop Cantwell contacted the Dominican Sisters of Mission San Jose, who were seeking to open a girls' boarding school in the Los Angeles area. In 1931 they purchased the abandoned resort, including the nine original buildings, hotel furnishings, and surrounding land at an auction for the unbelievably low price of $150,000.00. According to Sister Frances, FSHA's first principal, Mother Dolorosa, Sister Thomasinia and Sister Odelia travelled up the hill to take possession of their new school. They carried with them "only a statue of the Blessed Virgin and a single five-dollar bill." Just two weeks later the school opened for the first day of classes on September 2, 1931 with 200 students enrolled in grades one through twelve.

In the 1930s and 1940s, all students were boarders. It wasn't until the high school building was constructed in 1951 that the Academy began to accept day students. The new high school campus was complete following the construction of the auditorium in 1956. At about the same time, the school began to phase out the elementary grades, and in 1963 the elementary school was closed and the old elementary school building was later sold as a private residence.

Originally governed exclusively by the Dominican Sisters, the school today is a California, non-profit corporation governed by a Board of Directors. It includes both lay and religious leaders who seek advice in the areas of finance, development, and community relations from volunteer committees of alumni, parents, and friends. The Academy's ongoing desire for outstanding faculty and educational facilities is supported by a development program, which seeks voluntary contributions to support the annual and capital needs of the school.

AT A GLANCE

APPLICATION DEADLINE	December through January
OPEN HOUSES	Call school for dates
SCHOOL TOURS	Call school open house dates and tours and for deadlines
UNIFORMS	Yes
SUMMER SCHOOL	Yes
SEE MAP	B on page 285

FOUNTAIN DAY SCHOOL

Tel: 323-654-8958 • Fax: 323-654-5214
1128 N. Orange Grove Avenue • West Hollywood CA 90046
www.fountaindayschool.com

HEAD OF SCHOOL	MARY NOUSAKAJIAN
GENERAL MANAGER	ANDREW RAKOS
TYPE OF SCHOOL	CO-ED DAY SCHOOL
GRADES	PRE-K

- ENROLLMENT: 118
- NEW FAMILY FEE: $650
- BOOKS: $125-$450

- APPLICATION FEE: $65
- TUITION: $1,250 MONTHLY
- FINANCIAL AID IS AVAILABLE

As you enter the FOUNTAIN DAY SCHOOL, you walk past a "peace pole." There are three thousand of these around the world, and Fountain Day has number one. There is a definite kindred spirit to the environment. "Mr. Andrew," my utterly charming tour guide (and the school's general manager), teachers and administrators (and me!) are addressed as Miss or Mister, and your first name to continue the family type feel and relationship. This gem of a school was inspiring. That is how I knew I had stumbled upon something truly special, and by the time I completed the tour, I was excited and energized, and wanted to attend the school myself!

The campus itself is impressive. They are constantly improving and evolving as a campus and community. There is a pool for swimming lessons (summertime only), a science yard, a completely revamped playground, and a brand new parking lot, with a turn-around for parents to drop-off/pick-up their children. This is not a traditional drop-off, the school doesn't really encourage just dropping your child at school, but creating the transition into the school day with them when you are 'leaving' them at school. "We guide them into the things that make the family stronger and united", says Mr. Andrew. Fountain Day school really services the working parent, and understands that need for flexibility and support.

The curriculum includes yoga on Wednesdays, dance on Thursdays and exotic animals that come to visit! They also have the latest media technology, including computers and projectors. There are also two full time cleaning staff, two full service kitchens, and Whole Foods provides the all organic food and snacks! Though the school is non-denominational, they pray at lunchtime. Children eagerly greeted me and proudly showed me what they were working on. There is a definite confidence and full-self expression in this huge extended "family." As I completed my tour, I was given a "Kitchen Keepsakes" from the Fountain Day Family cookbook, which parents receive on their tour! Family recipes, I'm sure!

As of fall 2008, Fountain Day only goes through kindergarten. There was an increasing demand for preschool by parents and Fountain Day wanted to meet that need.

If you're looking for a fabulous school, this is it!

HISTORY

Fountain Day School was founded in 1957 by Ms. Evangeline Brooks. It began as a pre-school for working families and single mothers who found themselves in need of childcare. Ms. Brooks was a big-hearted woman who cared for children as if they were her own. The original building included her personal apartments upstairs. Often in those days, Ms. Brooks would end up babysitting children late into the night.

48 years later the school had a student population of 118 students. In the fall of 2008, Fountain Day went back to being a preschool also offering a Kindergarten program. Fountain Day School is now operated by her daughters Ms. Mary and Ms. Jane.

AT A GLANCE

APPLICATION DEADLINE	Preadmission is in December
SCHOOL TOURS	Tours provided, usually on Tuesdays, call first
UNIFORMS	Yes
BEFORE AND AFTER SCHOOL CARE	Available 7:30am-6pm and inclusive in tuition
SEE MAP	C on page 285

FRIENDS WESTERN SCHOOL

Tel/Fax (626) 793-2727
524 East Orange Grove Blvd. • Pasadena, CA 91104
www.friendswesternschool.org

HEAD OF SCHOOL	PETER DAY
TYPE OF SCHOOL	CO-EDUCATIONAL DAY SCHOOL
GRADES	K – 5

- ENROLLMENT: 26
- ACCREDITATION: NONE
- MATERIAL FEE $60
- MEMBERSHIP: FCE

- TUITION: $8,000
- APPLICATION FEE: $50
- YEARLY REGISTRATION FEE: $630
- FINANCIAL AID IS AVAILABLE

Not many schools can boast that their enrollment tripled in just one year, but FRIENDS WESTERN SCHOOL did just that. This very special Quaker school is now in its' seventh year with more than 26 students. It really feels like a school now. Peter Day, the head of the school tells me, "As we add new students, it is important us to maintain diversity in many aspects. Economic diversity is very important to our school. Our scholarship students are among our best and brightest, and we hope to be able to accept children based on who they are, how they learn, and their magnificent gifts, instead of whether or not their parents can afford the tuition."

The school is located on the grounds of the Orange Grove Friends Meeting house in Pasadena. The two-story building that serves as the school is surrounded by trees and a wonderful playground full of climbing equipment and different areas to play in. Upstairs in the schoolroom I was delighted to see how well organized it was. There are books galore, a brand new internet-ready computer, brightly painted walls, and a very well designed area for the students to study in - there's even a built-in low-cushioned area, where kids may relax.

Who are Quakers?
George Fox founded the Religious Society of Friends 400 years ago in England. The most fundamental belief of Quakerism is that there is a part of God within everyone. There is an Inner Light within us that will guide us if we listen to it. Although Friends have no formal creed, out of experience they have developed 'testimonies:'

> "The Peace testimony (Harmony) goes far beyond the simple idea that war is wrong. It is a commitment to try to solve conflicts without violence or threats. The testimony of Simplicity is a commitment not to live beyond their needs. This doesn't mean that they live spartan and monastic lives. Friends go to movies, have VCRs, and enjoy a good meal like the rest of us but feel that living a life of excess and conspicuous consumption gets in the way of the true joys of life. Simplicity also applies to speech and behavior. It means saying what they mean, being honest and fair, and acting in moder-

ation.

Equality is the oldest of Friends' testimonies and is the idea that all people are equal in God's eyes. It has led to a conscious effort to eliminate all words and behavior that arise from distinctions such as class, race, sex, or social status. Equality also means that for nearly 400 years women and men have shared in the leadership in Quakerism and from the beginning, Friends educated girls as well as boys."

Friends have a long and respected tradition of educating children to approach problems with knowledge and creativity, and to treat their fellow humans with respect and compassion, while maintaining high academic standards.

There is a daily silent worship held in the beautiful Victorian Meeting House that allows the children to begin the school day with a few moments of centering and reflection. Multi-age grouping allows the children to advance at their own pace in each academic subject. Physical education focuses on developing physical intelligence rather than solely learning rules for games. Students may participate in dance, gymnastics, martial arts, or other rigorous activities. Music is taught three times a week using percussion instruments.

During a typical day there will be a central theme: growth, point of view, character, and turning points. For example, if the theme were growth, the children might plan and build a flower box, work in the garden, measure and graph how high their flowers have grown, pretend to be a plant, sing a growing song or read a book together about gardens. They might write about their observations on growth, add things like charting their heights and foot sizes and observe the changes. Students might talk about how characters in a story grow, or perhaps create a computer model projecting the growth of a community.

In seventh grade, the students will serve in the community, as their social studies class. They will be set up in intern-like situations with time to work in the community and to discuss their services back in the classroom with their classmates. This will allow them to compare their theories of society to their actual experience.

As Robin explained it: "Because Friends Western School is a small school, we can give your child personal attention and teach in the way your child learns best. We design our instruction to balance skills and challenges so that each student experiences success. Each person in our learning community is treated with respect and compassion. We will do our best to discover and develop your child's unique intelligence. We believe that all children have unique talents. What gift does your child have?"

There are no hidden extra fees at this school, so families are expected to participate in at least one annual fundraising event per year.

Robin told me that parents interested in helping to start a middle school for next year can call her.

Recent additions are a new classroom for the younger students, and a weekly ceramics class taught by a parent, a ceramist herself. Their Outdoor Education classes are also taught by a parent, a geologist who is tired of teaching college students. She includes botany, geology, ornithology, maps and orienteering as well as useful skills such as planning what to wear according to the weather. If you are currently home schooling your child, Friends Western School is interested in including those children in selected instruction and activities. This allows these children some socialization and group learning, which are often difficult to incorporate at a home school.

While Quakerism is in the liberal Christian tradition, there are Friends who also draw from other faiths and practices. Families of all faiths are welcome among Friends.

Most of the children are gifted in one way or another, and three of them have identified learning disabilities. Several children are children of color or multiracial. One girl has two moms. Having been to many of these meetings with my own children, I would suggest prospective students and their families attend a Meeting for Worship at the Orange Grove Meeting in

HISTORY

The school was founded in 2002 by Robin Durant who had been an educator for 14 years, teaching in the Alhambra and Pasadena school districts.. In addition, Ms. Durant had her multiple subjects teaching credential through Pacific Oaks College, and a specialist credential from CSULA. She has worked in both public and non-public settings, and has been a Quaker all her life. In 2008, Peter Day became head of school.

AT A GLANCE

APPLICATION DEADLINE	Check with the school in the fall
OPEN HOUSES	Monday through Thursday after 3pm
AFTER SCHOOL CARE	Yes
UNIFORMS	No
SEE MAP	B on page 285

GLENDALE MONTESSORI

Tel: (818) 240-9415 • Fax (818) 240-8089
413 W. Doran • Glendale, CA 91203

HEAD OF SCHOOL	ARNOLDA C. UTRECHT
PRINCIPAL	GENA VENARDI
TYPE OF SCHOOL	CO-EDUCATIONAL DAY SCHOOL
GRADES	PRE - 2

- ENROLLMENT: 50
- ACCREDITATION: AMS/NCME
- MEMBERSHIPS: AMI/AMS/NCME
- FINANCIAL AID IS NOT AVAILABLE

- TUITION: $900/MONTH
- APPLICATION FEE: $200
- NEW FAMILY FEE: NONE

GLENDALE MONTESSORI is such a wonderful little gem that I am tempted to keep its where-abouts a secret. At first glance, the school appears to have an urban setting, with a paved front yard and three classroom buildings grouped around a common courtyard. However, if you look behind the caretaker's bungalow in the adjoining lot, you'll discover that the entire space has been converted into a shaded play-yard with several climbing structures and loads of (dust-free) sand to romp in. The children at GMS are blessed, and here's why. They have outstanding teachers, many of whom have been with the school for over ten years. The class-room environments are cooperative, peaceful, clean, and well-stocked with materials that are state-of-the-art. At GMS one thing is very clear: All of the school's resources go back to the students with the goal of providing the best education possible. The children are the focus. The only down-side to GMS is that it stops at second grade, and although many parents have tried to convince Mrs. Utrecht to expand, she feels that the school is just fine the way it is. She runs the school with an understated grace, in a reserved but always approachable man-ner.

Mercifully absent is the non-stop plea for funds over and above tuition that is standard issue at some private schools in Los Angeles. GMS does not do fundraising. It does not heckle par-ents to put in X amount of volunteer hours per semester, although it is open to parents par-ticipation in special events.

There are two fully-accredited teachers in each classroom, which translates to a 1:12 teacher to student ratio. All teachers have completed special Montessori training in addition to their regular credentials. There are four multi-age group classrooms with students from age 3 to 6 representing pre through Kindergarten work. The largest classroom is divided in half to house the first/second grade program. (One mother with a highly gifted child loved this program so much that she didn't want him to leave after second grade. The first/second grade teachers designed a program for the child to continue at GMS for third grade!)

The beauty of the Montessori program is that it allows children to work at their own pace and developmental level. There is no need to rush a child who is not ready to grasp certain concepts, or to hold back a gifted child who is ready to fly past his age appropriate work.

The method of teaching at GMS is sensorial as well as concrete. When a child gets to the point where he/she is writing numbers for example, that final step represents many preliminary ones such as writing the number in sand or tracing a sandpaper number with his finger.

There are specialist teachers for Spanish and music. Children aged 6 and up are given a recorder and meet for instruction once a week. Each Halloween the whole school dons costumes for a parade around the block (chaperoned by teachers and parents), an event enjoyed by all.

The attending families represent a wonderful mixture of every culture present in Los Angeles. Once each spring the school holds a luncheon inviting the students to bring a favorite or traditional family dish. The banquet table goes on for miles and is filled with the most extraordinary and delicious food. It is not only an opportunity for the children to set all the tables and play host to their families, but a great chance for parents to visit, break bread, and get a sense of the school community.

HISTORY

Glendale Montessori was opened in 1971 by Arnolda C. Utrecht, and expanded in 1989 to include the bungalow (now the caretakers' cottage) and adjoining property.

AT A GLANCE

APPLICATION DEADLINE	March
PROSPECTIVE PARENT ONE HOUR TOURS	September-June, call school to schedule
UNIFORMS	No
AFTER SCHOOL CARE	No
SEE MAP	B on page 285

GLENDALE MONTESSORI ELEMENTARY SCHOOL, INC.

Tel: (818) 243-5172
1212 N. Pacific Avenue • Glendale, CA 91202
www.glendalemontessorielementaryschool.com

HEAD OF SCHOOL	NINA O'BRIAN
TYPE OF SCHOOL	CO-EDUCATIONAL DAY SCHOOL
GRADES	K - 6

- ENROLLMENT: 52
- BOOKS/MATERIALS: $300
- INSURANCE FEE: $300

- TUITION: $950 MONTHLY
- MEMBERSHIPS: NCME
- FINANCIAL AID IS NOT AVAILABLE

GLENDALE MONTESSORI ELEMENTARY SCHOOL is located on Pacific Avenue about a half-mile north of the 134 Freeway. Although it shares a name with the Montessori on Doran Drive, it is a separately run, separately owned school.

The school rents its building from Temple Sinai, which occupies the lot next door and shares a parking lot with the school. There are three large classrooms, each housing combination classes of first/second, third/fourth, and fifth/sixth. There is also an art/music room, a basketball court, volleyball area, and a school garden.

The strong suit of this school is its teachers. They are passionate and deeply involved. The curriculum is both traditional and experiential, and the atmosphere is of a closely knit family community. At the helm of this community is director Nina o'er, a sharp, easy- going woman with a great love for the school, which she runs with the teachers.

The focus at GME is on the quality of education. For parents who cringe at the emphasis on fundraising and the materialism of many private schools, GME is a breath of fresh air. Although this is a basic campus, the school has all it needs to offer students a great education. the scores of its recent sixth grade graduates were on a par with ninth grade test levels.

I asked one mother who is sending her son to the school this fall if it was an issue to her that GME was not as fancy as the private school from which he was transferring. She answered:

"Not at all. Our son gets enough exposure to excessive living because my husband is in the entertainment industry. We want to do all we can to keep my son's values in the right place. What is important to us is the quality of education that he's actually getting, not what it looks like he's getting."

The students work as a group, as well as independently at their own level, and often work a grade level ahead if they need more of a challenge. The student/teacher ratio is 12:1, which gives each student the individual attention he/she needs. The school takes many field trips with parents going along as drivers and chaperones. A couple of years ago students did some of their own fundraising to finance a school trip to Washington.

The school is deeply committed to the community around it, and makes good use of the parks and public libraries that are within walking distance of the school. Every Friday, for example, the children have their lunch at the local park and afterwards play games on its acres of grassy lawns.

There are specialty teachers for art, music, Spanish and P.E. The school has after school classes in art and provides an after school daycare program.

Philosophy of the Teachers at GME

1. The total child must always be considered: home environment, school environment, body, mind, spirit – physically, mentally, emotionally, socially, and academically.
2. We have chosen to be a Montessori school rather than a traditional school. Therefore, our classes will be run as Montessori classes rather than traditional classes.
3. We choose to be a more academically-oriented Montessori school within the framework of what constitutes 'Montessori.' However, we will never sacrifice the spirit of the student for acquisition of academic ability.
4. We guide students in areas of behavior and attitudes, and recognize that these students are not our children, but come with their own personalities, likes, dislikes and values.
5. The school has a small list of rules established for the safety and security of all. Additional rules set up within the classroom pertaining to daily routines will be kept to a minimum, as we feel that excessive rules lead to dependence, not independence. We encourage students to learn to think for themselves and to solve problems in original and creative ways.
6. Students are encouraged to be assertive and to express their disapproval in a respectful way. We try to create a safe atmosphere where students are listened to and feel free to express their own view points.
7. Teachers encourage and inspire students to do not only the minimum, but also their best. Teachers do not coerce or attempt to break a student's spirit.
8. All levels of learning will be considered. Written reports and other written assignments are essential, but are not the only products of learning.
9. Basic facts in arithmetic will be presented, practiced, and given due attention in all classes; testing in various forms and without stress will be done. Ultimate accountability will occur at the beginning of the fourth grade age/ grade level. Parents may be asked to work on basic facts at home.
10. We will teach accountability gradually and in small doses at first. Students will be taught what it means as well as what their responsibilities are.

Discipline Policy

Parents will be informed of any negative and harmful behavior observed in their child's interactions with others and will be expected to cooperate in eliminating that behavior within a definite period of time. We will ask for the parents' input regarding ways to solve the problem. If the behavior isn't changed within the defined period of time, then the student will be asked to withdraw from the school.

Parents will be informed when students are falling behind in their work. We will meet with parents to discuss what can be done to solve this problem, both at school and at home. Parents will be asked to submit their preference for dealing with the situation in writing. The plan will then be put into action at home and at school.

HISTORY

Glendale Montessori Elementary School was opened in 1976 by Arnolda C. Utrecht. Mrs. Utrecht sold the school in 1986 to its current director Nina O'Brian, who had been a teacher at the school from its early days.

AT A GLANCE

APPLICATION DEADLINE	Open enrollment
OPEN HOUSES	Call school for dates
SCHOOL TOURS	On an as-needed basis
UNIFORMS	No
AFTER SCHOOL CARE AND ENRICHMENT CLASSES	Yes
SEE MAP	B on page 285

THE GOODEN SCHOOL

Tel: (626) 355-2410 • Fax: (626) 355-4212
192 N. Baldwin Avenue • Sierra Madre, CA 91204
www.gooden.org

HEADS OF SCHOOL	PATRICIA PATANO
DIRECTOR OF ADMISSIONS	MARIANNE RYAN
TYPE OF SCHOOL	CO-ED DAY SCHOOL
GRADES	K - 8

- ENROLLMENT: 175
- ACCREDITATION: CAIS/NAES
- MEMBERSHIPS: ERB/LACS
- NEW FAMILY FEE: $200
- LIMITED FINANCIAL AID IS AVAILABLE

- TUITION:
  K-5: $11,000
  6-8: $11,400
- APPLICATION FEE: $75
- YEARLY REGISTRATION FEE: $650

The GOODEN SCHOOL has such a quaint, small-town feeling to it that you'd believe you were on a movie set. This is an Episcopal school where the children attend regular chapel services held in a beautiful, old stone church across the street.

This is not a place where you'll find huge group tours alongside parents wielding cellular phones, it is more personal and applicant-specific than the larger schools. The staff was warm, friendly and a little bit curious about what a parent from Hollywood was doing wandering around their quiet little village (a southern California version of "Mayberry RFD").

The curriculum is traditional: reading, writing, math and social studies. The teacher to student ratio is 1:18 in elementary and 1:14 in grades 6 to 8. Teachers are described as having college degrees with related experiences.

Here is the Gooden Philosophy taken from the school literature:

"The educational program is built on high standards of academic excellence in a caring, Christian environment. Classes are small, which allows each child to receive individual attention. This warm, supportive atmosphere fosters a special relationship between student and teacher.

Gooden is affiliated with the Episcopal Church, and our principles and standards of behavior reflect a Christian outlook. While participation in chapel services is required, membership in the Episcopal Church is not expected. Children of many faiths and backgrounds attend the school."

There is an on-site library with 2,500 plus volumes, a computer lab with seven machines, and one computer in each classroom. The curriculum is complimented by classes in art, music, and physical education. Spanish is taught in grades 1 to 5 and offered as an elective (as is Latin) in grades 6 to 8. Field trips are scheduled for all grades.

Parent participation is encouraged in the yearly events, (the annual Holiday Party, Shrove Tuesday Pancake Supper and the Barn Sale) as well as in the annual giving campaign, which raises funds for enrichment programs at the school.

As far as life after junior high, Gooden states that, "Most graduates are accepted at their first choice college preparatory high school." This is an area always worth closer inspection at any school that ends at sixth or eighth grade. Choose a potential high school and ask, "How many of your students applied here last year, and how many of those applicants were accepted?"

It may seem like a long way off, but you don't want to be stuck later on if the elementary school you choose for your child does not sufficiently prepare him/her for senior grades.

HISTORY

The Gooden School was established by The Reverend and Mrs. Spencer P. Edwards Jr. It bears the name of the Right Reverend Robert B. Gooden, a longtime Episcopal Bishop. Bishop Gooden served as Headmaster of Harvard School for many years, and in that role was considered the patron of Episcopal Schools in Southern California. He maintained a life-long interest and involvement in education and remained active in affairs of this diocese throughout his life. The Bishop dedicated The Gooden School in 1975 in his 101st year.

AT A GLANCE

APPLICATION DEADLINE	January 30
OPEN HOUSES	11/15 & 1/11 from 1-3:30 p.m.
SCHOOL TOURS/ORIENTATION	Call Marianne Ryan at extension 23
UNIFORMS	Yes
BEFORE AND AFTER SCHOOL CARE	$5 an hour
SEE MAP	B on page 285

HARVARD-WESTLAKE

Middle School:
700 N. Faring Road • Los Angeles, CA 90077
(310) 274-7281 • Fax: (310) 288-3331

Upper School:
3700 Coldwater Canyon• North Hollywood, CA 91604
(818) 980-6692• Fax: (818) 487-6624

www.hw.com

HEAD OF SCHOOL	THOMAS C. HUDNUT
DIRECTOR OF ADMISSIONS	ELIZABETH GREGORY
TYPE OF SCHOOL	CO-ED COLLEGE PREP DAY SCHOOL
GRADES	7 - 12

- ENROLLMENT: 1,550
- ACCREDITATION: WASC
- NEW STUDENT FEE: $1,500
- MEMBERSHIPS: CAIS/CSEE/NAES/NAIS/WASC
- TUITION: $25,000
- APPLICATION FEE: $125
- FINANCIAL AID IS AVAILABLE

In case you are new in town, HARVARD-WESTLAKE is considered to be one of the top private schools in Los Angeles. What used to be the Hollywood Country Club back in 1937 is now home for Harvard Westlake's upper school, which occupies 22 acres in North Hollywood's Coldwater Canyon and it's gorgeous. The middle school is comfortably nestled close by in Bel Air, and there are big plans to expand it.

Competition to get into this school is tough since there are many more applicants than there are spaces. The program at this school is clearly designed for students who are highly motivated and independent learners. Your child needs to have extremely good study habits in order to survive here. The Harvard-Westlake experience is not for everyone. I have known some very able students drop out and leave because the pressure was simply too much. But then there are the others who stay and blossom into future world leaders!

The Admissions process is rigorous but well thought out. If your child excels, for example in soccer, then the school might arrange that he or she be interviewed by the soccer coach. Don't feel left out, you will have your own interview too!

The school will hold a number of 'Parent Coffees' for applicant parents. This is where you are handed the curriculum guide which is almost as thick as this book and will become your favorite bedtime reading! These informal gatherings are where you hear the Director of Admissions, and the Headmaster speak, and it's here that you can ask questions. There is a sibling and legacy policy, but admission is not automatic.

There are 211 faculty members, all degreed, and the facilities are amazing. There are eight academic halls, two lecture halls, two libraries, three gymnasiums, football/soccer fields, one track and one auditoriums. Besides having two orchestra rooms, there are Instrumental rehearsal studios, two electronic music studios and additional fully-equipped MIDI stations, and music practice rooms. Two art centers boast ceramic studios, two photography labs. Computer lab are available throughout both campuses. A seven lane Olympic-size swimming pool is a further enhancement.

Harvard-Westlake has its fair share of celebrity families but it also strives to include a student/parent body which is diverse, socio-economically, culturally and geographically. Harvard-Westlake parents are told that the tuition doesn't cover all of the costs. Parents give what they can, and if you look at the school's annual report, you will see a long list of donors. Some give a few hundred a year while others tens of thousands.

Middle school students are required to take three years of English, foreign language, history/social science, science, math, computer science, P.E., as well as human development, performing arts, visual arts and communications courses. Emphasis is placed on the Classics. Seventh graders take an introduction to language course and can choose from Latin, Russian, French or Spanish.

Sports is big at Harvard-Westlake, and competition is fierce. In addition to interscholastic sports in the traditional teams, there are other sports offered such as: Jiu Jitsu, fencing, equestrian team, aerobics and dance production. Ninth graders are encouraged to choose a sport very carefully since trying-out'for a team does not guarantee a place and they should have another P.E. class picked out as a backup.

All middle school students must participate in community service (12 hours a year), and there's a magazine called Reach which the students publish themselves.

The upper school students are required to complete three years of English, two years of history/social studies, two years of math (though three is recommended), and two years of laboratory sciences. a foreign language is studied up to level III, or two years of modern language and two years of Latin may be substituted. Students take two semesters of visual and/or performing arts in addition to five trimesters of physical education. For good measure, students do three years of community service, a semester of social service and health and human development.

Be warned that homework is given to the tune of two to three hours per night for Grades 7 and 8 and count on three to four hours for grades 9 through 12.

If your child shows an aptitude for the sciences, then you're in the right place. The Munger Science Building is choc-a-block full of the most sophisticated equipment, which includes a scanning electron microscope, an infrared, ultra violet and visible light spectrometer, as well as a gas chromatograph and a NMR spectron. Students can study Oceanographic Biology, enroll in a SCUBA certification (NAUI) program, while learning the physics, chemistry and geology of the oceans. Meanwhile back in the math department, once students have completed their basic math courses, there are advanced level classes offered in calculus, linear algebra and math competition.

The Performing Arts Department is an integral part of the program with courses given in theatre and drama. Your child might be happier 'behind the scenes' you say – no problem, there's a course entitled 'Technical Theater'. With a full-time set designer, part-time box office manager and professional level lighting, your child's school theater production can be quite the night out!

The music department offers a vast number of classes. The music room is home to rows of cellos and just about every other string instrument you can think of as well as five kinds of drums, horns and a piano. Students really enjoy this department and meet there daily to play and record all styles of music.

HISTORY

In 1989, Harvard, a boys' school founded in 1900 as a Military Academy, and Westlake, a girls' school founded in 1904 as a college preparatory school merged and Harvard-Westlake was born. The school's present headmaster, Thomas C. Hudnut has been with the school since 1987. Under his leadership the Munger Science Center was completed and is considered to be one of the most sophisticated science centers at any level.

AT A GLANCE

APPLICATION DEADLINE	January 22
OPEN HOUSES & TOURS	Call school for dates
ISEE	Yes
UNIFORMS	No
SUMMER SCHOOL	Yes
BUSING	Yes
SEE MAP	D on page 285

HIGH POINT ACADEMY

Tel: (626) 798-8989 • Fax: (626) 798-8751
1720 Kinneloa Canyon Road • Pasadena, CA 91107
www.highpointacademy.org

HEAD OF SCHOOL	JOHN T. HIGGINS
DIRECTOR OF ADMISSIONS	MARLYENE E. SCHWARTZ
TYPE OF SCHOOL	CO-ED DAY SCHOOL
GRADES	K - 8

- ENROLLMENT: 350
- ACCREDITATION: CAIS/WASC
- MEMBERSHIPS: ERB/CAIS/NAIS/WASC
- FINANCIAL AID IS NOT AVAILABLE

- TUITION: $10,500
- APPLICATION FEE: $90
- STUDENT BODY FEE: $750

HIGH POINT ACADEMY is located in northeast Pasadena where it borders Altadena at the base of the foothills. The main building has an outside balcony walkway for access to the upper classes. There is a spaciousness to the surrounding land, a feeling of being in the high desert. Huge eucalyptus and pine trees shade the two outside play yards and basketball courts, and down below is a well-groomed soccer field.

The school's facilities include twenty classrooms, two play areas, P.E. locker rooms, a football/soccer field, a computer room, and a library. In the last seven years all of the classrooms and the school office have been enlarged and/or re-modeled. A state-of- the-art science lab and an art/music room have also been added as well as a new arena-type seating area to the athletic field.

Kindergarten observation takes place by appointment, and parents shuttle between the two classes to watch quietly while the teacher goes through the normal schedule. This is a good time to see the 'Carden Method' of teaching in action. The teachers in kindergarten through third grade are trained in the method first developed by Mae Carden in 1934. Simply stated, the Carden Method is a phonic based method of teaching reading. A simple example:

> a + = a and another vowel says "a" as in gate
> a   = a alone says "a" as in mat

These are called vowel controls and help the children learn to decode the words for reading. During the information meeting, the teacher will talk about Carden phonics and answer parents' questions. Children in third grade are transitioned into more traditional phonics and dictionary markings.

The school's philosophy is:

> "High Point Academy strives to awaken in each child the joy of learning and to educate by emphasizing the acquisition of basic skills to master all subjects. The rigorous acad-

emic curriculum stresses command of both the written and oral language and mathematical concepts as tools for analytical thinking. The school provides a safe and nurturing environment which enables the child to flourish academically, emotionally, morally, socially, and physically. Through careful fiscal responsibility and resource management, High Point Academy seeks to make this quality education economically accessible to as many families as possible. With faculty and family support, the school's program develops in our students the ability and desire to pursue and organize knowledge throughout a lifetime."

The Kindergarten curriculum includes: manuscript printing, beginning reading (phonetic approach), vocabulary, high frequency sightwords, learning to tell time, addition, subtraction and counting, identifying coins, foundations for spelling phonetically, daily physical education (every day), music, computers, library, art and French twice per week.

High Point is a structured, traditional academic school. There are specialists in art, music, computer, library, French and Spanish. Each year there are drama productions in kindergarten through third grade. The school often uses the church facility across the street for events such as plays and assemblies.

I was very impressed with the website. It is easy to navigate and has so much information for the children to use as a research tool.

High Point's primary and elementary program is designed to give students a well-balanced academic schedule for core subjects while also preparing them for the challenges of junior high and high school. The junior high program has a strong academic emphasis that offers students a comfortable transition to high school.

In the the special curricular offerings students receive a variety of enrichment programs each week. All students in kindergarten through eighth grade have a daily physical education class. They also have (on a rotating basis) art, music, computers, and library time. Students in kindergarten through fifth grade have French twice a week, while sixth grade students can choose either Spanish or French. For a nominal fee, band is offered once a week after school to interested students, as well as science and chess classes.

Students in grades 7 and 8 can participate in an after-school sports program. They also take either French or Spanish daily. High Point belongs to the prep league which offers students an opportunity to compete in a variety of major and minor sports.

High Point Academy has 26 full-time and three part-time teachers, three extended care personnel and a librarian. Forty percent of the staff hold M.A. or M.S. degrees. All other members hold either B.A. or B.S. degrees, with many also holding California teaching credentials.

Dollar for dollar, this school offers good value. This is due to sound fiscal management and a board policy that tuition covers all operating costs.

HISTORY

High Point Academy is an independent day school for boys and girls grades K-8 founded in 1965. It is located in northeast Pasadena. Students come from Pasadena, Arcadia, Sierra Madre, Monrovia, Altadena, and other neighboring communities in the San Gabriel Valley. The school has a non-discriminatory admissions policy.

AT A GLANCE

APPLICATION DEADLINE	K: 12/17, grades 1-8: 1/9. All prospective parents are encouraged to attend an information session held either in the fall or in January. A classroom visitation day without your child before mid-January is strongly encouraged.
	Yes
UNIFORMS	
AFTER SCHOOL CARE	Yes until 6:00 pm
4 WEEKS SUMMER SCHOOL	Yes
	B on page 285
SEE MAP	

THE HOLLYWOOD SCHOOL HOUSE

Tel: (323) 465-1320 • Fax: (323) 465-1720
1248 N. Highland Avenue • Hollywood, CA 90038
www.hollywoodschoolhouse.org

HEAD OF SCHOOL	STEPHEN BLOODWORTH
ADMISSION DIRECTOR	ROBIN MCALPINE
TYPE OF SCHOOL	CO-EDUCATIONAL DAY SCHOOL
GRADES	PRE - 8

- ENROLLMENT: 255
- ACCREDITATION: WASC
- EXTENDED CHILDCARE AS NEEDED
- MEMBERSHIPS: ISAMA/ERB, NAEYC
- ENROLLMENT FEE: $1,000
- APPLICATION FEE: $75
- FINANCIAL AID IS AVAILABLE

- TUITION:
  PRE: $11,361
  K-4: $12,340
  5-8: $12,629
- NEW FAMILY FEE: $1,000
- TEXTBOOKS: (6-8) $400
- SPECIAL PROJECTS FEE: $250

The HOLLYWOOD SCHOOL HOUSE, formerly The Hollywood Little Red School House, is situated on Highland Avenue near Fountain. From the outside, it looks exactly like its old name, a very quaint, very small, and very red school house, but when you enter the campus you realize why they changed the name. It has grown considerably over the years. The campus extends back an entire city block and is over half a city block in width. It also has its own 35 foot pool. When you arrive at the front desk, you must sign in before they buzz you into the main school through a locked door. Once in the school, you realize how deceiving the front of the building is...it goes on and on.

There are four separate buildings: Building I houses the preschoolers and the administration offices. Building II is the home of junior kindergarten and the kindergartners; Building III accomodates the elementary and middle school grades. Building IV contains a very well stocked library, a dance studio, an up to date computer lab, and classrooms for third-and fourth-graders.

I have been told by a number of people whose children attend the school that, if there is trouble out on the streets, they send their security people out to deal with it! I felt incredibly safe every time I went to pick up my neighbor's children. They have a state-of-the-art security system installed, and there is a heavy presence of staff out on the playground at all times. In fact, I saw a young boy sitting alone one day, and it wasn't long before one of the staff was right there beside him asking if everything was okay. It was reassuring to see that sort of concern. The child jumped right back up and began playing shortly after.

There is a delightful preschool playground filled with playhouses and climbing equipment, surrounded by flowers and plants. The courtyard playground has plenty of shade while the back-gate playground is a large area in which the kids play basketball. Every time I have visited the school, I have been delighted to see the level of interaction between child and teacher. The kids really do seem to be very happy here – lots of smiling faces.

The teachers at Hollywood Schoolhouse bring a variety of experience and educational specialities to the program. They meet all state requirements and have further training in Early Childhood Education. In addition, the staff's continuing education is assured through in-service training, college courses, workshops, and professional conferences.

From the school brochure:
"The mission of the Hollywood Schoolhouse is to attend to the intellectual, psychological, social, and physical needs of the students so that they will become responsible, literate, thinking, contributing citizens who are technologically prepared for the twenty-first century. The school environment provides the warmth and care that nurtures a child's self-esteem and positive self-image. The school has developed a program that ensures an opportunity for individualized academics, while fostering creative learning through a fine arts curriculum. The school recognizes that each individual possesses special characteristics and talents. Our commitment to individualized growth is reflected in our small class size. Success at the Hollywood Schoolhouse is measured by the ability to confront new situations with confidence, assess information creatively and analytically, and act on that information intelligently.

We believe that:

- All students can succeed academically when given the opportunity to learn in a balanced program which includes directed/undirected, individual, and cooperative activities.
- Students should be taught environmental awareness, including a basic knowledge of and respect for all life.
- Students should be life-long learners who are encouraged to strive for personal excellence.
- School is an integral part of the community, and everyone (parents, teachers, children, and administrators) must work together to build a strong, caring, and stimulating community environment.
- Change is positive and new ideas and experiences provide opportunities for growth and creative thought.
- Diversity is a strength and by enhancing each student's self-esteem, all students will achieve their highest potential.
- Instruction should be culturally responsive, free of bias, and compatible with the values of students' own cultures.
- All students possess multiple intelligence and should be taught strategies to enhance their strengths and compensate for their weaknesses.
- All students must develop skills that will prepare them to meet the future and allow them to function in a technologically changing society.
- Students learn best from hands-on, child-centered, curricular experiences that encourage them to explore their world creatively and analytically.
- Students learn best from passionate and enthusiastic teachers.
- All students should be guided into becoming self-determined citizens who do what they believe is right and are able to make responsible choices."

The elementary and middle school offers the following academic subjects:

Language Arts: reading, vocabulary building, comprehension and rate building, creative writing, oral language, grammar, spelling, dictionary skills, listening skills development and literature.

Mathematics: concepts, computation, problem solving, graphs and tables, practical application.

Science: experimentation, concepts and data collection, reporting and practical application of natural, earth and life sciences, physics and chemistry.

Social Studies: historical concepts and patterns, current events, understanding maps and using maps, critical thinking skills, reporting and practical application, multi-cultural studies.

Library - The students visit the library at least once a week. The library also has after-school reading and writing programs, and mentorship programs.

Computers - The commitment to state-of-the-art technology includes networked computers with color printers in every classroom. The world wide web and interactive-tele-learning is accessible. They also have a mobile computer lab featuring "alphasmarts."

Fine Arts: art, dance, music, drama.

Spanish and Physical Education - Part of the regular weekly curriculum, swimming is a part of P.E. during warm weather months. Classes are taught by specialists.

Once a parent has visited the school and filled out an application, his/her child may be invited to spend time at the school. The visit gives your child the opportunity to interact with the teachers and students, and experience the school day first-hand. Using standardized assessment tools, an individual evaluation of the student's current academic skill level, plus social, verbal, and physical skills, are all carefully noted and assessed.

While the child is experiencing "a day in the life", the parents will meet with a member of the Admissions Committee. It is very important for both parents to attend this interview. The director maintains that the match between a school's program and the needs of the student and the family are paramount. The interview process gives you the opportunity for personal dialogue and helps in assessing the appropriateness of the program for your child. All qualified applicants are considered equally based on their commitment to a multi-cultural, socioeconomic student population, and a balance of boys and girls in their classes. But please know that the completion of all of the above steps does not guarantee admission.

This school is smaller than most, but with its caring and dedicated staff, It is to be recommended, especially to working parents who want not only a good education for their children, but also need after school care.

HISTORY

The Hollywood Schoolhouse, (formerly the Hollywood Little Red School House, and originally the Small Fry Nursery School), was established in 1945 by Ruth Pease on Highland Avenue in the heart of Hollywood. The school was a response to the county's request for help in meeting the child care needs of the post-war community. For more than 23 years, it served the area by providing pre-school activities for 20 children. However, by the 1960s the need for child care was growing. To meet the need the school expanded, and in 1968 the current preschool building was constructed with enrollment more than doubling to 50 children.

As years passed, the school prospered. Still, the ever-burgeoning demand for quality child care and an enhanced educational program beyond the early formative years, enlarged. To serve that demand, the Elementary Division was born in 1984. The campus expansion included the first elementary building with classrooms, a computer lab, and library. Two years later, a 35-foot swimming pool was installed, and in 1987, the new kindergarten building, as well as an art and science workshop, were unveiled. Most recently, a new building was added with classroom space, a multi-purpose room, a computer laboratory (with full internet access and multimedia capabilities), and a fully equipped kitchen facility. In 2002, the school became 'non-profit' with a board of directors.

Most recently they have added a new art studio, two new playground areas, an up-to-date technology program in each class and a new library program. As part of their Science curriculum the students maintain a community garden.

AT A GLANCE

APPLICATION DEADLINE	January
OPEN HOUSES	Thursdays 9/25-1/15 except winter holidays
ISEE TESTING	Required for 6-8th grade
UNIFORMS	No
BEFORE AND AFTER SCHOOL CARE	Yes
OPTIONAL LUNCH PROGRAM	$5 day or $80 per month
SUMMER CAMP	Yes
SEE MAP	C on page 285

IMMACULATE HEART MIDDLE & HIGH SCHOOL

Tel: (323) 461-3651 • Fax: (323) 462-0610
5515 Franklin Avenue • Los Angeles, CA 90028-5999
www.immaculateheart.org

PRESIDENT	JULIE ANNE MCCORMICK
HIGH SCHOOL PRINCIPAL	VIRGINIA HURST, IHM
DIRECTOR OF MIDDLE SCHOOL	ANNE PHELPS
ADMISSIONS DIRECTOR	KRISTY NISHINA
TYPE OF SCHOOL	CATHOLIC, ALL GIRLS DAY SCHOOL
GRADES	6 - 12

- ENROLLMENT 750
- ACCREDITATION: MIDDLE SCHOOL—WASC
- ACCREDITATION: HIGH SCHOOL—CAIS/WASC
- SCHOLARSHIP & FINANCIAL AID AVAILABLE
- TUITION $9,400 +FEES
- REGISTRATION FEE $500
- APPLICATION FEE $35

IMMACULATE HEART **Middle School** is a Catholic private school for girls, grades 6 through 8, located on the corner of Franklin and Western in the Los Feliz area. It's a great location surrounded by some of the largest homes in Los Angeles. Being a stone's throw away from Griffith Park, one has this feeling of not even being in the city once you enter the campus.

The middle school shares the rolling seven-acre hillside with Immaculate Heart High School, grades nine through twelve, and there's plenty of room for both. Each school is independently operated and has its own principal, director of admissions, faculty, curriculum, and program of activities. On occasion, though, the two schools will get together and share in celebrations. Please note that if you want your daughter to continue her education through the high school she must still apply to it as if it were a new school, entrance test and all.

It's a beautifully laid out campus, with gardens for students to use during the day or at lunchtime. There are pathways that wind their way through the property past the science building and student/faculty center, around the large playing field and four-lane competition-size swimming pool. There's volleyball and basketball courts and an impressive auditorium that serves as a gymnasium and performing arts center. My daughter pointed out the very charming, intimate chapel. Above it sits the dining room/cafeteria, where the children can enjoy lunch sitting outside on the patio perched high up on the side of the hill, with wonderful views over the city.

As we were walking through the grounds admiring our surroundings, we were greeted by a couple of girls who recognized my daughter from AYSO soccer. They could not have been more polite and bubbled with pride about their school.

The philosophy of Immaculate Heart is firmly rooted in Christian principles based on a primary belief in God. They also view technology as an essential educational tool and have a very in-depth computer program that integrates computers into the students everyday lives.

The library and audio-visual center serve both the middle and high school students and faculty. It's a wonderful place bursting with state-of-the-art equipment. The school's deep belief that the Library Information Center is essential to the learning process is plainly apparent when you enter this well organized, large and airy building. Here the students are encouraged to use both computers and the virtual library to help them in their studies.

Immaculate Heart Middle School's curriculum is designed to provide a sound academic foundation and allow the student to move with confidence into a strong college-preparatory high school program. Honors classes are offered in English, literature and mathematics. Students may qualify for membership in the California Junior Scholarship Federation as well as for a listing on the principal's Honor Roll.

Curriculum Components: Computer science, mathematics, religious science, Spanish, English, science, literature, social studies, art and physical education. Electives include: chorus, computer lab, dance, drama, leadership, newspaper, speech, and the Yearbook.

There are also many field trips planned throughout the year to places such as: The Will Geer Theatricum Botanicum, LACMA, the Museum of Tolerance, and The Norton Simon Museum. Recent two-day trips have been to San Francisco, Sacramento and Catalina Island. Sixth graders experience a three-day outdoor educational trip. In the annual Celebration of Cultures, students recognize and embrace their cultural diversity through music, dance, stories, and a vast array of international foods.

There is a Father/Daughter picnic and Mother/Daughter luncheon and only one fund raising event per year, which is a 10K walk. It is a great way for the kids to raise money for their school, and for children and their parents to get some serious exercise!

The average class size is only 22 students, and with 41 full-time faculty members there is a student/instructor ratio of 1:16, which means lots of extra attention. There is a school psychologist on staff to help students resolve personal problems. In the middle school, the homeroom teacher, along with the school director, oversees the academic progress of each student.

If it's the Middle School you're interested in, then there's an open house in early December. But if you miss it, don't worry, you can fill out the application and student essay form and return it to the Admissions Office by early January. For seventh grade, the application due date is early February.

Immaculate Heart **High School's** curriculum offers students a wide choice of classes in addition to those required for college admission. A typical freshman program of studies might include: religious studies I, English I or honors English I, algebra I or honors algebra I, or geometry or honors geometry; French I or Spanish I, and world civilizations I.

Honors classes are also offered (after the freshman year) in Spanish, French, chemistry, algebra, geometry, biology, physics, world civilization, design layout and advanced art. Students are encouraged to participate in advanced placement classes which qualify them for college credit and include: English, calculus, U.S. history, U.S. government, comparative government, Spanish and studio art.

The Visual and Performing Arts program offers studio arts, chorus, speech, and drama. The school is proud of their drama troupe, "The Genesain Players," who present major productions yearly. The school competes in CIF volleyball, cross-country, basketball, tennis, swimming, softball, soccer, and track.

As with the middle school, there is a school psychologist available on staff to help students resolve personal problems, and an academic counselor who supervises the progress of each student.

When it comes time for your daughter to find a college or university, there is a college counselor who helps in the research and application processes, plans college admission informational programs for parents and students, and coordinates the visits of college representatives to the school. I was impressed to hear that 98 percent of Immaculate Heart's high school graduates enter many prestigious colleges and universities immediately after graduation.

If you are looking at ninth grade, your child is invited to attend an academic playday. Each year in November, the faculty and students present a 'playday' for eighth grade girls to acquaint them with the campus and members of the school community. The half-day event features student-led campus tours and informal workshops followed by a barbecue. It's a great way for your child to see the school and experience a day in the life of a high school student at Immaculate Heart.

HISTORY

The school was founded in 1906 by the Sisters of the Immaculate Heart of Mary, a Catholic religious order of women who trace their origin to Olot, Spain. In 1996, Ruth Anne Murray, IHM, stepped down from the position of principal to become President of Immaculate Heart High School, and Virginia Hurst, IHM, became the new principal. A new sixth grade class was added to the middle school and Immaculate Heart celebrated its 100 year anniversary in 2006. To see more, visit their website. The children have worked very hard on a most impressive look at Immaculate Heart's long history. It's also a great way to take a 'virtual tour' around the campus.

AT A GLANCE

APPLICATION DEADLINE	Call school for date
OPEN HOUSES	December 7
ENTRANCE EXAM	December 13
UNIFORMS	Yes
SUMMER SCHOOL	Yes
SEE MAP	D on page 285

LAURENCE SCHOOL

Tel: (818) 782-4001 • Fax: (818) 782-4004
13639 Victory Blvd. • Valley Glen, CA 91401
www.laurenceschool.com

HEAD OF SCHOOL	MARVIN JACOBSON
ASSOCIATE HEAD	LAUREN WOLKE
TYPE OF SCHOOL	CO-EDUCATIONAL DAY SCHOOL
GRADES	K - 6

- ENROLLMENT: 275
- ACCREDITATION: CAIS/WASC
- NEW FAMILY FEE: $1,750
- ENROLLMENT DEPOSIT: $1,500

- TUITION: $18,900
- APPLICATION FEE: $125
- SIBLING APP. FEE: WAIVED
- FINANCIAL AID IS AVAILABLE

LAURENCE SCHOOL is located on Victory Boulevard in Valley Glen. It has beautifully landscaped grounds nestled in the heart of the San Fernando Valley. The campus is much larger now than it was when it was located on a one-acre site in Van Nuys, between a Jack-in-the-Box restaurant and an apartment building. the school is now double the size of the original campus.

The new facilities include a state of the art library, with reading and storytelling room, a science center, additional classroms with computers in every one. Included in this major campus expansion is a cutting edge Technology Center/Multimedia Lab,which utilizes a "smart board." This is an interactive board, the ultimate modern overhead projector! Students or teachers can type information on the board, and then print. It also features a touch screen for total interactive use. Students as young as second grade are using it. The fully equipped science center has multi-cultural gardens in which each class has a planting box. A 10,000 square-foot gym an indoor/outdoor theatre, plus a large athletic field complements the main playground.There is a full kitchen which can even accommodate school-wide special events. I also liked the fast, convenient and safe drop-off/pick-up area, and Laurence encourages carpools to ease traffic.

During our tour, the person who impressed me most was the kindergarten music teacher, a truly inspired artist and educator. Music is taught using the Orff and Kodaly techniques, and the children put on an outstanding demonstration using song and rhythm instruments. The children had an obvious warmth and respect for their teacher, and she had their focused attention even with more than fifty parents watching. Kindergarten students have Art and Music every day, and enjoy an impressive playground with rubber flooring and raised ski-slope type shapes. The playground includes misters for hot days. Students are also put into small groups at their age level. Perhaps ten will do art,and the remaining ten are places into even smaller groups to work on academics. Later the groups switch.

Laurence's educational philosophy is a good mixture of being warm and nurturing with a whole-child developmental approach, but also states that it has a 'strong academic curriculum.' The goal is to have children enjoy learning, which sets the pace for their academic experience throughout life. They proudly report that their graduates are routinely accepted into challenging prep schools such as Harvard-Westlake, Marlborough, Brentwood, Oakwood, and Campbell Hall. 97 percent of Laurence students get their first choice school. All graduating sixth graders speak at graduation, and write graduation letters that are posted and each year the sixtth grade class leaves a parting gift to the school, the beautiful fountain in one of the gardens.

I was most impressed by the sense of unity and oneness at the school , the deep feeling of community and family. The children all have "buddies"(for example a sixth grader with a first grader) and they get together once a week. Many extend the friendship outside of school with "play dates". Every family new to the school, gets a "host" family, to help teach them the ropes of Laurence and help them become acclimated. The families communicate year round. It is simply a very family oriented community, and a great deal of parent involvement. In fact, many people who work at Laurence have children there, or have had children there. It is as if the kids leave, but the parents don't!

Here is the philosophy as taken from the school brochure:

> "Since our founding in 1953, the philosophy at Laurence School is to encourage our kindergarten through sixth grade students to actively participate in a variety of learning experiences. Laurence's rich and balanced curriculum motivates students to understand important concepts, refine higher level thinking skills, engage in real-world discovery and connect learning to their everyday environment. Our innovative programs appeal to the multiple intelligence found in children and provide them with the opportunity to explore their special interests and talents. We take pride in our nationally acclaimed character education and community service programs. By fostering a child's personal and social, as well as academic development, Laurence School provides an intimate, stimulating environment in which to educate The Total Child."

There is an average of 18 students per class, with a student-teacher ratio of 8:1. There are specialists in music, physical education, art, computer, and Spanish. All specialists are experienced in their fields and all teachers are credentialed. A Red, White, and Blue assembly is held every Friday morning, with lots of American flags waving while students receive recognition for outstanding achievements, noteworthy participation, birthday celebrations and special events.

After school programs include art, musical theatre, school orchestra, and computers, in addition to intermural sports teams in basketball, soccer, and volleyball. There is a heavy theatre program at Laurence, and all students are comfortable speaking to adults, and speaking in front of a group. Other special programs include Kid's Court, which involves students in a simulated courtroom trial, and a celebration of the Elizabethan-era and Shakespearean literature. Student Council representatives hold town meetings, publish a student newspaper, and organize collection drives for a local food pantry.

In 1993, the school began a Character Education Program designed to teach the concept of values: honesty, respect, self control, good judgement, caring and responsibility. These values are continually reinforced in the classroom and at assemblies where children are recognized and awarded for their good deeds. The school was recently a recipient of an award from the National Character Education Partnership and received commendations for its community service programs, class meetings, and cross-age buddy programs.

Co-directors, Marvin and Lynn Jacobson, are very proud of their school, and lovingly refer to it as "our secret garden where children grow." Marvin Jacobson is still at the school on a daily basis, after all these years, and his philosophy that everything around children affects their learning is evident in the attention to detail, and the user friendly nature of basically everything on campus. the 11-page brochure with 20 different quotes, poems, and passages of recommendation from teachers, students and parents all reflecting a love for and appreciation of the school.

The brochure is full of happy, smiling faces, a true representation of our city's rich cultural blend. My general impression is that Laurence provides a very good, traditional academic education for its students, and all interested should go for a visit.

HISTORY

Director Marvin Jacobson opened the original two-room schoolhouse in 1953 as a special education school for children between the ages of 5 and 10. It continued teaching children with special educational needs until 1975 when it changed to a program for children with average to gifted intelligence.Laurence also has a sister school for physically challenged students.

AT A GLANCE

APPLICATION DEADLINE	January 16
OPEN HOUSE	October - January
AFTER SCHOOL CARE	Yes
SUMMER CAMP	Available month of July
UNIFORMS	Yes
SEE MAP	A on page 285

LOYOLA HIGH SCHOOL

Tel: (213) 381-5121 • Fax: (213) 368-3819
1901 Venice Blvd. • Los Angeles, CA 90006
www.loyolahs.edu

HEAD OF SCHOOL	FRANK KOZAKOWSKI
DIRECTOR OF ADMISSIONS	HEATH UTLEY
TYPE OF SCHOOL	ALL BOYS CATHOLIC DAY SCHOOL
GRADES	9 - 12

- ENROLLMENT: 1,210
- ACCREDITATION: JSEA/WASC/WCEA
- ANNUAL REGISTRATION FEE: $350
- FINANCIAL AID IS AVAILABLE

- TUITION: $10,960
- APPLICATION FEE: $70
- ACTIVITY FEE: $205

The LOYLA HIGH SCHOL campus is magnificent-looking, with handsome three-story brick buildings that remind one of the University houses in Cambridge, England, and a sweeping circular driveway that deposits you outside one of the finest Catholic all-boy schools in the city. Students at Loyola enjoy the spacious school buildings with wide corridors and large, bright classrooms overlooking the huge playing fields and gardens.

The campus is close to downtown and centrally-located, which is convenient for Loyola students who come from Malibu, Santa Monica, North Hollywood, Beverly Hills, Hancock Park, San Gabriel Valley, Whittier, Long Beach, Palos Verdes and Pasadena.

In any one year, this school may receive applicants from as many as 225 Catholic, public and private elementary schools. The competition is tough, last year they had 800 applicants for 300 slots. They generally give preference to Catholic boys, although they do take in about 14 percent non-Catholics each year.

Mission Statement (as taken from the school brochure):

> "Loyola High School of Los Angeles is a Catholic College preparatory school for young men who represent the racial, ethnic, and socio-economic diversity of greater Los Angeles. Drawing upon the Jesuit tradition, Loyola is committed to the development of the whole person through a challenging educational experience of academic, co-curricular, and religious opportunities. By teaching as Jesus taught, Loyola is dedicated to inspiring its students to develop as conscientious leaders and agents of change who are intellectually distinguished, morally courageous, and compassionate in service to others."

The average student/teacher ratio is 15:1, so your child won't be lost in huge lecture-size classes and will have plenty of individual attention. This is a traditional school which offers many advanced placement courses (see below). If your child enrolls in these classes, and then passes the exams set by the College Entrance Examination Board, he will receive college units, which may earn him credit and/or advanced placement.

In his freshman year your child will choose from the following subjects;– English I, algebra, accelerated algebra, foreign language with a choice of Spanish, French, German, and Latin, Honors Spanish, theology, global studies, global science, biology, physical education, touch typing/word processing.

His sophomore year will include: English II (British Literature), AP English language and composition, foreign language, Honors Spanish, geometry, theology, community service project, western civilization, biology, health, Earth science, AP environmental science, honors French.

In his junior year: English III, AP English language and composition, foreign language III, honors Spanish IV, algebra II, honors algebra II, honors pre-calculus, theology, community service project, U.S. history, AP U.S. history, chemistry, honors chemistry, AP chemistry, Earth science, fine arts (photography, painting, design, ceramics, music, drawing, chorus, acting workshops), AP environmental science, AP Latin III, honors French III.

Finally, in his senior year, your child must take at least ten courses in required and elective subjects. The required subjects are: English, mathematics, fine arts, foreign language IV, science, social studies electives, and theology. He must also complete a senior internship in community service.

Loyola is well known for its sports programs. It fields 11 varsity teams: football, cross country, and water polo in fall, basketball and soccer in winter, baseball, volleyball, swimming and diving, track and field, golf, and tennis in the spring. As a Loyola athlete, your son will have the chance to compete with and against some of the best athletes in southern California, often reaching the CIF finals and then winning those, too. However, if your son does not make it onto one of the interscholastic CIF teams, the school offers a wide range of intramural sports.

Your child is not expected to 'sail through' this very rigorous 4 years, and that's why they allocate each student a personal counselor and an academic advisor to help when needed. They take a personal interest in your child at Loyola, and that's an important reason why their students are so successful, extremely polite and well-mannered. Visiting the school is a delightful experience, and I thoroughly recommend it.

Another reason to consider this school is that 99 percent of their graduates go on to college immediately (97 percent of those to four-year universities). The most popular choices are the UC campuses, UC Berkeley, and UCLA, although many have gone on to a Jesuit college or university, to USC, and others to one of the Ivy League schools.

HISTORY

The school was founded 137 years ago and follows the Jesuit tradition of education, which spans over 450 years. There are 85 faculty members at Loyola, and of these, 10 are Jesuits.

AT A GLANCE

APPLICATION DEADLINE	January
OPEN HOUSE	Call school for dates
UNIFORMS	No, but there is a dress code
SEE MAP	C on page 285

LILA – LYCEE INTERNATIONAL DE LOS ANGELES

Tel: (323) 665-4526 • Fax: (323) 665-2607
4155 Russell Avenue • Los Angeles, CA 90027
(other locations in Tarzana, Orange, Pasadena)
www.lilaschool.com

HEAD OF CAMPUS	ELIZABETH CHAPONOT
ADMISSIONS COORDINATOR	MUY SUN
TYPE OF SCHOOL	BILINGUAL (FRENCH/ENGLISH)
	CO-ED DAY SCHOOL
GRADES	PRESCHOOL - 12

- ENROLLMENT: 350
- DISCOUNTS FOR MORE THAN ONE CHILD
- ACCREDITATION CAIS/WASC/ FRENCH MINISTRY OF EDUCATION, INTERNATIONAL BACCALAUREATE- GENEVA

- TUITION:
  PRE-5: $10,900
  6-9: $11,900
  10-12: $13,600

The FRENCH-AMERICAN SCHOOL OF LOS ANGELES OR LILA (Los Feliz campus) has come a long way in the years since it opened. When I first visited the campus in 1990, it was a run-down facility with a barren dirt play yard struggling to get on its feet. Now it is a thriving place of learning, with full classrooms, bright play equipment and grassy fields outside.

The campus sits on six green acres, and its classrooms are a collection of one-story octagonal buildings, which are now protected by the California Historical Society. There are huge eucalyptus trees throughout, and in the background towers the famous "Shakespeare bridge" built in the 1920s. These great, round buildings are divided into pie-shaped spaces, and because the windows go on uninterrupted for 360 degrees, (picture an airport control-tower) there is a wonderful feeling of openness and light. The kindergarten program is a traditional academic one, and all subjects are taught in French. The school goes up to the twelfth grade, but it doesn't feel like a typical high-school setting, perhaps because the classes are small. There are two outside play yards, a soccer field, and a basketball court. The three main (octagonal) buildings house the classrooms, library, offices, and a multi-purpose room. The school also uses temporary trailers for additional space.

Here is a description of the program taken from the LILA brochure:

"Our program requires children to follow a systematic, integrated curriculum in which courses in all major areas of study are taken every year. There are few electives, and each year's program represents a logical progression which starts from and builds upon the knowledge acquired during the previous year. We provide a comprehensive training in both French and English with an enriched curriculum in the humanities, sciences and the arts. Small classes permit the most effective instruction and personalized guidance."

The French "Brevet" is a French national exam taken at the end of ninth grade (which is the equivalent of American twelfth grade). If the student passes the "Brevet," he or she may go on to technical/professional schools in French, or continue at the school through twelfth grade and take another national exam called the French Baccalaureate.

At the school, they explain that when a student has graduated from the French school in twelfth grade, it is the educational equivalent of completing high school and the first year of college.

French exams are national exams taken under the supervision of the Cultural Services of the French Embassy.

Some American parents that I spoke with were concerned that LILA was too structured and academic for their children, and worried about their child's ability to handle only French being spoken. A few other families that I know absolutely adore the school, and can't say enough about how great it is for their children to know another culture and language.

HISTORY

In 1978, a group made up of French families and friends of French culture founded the French American School of Los Angeles (C.E.F.). It started with only five students, in a house on Victory Boulevard in the San Fernando Valley. Since then, C.E.F. has become the Lycee International de Los Angeles (LILA), the French American School, which now has four campuses in the greater Los Angeles area.

AT A GLANCE

APPLICATION DEADLINE	Ongoing as spaces are available
OPEN HOUSES & TOURS	Early September
SPORTS PROGRAM	Yes
UNIFORMS	No
BEFORE/AFTER SCHOOL PROGRAM	Yes
SEE MAP	C on page 285

MARLBOROUGH SCHOOL

Tel: (323) 935-1147 • Fax: (323) 933-0542
250 S. Rossmore Avenue • Los Angeles, CA 90004
www.marlboroughschool.org

HEAD OF SCHOOL	BARBARA WAGNER
DIRECTOR OF ADMISSIONS	JEANETTE WOO CHITJIAN
TYPE OF SCHOOL COLLEGE PREP DAY SCHOOL FOR GIRLS	
GRADES	7 - 12

- ENROLLMENT: 530
- NEW STUDENT FEE: $1,500
- ACCREDIDATION: CAIS/WASC
- MEMBERSHIPS:ABC/CAIS/CEEB/CIF/CLS/CSF/ERB/NACAC/NAIS/NAPSG/NCGS
- TUITION: $28,750
- APPLICATION FEE: $100

MARLBOROUGH SCHOOL is an independent day school offering young women an outstanding education. The four-acre campus includes a gymnasium and training room, seven science labs, a computer center, facilities for photography, painting and sculpture, a 75 foot six-lane pool, and several outdoor courts. The school built a new parking lot across the street, which was designed with a great deal of style and taste.

There is a 22,000-volume library offering over 90 periodicals and newspapers, and it is connected to UCLA's card catalog (ORION). The Performing Arts Annex includes two dance studios, a music room, a 100-seat performance theater and a 500-seat auditorium.

A girls' school education is not for everyone. One father, whose daughter was accepted at Marlborough, was tearing his hair out because she refused to go. He tried to convince her that it was the opportunity of a lifetime, while she insisted that a co-ed experience was the only one for her.

The benefits of a single sex education for our daughters are well documented. Marlborough grads say that it helped them to develop leadership skills, self confidence and enabled them to focus on their goals. Research sponsored by the Women's College Coalition has found that graduates of single sex women's schools are six times more likely to sit on the boards of fortune 500 companies than women attending co-ed schools. The Coalition also found that 41 percent of the women who ran for U.S. Senate were graduates of women's colleges. This is an amazing figure, since it only represents two to three percent of the women in this country.

Academic Life

Each year, Marlborough offers 150 courses, including 26 advanced placement courses. The average class size is 13, which allows for intimate discussion and debate. In the middle school, students sign up for five courses each term, plus physical education and fine and performing arts. The curriculum includes projects that are interdisciplinary. For example, seventh graders incorporate art, English and history in their study of Los Angeles.

Seventh graders: English, physical education, foreign language, re-algebra (or algebra), intro to US History, Exploring Science I, fine and performing arts.

Eight graders: English, physical education, foreign language, algebra or geometry, global studies, exploring science II, fine and performing arts.

Ninth graders: English, algebra, physical education/health, ancient civilization to 1500 AD, fine and performing arts, foreign language, geometry exploring Science III or chemistry.

Upper School Grades 10 - 12
Minimum graduation requirements, as defined by the academic program in grades 10 through 12, include three years of English, foreign language through level III, two years of mathematics, two years of laboratory science, European History or modern world history and US History, and four semesters of fine and performing arts in grades 9 to 12. In addition, students must complete six semesters of physical education in grades 9 to 12 and demonstrate proficiency in typing. Most students at the school exceed these basic requirements.

At Marlborough, it is a long-standing tradition that 100 percent of graduates matriculate at four-year colleges and universities.

Advanced Placement Courses (AP)
These are classes that prepare students for the Advanced Placement examinations administered by the College Board. Marlborough offers the following AP courses: art history, calculus AB & BC, european History, French, studio art, chemistry, biology, Latin, physics, computer science, US history, Spanish, English, modern world history, environmental science, statistics, government.

There is an extensive college counseling program at Marlborough that begins in the sophomore year and shepherds both the student and her family through the application process.

There is also a College Counseling Resource Library which offers hundreds of college catalogs, guides, video cassettes, and computer software including the College Board's ExPan program. Within the Resource Library is an area for meeting with college representatives (more than 100 visit each year), and an area for quiet study.

Student Government
Student government is an important means of cultivating leadership qualities in young women. Each class elects a Class Council that includes a president, vice president, secretary, treasurer, athletic representative, fine arts representative, and community service representative. Class Council members work as a team to facilitate weekly class meetings and organize class activities, including class traditions such as Colors, Banner, and Mascot presentations.

Each graduating class designs a Banner using elements and ideas that tell a visual story of what the group is all about and what they have experienced in their years at Marlborough. It is so impressive to walk through the hallways where banners dating back to the turn of the century are on display. Now that's tradition!

Marlborough offers classes in photography (complete with dark room), video production, and ceramics (there are several kilns). Displays of the remarkable artwork in its own art gallery are located in an atrium/lounge area at the center of one of the campus buildings.

Philosophy

Marlborough School provides a learning environment where young women develop self-confidence, creativity, a sense of responsibility and moral decisiveness. The school's program encourages students to discover their potential, to think critically, and to develop intellectual curiosity. Students learn to set priorities, develop decision making skills, and value the process of the educational experience. Marlborough believes that for women, academic excellence, leadership skills and confidence flourish best in a school exclusively devoted to their education. The Marlborough community enables each student to develop her fullest potential so that she may contribute in a global society.

HISTORY

Marlborough School was founded in 1889 as Mrs. Mary S. Caswell's School for Girls by Mary S. Caswell. A former resident of Maine, Mrs. Caswell brought her 20 years of East Coast educational experience to Los Angeles. In 1916, Mrs. Caswell moved her school to the (then) far western edges of the city at Third and Rossmore. The new buildings were surrounded by barley fields, with the nearest paved intersection at Third and Arden.

Upon Mrs. Overton's retirement in 1948. She and her husband, Kenneth (the school's business manager), established the Marlborough School Foundation and sold the school to the Foundation trustees in 1960, at which time the school became a non-profit organization.

Marlborough's future under the current Head of School, Barbara E. Wagner, is bright and secure as she guides the institution with Mrs. Caswell's vision for the highest quality women's education available in the United States.

AT A GLANCE

APPLICATION DEADLINE	January 15
OPEN HOUSES	10/25 & 11/22 from 9-noon. RSVP.
UNIFORMS	Yes
ISEE	Required
CO-ED SUMMER CAMP	Very varied
SEE MAP	C on page 285

MARYMOUNT

Tel: (310) 472-1205 • Fax: (310) 440-4316
10643 Sunset Blvd. • Los Angeles, CA 90077
www.mhs-la.org

HEAD OF SCHOOL	DR. MARY ELLEN GOZDECKI
DIRECTOR OF ADMISSIONS	ERICA HUEBNER
TYPE OF SCHOOL	CATHOLIC, INDEPENDENT
	ALL GIRL DAY SCHOOL
GRADES	9 - 12

- ENROLLMENT: 420
- ACCREDITATION: CAIS/NAIS/NCEA/WASC
- BOOKS & UNIFORMS: $850
- FINANCIAL AID IS AVAILABLE

- TUITION: $20,900
- APPLICATION FEE: $100
- NEW FAMILY FEE: NONE
- UNIFORMS: $250-$300

Marymount is located on Sunset Boulevard across the street from UCLA. My daughter and I drove down there one afternoon from Hancock Park. The traffic was light and it only took us about 20 minutes door-to-door. I began to see why parents might choose to send their children to school on the other side of town, but then I wasn't driving in rush hour and sitting bumper to bumper with several hundred other frustrated mother/chauffeurs!

We turned up the steep driveway and parked right outside the school. It's an impressive looking building – manicured lawns abound. Built on five-and-a-half acres, the original buildings were declared cultural historical monuments in 1982. In addition, the campus is home to the Marian Hall Library and Learning Center and the Pavilion, a sports complex that includes a state of the art gymnasium and weight room. Athletic facilities also include a soccer field, tennis courts, and an Olympic-size swimming pool.

We were greeted by Sharon Stephens, a very warm and welcoming Director of Admissions. My daughter immediately felt at home, and we were invited to take an impromptu tour of the school.

Hand-carved wood, frescos, stained glass and expansive lawn are some of the things that create the stately elegance of this Spanish Colonial Revival architecture. They even have a three-hole golf course which borders onto a private club on the Westside, so it gives the impression of being somewhere out in the middle of the country. It's an idyllic setting on Sunset Boulevard.

The classrooms are big, bright, and airy with lots of space. I could imagine running through the corridors of this school feeling like quite the special daughter, especially when I looked at the wonderful walls of photographs depicting beautifully clad girls in their graduation robes.

My friend's daughter was accepted into Brentwood and Marymount. We all thought for sure that she would choose Brentwood because it was mixed and had a tad more cache to it . . . but she opted for Marymount. I asked her why, and she told me that she wanted to concentrate on doing well in school and that she would be too distracted by the boys at Brentwood.

Admissions are selective. Drawing from communities as far away as the South Bay to the San Fernando Valley, and from central Los Angeles to the Westside, the student body reflects a broad spectrum of ethnic, economic and religious backgrounds.

The average class size is 15, with a student/teacher ratio of 8:1. There are 60 faculty members, all of whom hold a B.A. or B.S. degree. Typically 99 percent of Marymount's graduates go on to universities and colleges that include: Amherst, Barnard, Brown, Columbia, Duke, Georgetown, Harvard, MIT, NYU, Princeton, Tufts, UC Berkeley, UCLA, Notre Dame, USC, Vassar and Yale.

Marymount offers a rigorous and challenging academic program. The students must complete a minimum of six courses per semester. Requirements include four years of English and theology, at least three years of foreign language, mathematics, science, social studies, three semesters of visual and performing arts, three semesters of physical education, and one semester of computer science.

There are Honors courses at every grade level and in every subject and 16 Advanced Placement (AP) classes. There are independent study projects. A very healthy 64 percent of the student body is enrolled in honors or AP classes.

Each year, the college board names several Marymount students as AP Scholars in recognition of their exceptional achievement on the college-level AP examinations. In addition, each fall several Marymount seniors are selected as scholarship winners, a National Merit Finalists, semifinalists or commended students. This places them in the top five percent of the over one-million students who take the qualifying exam - very impressive.

Important in the review of a school are the elective courses offer. At Marymount they offer a wide range of self-expression in diverse areas such as oceanography, engineering and robotics, music, drama, art, photography, physical education, journalism and yearbook. At each grade level, the Guidance Department coordinates with the Human Development Program, enabling each student to develop her personal resources and helping her to make the right decisions in life issues. Students are encouraged to maintain balance in their lives by participating in co-curricular activities and, as you can see, they are have a wide choice of clubs, student organizations and athletic teams in which to take part.

Speaking of athletics, Marymount fields 22 sports teams, including baseball, crew, cross-country, equestrian, fencing, golf, soccer, softball, swimming, tennis, track and field, volleyball and water polo. Last year Marymount won their second consecutive State Championship in volleyball; the first CIF-Southern Section Championship in volleyball, three Varsity Sunshine League Champion teams in volleyball, soccer, and track, and Junior Varsity Sunshine League Champion teams in volleyball, tennis and freshmen volleyball.

If your child is interested in the performing arts, she may participate in the fall play, the spring musical, the Marymount Singers choral group, the handbell choir, the orchestra, the pop bank, the jazz/rock ensemble, and the annual student produced talent benefit.

In the publications department, the school offers an award-winning student newspaper, *The Anchor*, and the literary magazine, *Sunset*, winner of a gold medal from the Columbia School of Journalism.

Other clubs include: French Club, Spanish Club, Art Club, Science Pre-Med Club, Creative Writing Club, Mock Trial, Marymount Ambassadors, Model United Nations, History Club, Action!, The Film Club, The Book Club, Rainbow Coalition, Current Affairs Club, National Honor Society, Spirit Club and Amnesty International.

You as parents are expected to support the Marymount Annual Fund Drive. Last year 91 percent of the parents participated. Money goes to faculty salary and benefits, daily bus transportation, and contributes to the academic and co-curricular program that is so extensive at Marymount. Plans are underfoot to improve student restroom and eating/study areas.

Recently, funds from the Board of Trustees have helped to redesign and refurbish the parking facilities and to create a beautiful new Pavilion Courtyard. New computers have been acquired so that every classroom has them. New security lighting was also installed to help maintain the safety of the campus.

HISTORY

Founded in 1923 and rooted in the tradition of the Religious of the Sacred Heart of Mary, Marymount High School is a Catholic, independent, college preparatory school for girls.

AT A GLANCE

APPLICATION DEADLINE	January 12
OPEN HOUSES	Sunday, November 23 from 1 - 4:00 p.m.
UNIFORMS	Yes
ISEE TESTING	Yes
SUMMER SCHOOL	Yes
SEE MAP	D on page 285

MAYFIELD JUNIOR SCHOOL OF THE HOLY CHILD

Tel: (626) 796-2774 • Fax: (626) 796-5753
405 S. Euclid Avenue • Pasadena, CA 91101
www.mayfieldjs.org

HEAD OF SCHOOL	JILL BROWN/BRIDGETT KELLY-LOSSADA
DIRECTOR OF ADMISSIONS	AVERYL THIELEN
TYPE OF SCHOOL	CATHOLIC CO-ED INDEPENDENT DAY
GRADES	K - 8

- ENROLLMENT: 486
- ACCREDITATION: WCE/NAIS/CAIS/WASC
- MEMBERSHIP: ISAMA
- FINANCIAL AID IS AVAILABLE

- TUITION: $14,235
- NEW FAMILY FEE: $2,500
- APPLICATION FEE: $100

MAYFIELD has a large, attractive campus with an athletic field,hard court play areas and a primary playground. The elementary and middle schools have science and foreign language labs as well as art studios, performing arts center and a beautiful well-stocked library. Students have an indoor gym and there is a school chapel.

The campus has an old-fashioned air about it with a collection of buildings from the 30s, 60s, 70s, and 90s as welll as modern structures. The classrooms are large and bright with lots of windows. The feel of the campus has changed slightly with the South Campus Expansion. Last year the new Primary Center opened to house K to second grade classes. It also includes a hands-on science center and elementary art lab. The new Performing Arts Center replaced the old auditorium, and the old convent buildings were transformed into Connelly Hall with new offices. There is an underground parking facility under the new complex. The Multipurpose Building houses the gym, art studio, chapel and P.E. offices all on one level. The lower level houses the Kids Club After School Program and music rehearsal rooms.

The library is located in the Pike Resource center and is beautifully laid out with lots of large, round tables. It has a lower level, with pillows on the floor for a more relaxing read. Above this reading area is a large, round window allowing lots of natural light to come.

Mayfield is a Catholic school committed to the philosophy of Cornelia Connelly, (founder of the Society of the Holy Child), who believed in the spirit and talents of the individual. The school provides a traditional academic and religious education challenging each child to reach his or her potential.

There is also an emphasis on athletics. The competetitive sports programs for seventh and eighth grade boys and girls include: volleyball, basketball, soccer, track, softball,l, golf, and swimming. A tennis program takes place once a week from September through May.

The school is run by a board of directors and the Society of the Holy Child Jesus. There are additional committees for finance, educational planning, building and grounds, and the executive committee. There are specialists in art, technology physical education, music, drama, French and Spanish. The average class size is 17 with a student/teacher ratio of 12:1

Mayfield Junior School implements the philosophy of the Holy Child Schools. School personnel are committed not only to the religious and educational development of each child, but also to maintaining a sense of community and family spirit.

Here is the definition of a Holy Child school, from the brochure:

> The educational philosphy of Mother Cornelia Connelly seeks to educate the whole child,Thus, a Holy Child school educates the body, mind, and spirit in a context which is values-based and responsive to individual needs. Instruction takes place in a learning climate based on trust and reverance for the uniqueness of the individual.

I was particularly interested to hear about the Reach Out Program that includes individual classes, parents, and the outside community. With a constant emphasis on learning to be there for others.

HISTORY

Mayfield Junior School was founded in 1931, and named after the Holy Child School in Mayfield, England. It was founded by the Sisters of the Holy Child Jesus and dedicated to the educational philosophy of Mother Cornelia Connelly, a tradition and a history which began in England in the year 1856.

AT A GLANCE

APPLICATION DEADLINE	Applications available in October for next academic year
OPEN HOUSE DATES	Fall and early winter, call to make a reservation
UNIFORMS	Yes
AFTER SCHOOL CARE	Yes
SEE MAP	B on page 285

MIRMAN SCHOOL is located on Mulholland Drive's private school row, which includes Curtis, Berkeley Hall, Westland and Steven S. Wise. It is a beautiful setting with views of the San Fernando Valley to the north and West Los Angeles to the south. The current facility has received architectural awards from the Westwood Chamber of Commerce and the Southern California Chapter of the American Institute of Architects.

The campus includes ten lower school classrooms, eight upper school classrooms (including a science lab and a computer/research library), an art center, a music room, a lower school computer lab, amphitheater, library, and a large auditorium. There are volleyball, basketball, and handball courts as well as a baseball diamond, running track and climbing equipment.

This is a school that is very specific in its purpose which is to give children with high IQ's the opportunity to reach their intellectual potential. Your child must score in the 99 percentile on selected IQ tests before you can officially begin the admission process. So the first step for entrance is an IQ test, to be administered by a certified educational psychologist using the Stanford-Binet LM (score 145) or the WISC (score 138) IQ test. The school maintains a list of testers in both the valley and LA for the convenience of parents, but any qualified and experienced psychologist may administer the test and submit the results to the school.

The philosophy as written in the school brochure:

> "The school recognizes that the innate intellectual potential of the child is not enough to ensure the actualizing of these talents; there must be nurture to maximize nature. Having recognized that gifted children learn differently, the school is committed to providing an academically appropriate learning environment that is stimulating, secure, and joyful, with an age-appropriate social and emotional setting in which gifted children can maximize their potential."

At Mirman the belief is:

- "That while we are equal as human beings with equal legal, civil and political rights, we are not equal in our talents or our 'native capacities.'
- That America has made very little progress in providing education suited for children with unique capacities, and that rather than admit to or take responsibility for assessing differences in talent, often prefers to accept mediocrity.
- That there has always been an elite in other fields such as art, music, and athletics, why not in education?"

There are no grade levels. The children are divided by age and at the elementary level there are two groups at each age. Classes are scheduled in such a way so that children can move up a level when they are ready. For example, the entire lower school has math at the same time of day so children can move to other classrooms for math instruction if their skills are beyond the range taught by their homeroom teacher. A six-year-old might learn math with the seven or eight-year-olds, read with the third grade group, and then return to age-mates for the rest of the day.

The requirements and expectations are high at Mirman. The brochure states that absenteeism and tardiness will not be tolerated. Children must be free of 'emotional disturbance.' Students are generally working at least one or two years above 'grade level,' and in some parts of their curriculum, considerably more. At Mirman there is a commitment to provide for the children material they are ready to learn when they are ready to learn it.

In the lower school (ages 5 to 9) the classroom teacher works with the children in language arts, reading, math, social studies, and general studies. The teacher has an aide in the morning to assist in individualizing the curriculum and work with small groups. In addition, there are specialists in science, Spanish, computer, art, music, and physical education two or three times each week.

There is an after school mentor program for further exploration in art, music, chess, drama, rocketry and science, physical education, and the Great Books.

At the upper school level, the 10 to 14 year olds follow a departmentalized program with academic solids, electives, independent study, community service and school dances. The curriculum includes: reading, spelling, English, geography, math, language arts, and study skills. History, Spanish, anthropology, art, music, physical education, theater arts, and Latin are also studied. All students may select from an elective pool of orchestra, choir, Olympics of the Mind, calligraphy, computer, art, science or speech.

All 30 teachers and specialists are credentialed, and many have been master teachers or gifted coordinators in school districts across the country. They are secure in their professional competence and personality to be able to accept and enjoy bright children, and neither resent the gifted child nor regard him as a threat.

Director of Admissions, Leslie Geffen, has had over 15 years experience working in counseling and administration of an Honors Program at UCLA. She is the daughter of founders Dr. and Mrs. Mirman and the proud parent of two Mirman School students.

The school remains one of the few in the country devoted specifically to highly gifted children. The Mirmans' legacy continues to influence and inspire educators, parents, and generations of children.

HISTORY

Beverly and Norman Mirman founded the school in September, 1962, out of their love for children and a deep concern for their education. Dr. Mirman received his doctorate in elementary curriculum and administration from UCLA and completed his doctoral study in the area of gifted child education.

He holds the State of California Life Diploma in the general elementary teaching field as well as a General Secondary teaching credential and the Elementary Administrator's credential. He is past President of the National Association for Gifted Children and is one of the founders of the California Association of the Gifted.

Mrs. Mirman is co-founder and co-director of The Mirman School. She attended Brooklyn College and the University of Tampa, her graduate studies at UCLA were early childhood education.

AT A GLANCE

APPLICATION DEADLINE	January 2
INFORMATIONAL EVENINGS	10/16 and 10/13, 9-10am. Please RSVP.
TESTING	IQ of 145 or higher is required for admission.
IQ TEST DATES	1/10, 1/31 & 2/7 at 10:30 a.m.
UNIFORMS	Yes
SEE MAP	D on page 285

NEW HEIGHTS PREPARATORY SCHOOL

Tel: (818) 993-3800 • Fax: (818) 885-1663
8756 Canby Ave. • Northridge, CA 91325
www.newheightsprep.org

PRINCIPAL	DAN WESLOW
ADMISSIONS COORDINATOR	HILDA JIMENEZ
TYPE OF SCHOOL	CO-ED DAY SCHOOL
GRADES	6-12

- ENROLLMENT: 100
- ACCREDITATION: NIPSA, WASC CANDIDATE
- ACTIVITY FEES: $450
- FINANCIAL AID IS AVAILABLE
- TUITION: $16,500
- APPLICATION FEE: $100
- BOOKS: $100-$450

For a relatively young school, NEW HEIGHTS PREPARATORY SCHOOL is a rising star in the southern California private school community. It's the San Fernando Valley branch of the New Visions family of schools co-founded by Herb Alpert and Dr. Paul Cummins. Crossroads School for Arts and Sciences opened in Santa Monica in 1971, then New Roads in 1995. After a 12-year collaboration between Igall Barka of HSIS Schools and Dr. Paul Cummins, New Heights was born!

This school has had some impressive results in their short history. I had the pleasure of meeting Dr. Cummins at an open house I was invited to. He spoke about the school and afterwards took us on a lively tour of the campus. He was so enthusiastic about NHPS and what is had to offer that I was a believer by the time I left! He told me that NHPS offers an intellectually demanding and creative curriculum that was founded upon five central commitments. These five commitments, which constitute the pillars upon which our school community is built, are: to academic excellence; to the arts; to the greater community; to the development of a student population of social, economic, and racial diversity; and to the development of each student's physical well being and full human potential."

The campus is quite small but growing fast. They recently finished building a second floor with ten new classrooms and solar power. They have plans to separate the middle school from the high school by building five middle school classrooms at 8736 Canby (where the old Performing Arts Center used to be). A new Performing Arts and Athletics Center will be built to house their stage, dance and musical productions, it will also double as a gymnasium because of its versatile design. Outdoor sports and performances will take place next to the Performing Arts Center on the campus' athletics fields.

I really like their integrative approach. Faculty and teachers make sure the children have a highly personal experience in their education. This college-prep school wants to make sure the lessons really stick, so they integrate curriculum by making it relevant to the kids. One way is through their arts program, which brings creative writing, visual arts, drama, music and dance into their core curriculum by discussing the role each has played in science, social studies and history. Through this context, art "...is used as a lens to see the world through." In every subject, students are taught to ask why, and to critically analyze anything in front of them to prepare them to make intelligent choices in life.

NHPS offers some very unique classes...like flying! Yes flying, which is after all, a mixture of applied physics and math. Students can receive college credit for this course, while having an incredible experience. This type of class represents the NHPS philosophy, which is based on a very hands-on approach. There are no AP classes yet but lots of Honors classes. They have great music classes and allow the kids to start their own sports teams, and offer equestrian and volleyball to name a few.

NHPS believes that their students are responsible for the betterment of his or her community. In their Core/Humanities program, students participate in community service projects intended to give something back. Student-led clubs and groups also participate in service projects that are relevant to their particular subject of interest. There's a very refreshing take on health, fitness and nutrition. The Human Development and Health program is just wonderful. In an era where children are dealing with obesity and illness, this one heads in the direction of personal growth. There are no junk or processed foods sold on campus, hurrah! Finally a school that can connect the dots: sugar and junk food at school = crazy unruly kids. Healthy food served on campus = calm kids that can concentrate. I cannot tell you how frustrated I have been at times knowing that my own kids were buying out of those awful vending machines that spew out candy and chips.

There is a "council" that discusses teasing, academic and social pressures. Parents tell me that their children look forward to coming to school. With this innovating curriculum and the strong support they offer the children, it's no wonder NHPS students are matriculating to their first college picks. Not only did ALL of the 2008 class get their first picks, but many of them were accepted under the ìearly acceptanceî program that many colleges offer now.

The school has strong financial backing so they can be selective and don't have to take in students that they don't think will do well, or are not necessarily the best fit. However, NHPS seeks to create a diverse student body and provide educational opportunities for low-income students. They achieve this by operating as a for-profit institution knowing that they can increase efficiency, discourage financial waste and utilize tax breaks to direct funds to their financial aid program thereby maintaining a minimum of 20 percent of low-income families on their rosters without having to rely on external donations.

When you look at a school, you look at leadership. Have a look at their teachers: 85 percent of NHPS teachers have a masters degree or better in their field of specialty, five out of fourteen NHPS teachers have prior experience at either Crossroads or New Roads – the two schools from which NHPS was modeled. NHPS searches far and wide to find good teachers, and they don't pick them from their resume alone. Teachers who apply must also send in a DVD of them in action! You get the feeling that NHPS is growing exactly how it should, with strong roots from a seed. Seeds are being planted all over the city. Please Paul, can you plant one here in Hancock Park?

P.S. There are many more boys enrolled, so NHPS is looking for girls if you have one!

HISTORY

New Heights Preparatory School, founded in 2006, is the result of a 12-year collaboration between Igaal and Hilda Barak of HSIS Schools and Dr. Paul Cummins of New Visions Foundation. It is the San Fernando Valley branch of the New Visions family of schools established in Santa Monica. New Heights Prep is a school for the arts and sciences. They found that many public schools, as well as some nonpublic schools, had not been responsive to the needs of parents whose concern is their child's whole well being. They set out to orient students back to the motivation they once had for school.

AT A GLANCE

APPLICATION DEADLINE	10/28 and 3/18
OPEN HOUSES	Once a month, call school for details
UNIFORMS	No
SUMMER SCHOOL	Yes
SEE MAP	A on page 285

NEW ROADS SCHOOL

Elementary School:
1512 Pearl Street • Santa Monica, CA 90405
(310) 479-8500 •Fax (310) 479-8556

Middle School:
1238 Lincoln Blvd. • Santa Monica, CA 90401
Tel: (310) 587-2255 • Fax: (310) 587-2258

Middle School:
3504 Las Flores Canyon Rd. • Malibu, CA 90265
(310) 456-1977 •Fax (310) 456-8027

High School:
3131 Olympic Blvd. • Santa Monica, CA 90404
Tel: (310) 828-5582 •Fax: (310) 828-2582

www.newroads.org

HEAD OF SCHOOL	DAVID BRYAN
TYPE OF SCHOOL	INDEPENDENT CO-ED DAY SCHOOL
GRADES	K - 12

- ENROLLMENT: 570
- ACCREDITATION: CAIS/NAIS/WASC
- MEMBERSHIPS: ERB/ISAMA
- NEW STUDENT FEE: $1,000
- APPLICATION FEE: $100
- TUITION:
    K-5 $19,040
    6-12 $23,652
- FEE FOR SUMMER SCHOOL
- FINANCIAL AID IS AVAILABLE

NEW ROADS SCHOOL in Santa Monica is an independent educational community currently set on four campuses. There are plans underfoot to create an educational village on the site where the High School is located, offering education all the way from preschool through to twelfth grade. Being able to grow up in a village-like community is something we are losing as our cities keep growing and children spend hours in travel time instead of play time.

K through 5
The Pearl campus K through 5 is a small jewel. Just opened and located at the corner of Pearl and 16th Streets in Santa Monica right across from Santa Monica College and just a few blocks away from the beach. The campus has comfortable classrooms, a well-stocked library, computer and science areas, and an art studio surrounding two play yards and gardens. They offer an innovative and creative developmental approach to education which includes language arts, math, science, social studies and Spanish. Other programs are music, visual art, drama, dance and P.E., as well as human development, environmental studies, ser-

vice learning and information technology. This is a wonderful home for discovery and exploration. Check it out!

Middle School

The Middle School is currently sharing a 27,000 square foot facility owned by the Santa Monica Boys and Girls Club. When I visited the school it was at the end of the regular school day and the gymnasium had been taken over by the children of the Santa Monica Boys and Girls Club. It was a little overwhelming at first, but I soon got used to it, and it was fun to see the building being used in such a positive way after school.

School Philosophy as taken from school brochure:

> "Born of a felt responsibility to prepare young people for the challenges and opportunities they face, New Roads School seeks to promote personal, social, political and moral understanding, and to instill in young people a respect for the humanity and ecology of the earth and the sensitivity to appreciate life's deep joys and mysteries.

> The School rests upon several fundamental commitments: to the development of a student population of social, economic, ethnic and racial diversity; to the development of each student's full human potential; to academic excellence and excellence in the arts; to behaving responsibly and honorably as an institution and serving the larger ecological and social community.

> It is our goal to provide a strong college preparatory program from which each student will develop a personal dedication to learning, a respect for independent thinking and an expanding curiosity about the world and its people. We believe that education must not be a race for the accumulation of facts, but a joint venture among students, parents, and teacher to develop habits of mind; habits of character; an ever expanding awareness of the human situation; and the tools needed for effective personal, social, political and moral participation. We consider certain skills to be essential for all graduates: to read well and write clearly, to express oneself effectively; to reason and question thoughtfully, soundly and critically, and to study successfully and with determination. To be truly supportive of young people, teachers and parents must themselves continue to learn so that they may perceive the young accurately and treat them wisely.

> We understand that there are many kinds of intelligence. As such our programs assist young people in developing and appreciating cognition, intuition, imagination, artistic creativity, physical expression and performance, sensitivity to others, self-understanding, and personal well-being. To neglect any of these areas is to limit students in the development of their full potential."

I felt it important to reproduce the school's philosophy in its entirety since it pertains to what we parents are striving to do for our children.

The middle school has six spacious classrooms, an art room, a large gym, meeting rooms and outdoor playing fields, The children take part in many after-school activities on the site, which is located near the beach, community arts resources, and the local library. Apart from the traditional core subjects the schoolexpects their students expect their student to be committed to learning, and so consider such affective skills as accountability and responsibility into their assessments of a student's performance. The school is very diverse in its ethnic and social background helping students to discover different people and communities. For

~ 153 ~

instance, in the middle school the students will study Spanish in a unique program that supplements classroom based Spanish instruction with more intensive immersion-type experiences, including visits to Spanish-speaking communities. They also work with the children on real world investigations, problem solving and exploration, in keeping with what will be major challenges in the future. Each week the teachers and students work in a collectively designed, holistic course of study called The Workshop for Social, Economic and Ecological Action. In high school, the students actually design and implement their own community service plans.

High School

The high school campus is near Overland Avenue on Olympic Boulevard. It is a welcoming place. When I attended the open house I was impressed by David Bryan, the Headmaster. He was very easy to talk to and had much to convey. He introduced us to one of his students who came into the room and, without any warning, began to recite a very moving and beautiful poem he had written, parts of which I can still remember. On the tour we visited the various class rooms and their teachers, all of whom made a very good impression, for they were enthusiastic and informative. I left the school that afternoon with an application for my son. Sadly, he was put on a waiting list and in the meantime accepted into another school.

Grades 6-12 Curriculum

MATH
Fundamentals, algebra, geometry, algebra II, pre-calculus and calculus.

SCIENCE
An integrated program of skills: computer studies, college preparation, individualized study, biology, chemistry, physics and advanced area studies.

THE HUMANITIES
English — genre studies (poetry, fiction, non-fiction, drama), vocabulary, grammar, diagramming, creative writing and essay writing, and ethical themes.
Social Science — chronology, thematic investigations, multi-cultural history and literature, application of composition skills to history essays.

WORKSHOP
Integrated curriculum, real world explorations and applications, social justice, inclusivity, ecological regeneration, community service.

FOREIGN LANGUAGE — Spanish, with In-class instruction, sister school in Mexico, cultural history, conversation and translation, Spanish I through AP Spanish Literature.

THE ARTS
Music — instrumental (flute, recorder, guitar, piano, strings, percussion, jazz), chamber music, music theory, choral, the piano academy.
Visual Art — painting, sculpture, book arts, film history & film production.
Drama and Writing — technique, improvisation, scene study, productions, creative writing, journalism.
Dance — jazz, ballet, hip hop, tap, modern.

PHYSICAL EDUCATION AND ATHLETICS
Yoga, team sports, golf, tennis, basketball, volleyball, fencing, track and cross country, baseball, softball.

HUMAN DEVELOPMENT

Diversity training, human development (mysteries/connections) combining a focused music studies curriculum with a college preparatory academic curriculum.

The Piano Academy is a middle and high school program for grade 6 to 12 students combining a focused music studies curriculum, with a college preparatory academic curriculum. If your child is serious about playing piano this could be the school for you since the School recognizes that aspiring concert and career pianists have special needs: such as) time to practice every day. A flexible school curriculum will allows them time, away from school, for concerts, recitals, tours, and competitions and a multitude of activities necessary to develop ability to concert performance level.

The Piano Academy is designed to meet all these needs. In cooperation with Crossroads School, New Roads will provide aspiring pianists with a unique year-round program. The program will also offer home stay at International House residences for international students and for local students who seek five or seven-day boarding situations.

Another very interesting aspect of the school is that New Roads has devised an Independent Studies Program (ISP) to enable students to find their own way of learning most effectively. Many parents would love their children to learn this way. I know I would.

New Roads students can participate in many after-school activities. There are art classes, music and drama production, homework tutorials, peer tutoring, student organized clubs and competitive athletic teams. Each campus makes an effort to accommodate students' interests at its facility. Students are welcome to participate in activities at either of the New Roads' campuses.

While admission is competitive, and there are many more applicants than openings, the student who is able to exhibit a genuine desire to be part of the school will help his or her chance of acceptance. Applicants must supply transcripts of previous academic work and two letters of recommendation from current teachers. The Independent School Entrance Examination (ISEE) is used for all applicants. New Roads' school code is 054243. Please request that ERB (Educational Records Bureau) send the test results to that number. Students will be notified of acceptance beginning in late March, and thereafter as openings occur.

HISTORY

New Roads School was established in 1995 by The New visions Foundation* as a model for education in an ethnically, racially, culturally, and socio-economically diverse community. to prepare young people for the challenges and opportunities they face, the school aims to promote personal, social, political, and moral understanding, and to instill in students respect for the humanity and ecology of the world in which they live. A non-profit, non-denominational institution, New Roads School is guided by a 25-member Board of Trustees.

*Paul Cummins is the Executive Director of New Visions Foundations. He used to be headmaster, and is now President of Crossroads School.

AT A GLANCE

APPLICATION DEADLINE	February
OPEN HOUSES	October through December
UNIFORMS	No
SUMMER SCHOOL	Mandatory Fee
SEE MAP	D on page 285

NOTRE DAME ACADEMY

Tel: (310) 839-5289 • Fax: (310) 839-7957
2851 Overland Ave. • Los Angeles, CA 90064
www.ndala.com

PRESIDENT	SISTER MARIE PAUL, SND
PRINCIPAL	JOAN TYHURST
DIRECTOR OF ADMISSIONS	YOLANDA OLENIACZ
TYPE OF SCHOOL	ALL GIRLS CATHOLIC DAY SCHOOL
GRADES	9 - 12

- ENROLLMENT: 480
- ACCREDITATION: CAIS/WASC
- MEMBERSHIPS: ASSA
- APPLICATION FEE: $65

- TUITION (CATHOLIC): $8,600
- (NON-CATHOLIC): $9,100
- YEARLY REGISTRATION FEE: $425
- FINANCIAL AID IS AVAILABLE

I visited NOTRE DAME ACADEMY one Sunday in the fall for one of their Open Houses. The school is nestled in a residential area of West Los Angeles, close to the Santa Monica Freeway. The Academy is a microcosm of the ethnically-diverse community it serves. Most of the students commute from as far north as Malibu and as far south as Palos Verdes. With varied ethnic, social and economic backgrounds this seems to make up what appears to be a progressive and talented student body. Ninety-three percent of the students identify themselves as Catholic.

Mission statement (as taken from school brochure):

"Notre Dame Academy educates young women to make a difference. In a caring and nurturing atmosphere, the Academy's value-centered program stresses the importance of personal spirituality, concern for the common good, and service to one another and to the community. Each student is encouraged to set realistic goals, to take confident steps to achieve them and to realize her leadership and service potential. The student sees herself as a worthwhile, esteemed and competent woman, able to make a positive contribution to her Church and the world."

The open house was a very well organized affair. The girls looked beautiful, all dressed in their Sunday best, and very helpful. We arrived in the auditorium, which was filled with booths the girls had set up showing off all the various clubs and organizations to which they belong. It was an impressive show of talent. We were then taken around the school in small groups and shown the students "at work" in their various classrooms.

We visited the computer labs, the art studio, and the Regal Theater, where students were singing, and watched experiments being performed. We then looked in on the Counseling Center and heard about all the resources available to the students to assist in the college selection process. The campus ministry program is the largest organization on campus and is extremely active. The campus ministry students plan school liturgies and retreats. Members of the HOPE (Helping Other People Everywhere) service organization coordinate extensive Christian service programs and work to raise money for various local and international charities.

Developing leadership skills and building a spirit of cooperation, unity and school pride are the goals of all the student organizations, including: National Honor Society, Student Council, Music Club, Queen's Council (a student service organization), Yearbook, L'Esprit, NDA International, Speech/Debate, WIMS (Women Interested in Math and Science), Journalism and the Environment Club.

I especially liked Mrs. Joan Tyhurst and Ms. Gina Liberotti who manned a table near the sign-in tables and were there to answer the curricular questions that all of us parents were so anxious to ask! Finally we were treated to the most delicious refreshments in the rather grand looking cafeteria on the lower level. It was a nice way for us to meet and talk to some of the students and the staff, which was thoroughly enjoyable.

Notre Dame Academy has a full and balanced program of student activities. Notre Dame also offers Advanced Placement and Honors Courses in Art, English, Foreign Languages, Mathematics, Science and Social Studies.

In order to graduate from Notre Dame the students must have completed a minimum of 240 semester credits, including the following specific requirements: religion (four years); English (four years); social studies (three years); foreign language (two years); laboratory science (two years); mathematics (three years); physical ed/health (one year); art, dance, drama, music (one year); computer literacy (one semester), dramatic Interpretation (one semester).

Students are provided with classroom instruction, workshops and one-on-one counseling sessions to help them throughout the college selection and admissions processes.

Ninety nine percent of graduates attend either a two or four-year college. Students have been offered admission to all the top colleges and universities around the country.

The sports program excels on every level and stresses the importance of good sportsmanship and team play on the road to victory. Their competitive teams have won numerous championships in volleyball, cross country, basketball, soccer, track and field, softball and swimming.

The school really believes in educating the whole person. With that in mind, it has academic advisors and personal counselors who are qualified professionals dedicated to recognizing and nurturing the uniqueness and potential of each student, assisting her to develop a strong sense of self as she grows from a young teenage girl into a mature young woman. "The best gift your daughter can receive is open communication and support from all of us working together as a team for her."

HISTORY

Notre Dame Academy is a Catholic private college-preparatory high school for young women fully accredited by the Western Association of Schools and Colleges and by the National Catholic Education Association. Founded in 1949, NDA is owned and operated by the Sisters of Notre Dame.

AT A GLANCE

APPLICATION DEADLINE	January 7
OPEN HOUSE	Call schedule for details
UNIFORMS	Yes
HIGH SCHOOL PLACEMENT TEST	January 26
SEE MAP	D on page 285

NOTRE DAME HIGH SCHOOL

Tel: (818) 933-3600 • Fax: (818) 501-0507
13645 Riverside Drive. • Sherman Oaks, CA 91423
www.ndhs.org

PRINCIPAL	STEPHANIE CONNELLY
DIRECTOR OF ADMISSIONS	COURTNEY RALPH
TYPE OF SCHOOL	CO-EDUCATIONAL DAY SCHOOL
GRADES	9 - 12

- ENROLLMENT: 1,150
- ACCREDITATION: WASC/WCEA
- FINANCIAL AID IS AVAILABLE

- TUITION: $10,200
- REGISTRATION FEE: $500

NOTRE DAME HIGH SCHOOL is on the corner of Riverside Drive and Woodman Avenue in Sherman Oaks. If you live in Hollywood it's a quick trip north on the 101, and the exit is conveniently no more than 30 seconds from the school's main entrance. The school's grounds are wonderful to walk through. It is beautifully kept with flower gardens, trees and places to sit and relax. The playing fields are vast. There is plenty of room to play every sport. Built in the late 40's, the architecture is "early California mission" and it's a sight for sore eyes It makes me want to go back to school.

While touring the campus, I spoke with the Director of Counseling who has been there for ten years. She said, "If you're looking for a well-rounded education for your child, this is the school. Everyone graduates and then goes to college. A few kids take a year off and go traveling."

Mission

"Incorporating the Holy Cross educational tradition in our school community, Notre Dame strives to provide each student with a rich academic background, a strong sense of self, a willingness to take risks for the sake of growth, commitment to family and community and an appreciation for the spiritual dignity of all persons."

Sixty-seven percent of the student body are Catholic and the school does give preference to Catholic students attending a Catholic school, secondly to Catholic students previously not attending a Catholic school, and lastly to non-Catholics. If you are Catholic and your child's grades have not fallen below a "C" in any subject, then he/she may be accepted.

There are 75 faculty members, with 36 holding master's degrees and two with Ph.D.s for a total of 96 staff members. Notre Dame offers a college preparatory curriculum with honors and advanced placement courses in art, English, foreign languages, mathematics, science, and social studies. An extensive elective program offers students courses in computer programming, acting, band, art, art history, journalism, speech, debate, advanced topics in biology, sports medicine, psychology of prejudice, law and society, sociology, and film and American history.

Graduation Requirements

- 4 years English
- 4 years religious studies
- 3 years mathematics
- 3 years social studies
- 2 1/2 years science
- 2 years foreign language
- 1 year fine arts
- 1 year physical education
- 1 semester computers

In addition to the academic requirements, students are required to complete 90 hours of community service by the time of graduation. Freshmen are required to complete 10 hours of service within their family. Sophomores must to complete 20 hours of service where they worship. Juniors will to complete 30 hours of service at Notre Dame, and Seniors are required to complete 30 hours of service anywhere in the local community. The campus ministry program provides a religious experience for students, faculty, and staff by providing spiritual, prayerful experiences on retreats, prayer services, liturgies and personal counseling.

Three levels of athletic teams, Freshman, Junior Varsity and Varsity levels, compete in 15 different girls and boys athletic events. During the school year, both the boys and girls will play in the Mission League. Their league opponents are Alemany, Chaminade, Crespi, Flintridge Sacred Heart, Harvard-Westlake, Louisville, Loyola, and St. Francis.

Notre Dame students are involved in a variety of extra-curricular opportunities. There are many different clubs on campus, ranging from the Japanese Animation Club to the Liturgical Music Club.

The Theater Department produces three very good plays every school year, and the Student Publication groups publish the school Newspaper, Yearbook, and Sports Guides. Forensics and journalism students travel around the country competing in tournaments and participating in conferences. Their award-winning Irish Knight Band competes in many parades, performs in concerts and supports their football and basketball teams. In addition to all of this, the school has an extremely active Associated Student Body group which organizes dances and other social events throughout the year.

The School has worked hard to provide the students with the most up-to-date technology to prepare them for the world. The Fritz B. Burns Center for the Arts and Technology opened in 2001, and has allowed the school to move closer to reaching its goal. In addition to two computer labs, all the classrooms have a computer for the teacher's use. The library also hosts 20 computers for student use. All the computers on campus are connected to the internet. In 2003 new classrooms were added to the Riverside Building.

One hundred percent of Notre Dame graduates will attend college. Seventy three percent will go to a four-year college, 20 percent to a two-year college and the rest will take a year off traveling.

This school is becoming a popular choice among parents looking for a reasonably priced college pre high school for fees are about a third less than other local private high schools. I highly recommend taking a closer look at this school.

HISTORY

Notre Dame High School is a private Catholic secondary school. Founded by the Congregation of Holy Cross in 1947, Notre Dame has been co-educational since 1983. In 1997 Notre Dame celebrated it's 50th Anniversary and in 1998 Mrs. Stephanie Connelly was appointed as principal. The school has the maximum six-year accreditation by the Western Association of Schools and Colleges, and is recognized as a National Blue Ribbon School of Excellence.

AT A GLANCE

APPLICATION DEADLINE	January
OPEN HOUSE	November
UNIFORMS	Yes
SUMMER SPORT CAMP	Ages 6-12
SEE MAP	A on page 285

THE OAKS SCHOOL

Tel: (323) 850-3755 • Fax: (323) 850-3758
6817 Franklin Avenue • Los Angeles, CA 90028
www.oaksschool.org

HEAD OF SCHOOL	MARY FAUVRE, PH. D.
TYPE OF SCHOOL	CO-ED DAY SCHOOL
GRADES	K - 6

- ENROLLMENT: 150
- ACCREDITATION: CAIS/WASC
- MEMBERSHIPS: CAIS/CSEE/NAIS/ISAMA
- TUITION: $15,821
- APPLICATION FEE: $100
- FINANCIAL AID IS AVAILABLE

The OAKS SCHOOL is located in the landmark Hollywood United Methodist Church where Highland meets Franklin. The church building is an architectural beauty, and there are massive, gothic-style arch-ways leading to a charming interior courtyard. The church rents most, but not all, of its space to the Oaks. It also rents to film and television productions and is home to the Court Theatre. So while on the parent tour, you might see a messenger searching for an office number or an actor on his way to an audition!

The classrooms and offices of the school are spread out in a labyrinth of winding halls and staircases. There are seven classrooms, a library and a gym. The children use a large basketball court/play area in the far corner of the church parking lot for outside recreation. The Zachary Fried Children's Library opened in the fall of 1999. A large learning center houses an extensive collection of books, computers, and a storytelling area.

The kindergarten class has a huge, bright room with lots of activity centers. There is a full time teacher, and two full time assistants. There are specialists in art, music, computer and physical education, as well as a full-time librarian. After school enrichment programs are offered each semester in a variety of creative and special interest subjects.

One thing that noteworthy about the school is its flexibility. The educational approach is developmental, and one suspects that from class-to-class the teachers are able to structure the curriculum in a way that suits their teaching style, and also fulfills the needs of their students.

There is an open, friendly, non-clique atmosphere about the Oaks that is refreshing. A fairly new school, it has a group of educators and parents working hard to keep it thriving. It is run by a Board of Trustees that is made up of parents, educators, and members of the community.

Here is the school's philosophy, as written in the brochure:

"We believe that children acquire knowledge best by taking responsibility for their own learning. We provide a safe, non-competitive educational environment where children are given the time to take risks, make mistakes and master skills. Small class size and flexible teaching strategies enable us to address each child's unique learning style and personal development. Our teachers offer a varied and challenging program within a supportive structure to generate growth, enthusiasm, a love of learning, and the confidence born of competence."

Some parents were concerned about the high-traffic area the school is in. It is located in Hollywood, which has a high incidence of crime and a high profile of homeless people walking about. One Oaks parent that I spoke with offered the following: "The school has always felt very secure and safe to me. Sometimes there are homeless people outside as the church is very active in helping the homeless. This is the real world, and I would rather have my son see it than isolate him from it."

HISTORY

In September 1986, eleven children from various preschools attended the first class of what was to become The Oaks School, on the premises of St. Thomas Church. The school was founded by the Head, Deborah Wyle, and concerned parents seeking to bring quality progressive education to the area. In April of 1987 The Oaks incorporated as a non-profit educational institution and moved to the Hollywood United Methodist Church. A 19-member Board of Trustees that includes parents, educators, and members of the community governs The Oaks. Families of all races, religions, cultures, and socio-economic status are welcome.

AT A GLANCE

APPLICATION DEADLINE	End of January. For Kindergarten, your child must be age 5 by 10/1
PROSPECTIVE PARENT ORIENTATION	November 5, and January 11
UNIFORMS	No
BEFORE AND AFTER SCHOOL CARE	Yes
SEE MAP	C on page 285

THE OAKWOOD SCHOOL

Elementary Campus:
11230 Moorpark St. • North Hollywood, CA 91602
(818) 752-4444 • Fax: (818) 752-4466
Secondary Campus:
11600 Magnolia Blvd. • North Hollywood, CA 91601
(818) 752-4400 • Fax: (818) 766-1285
www.oakwoodschool.org

HEAD OF SCHOOL	JAMES A. ASTMAN, PH.D.
DIRECTOR OF ADMISSIONS	
ELEMENTARY:	NANCY GOLDBERG
SECONDARY:	JULIA COLEY
DIRECTOR/DIVERSITY & OUTREACH	LIDA ROSE-WINTERS
TYPE OF SCHOOL	CO-EDUCATIONAL DAY SCHOOL
GRADES	K - 12

- ENROLLMENT: 764
- PARENT ORGANIZATION DUES: $50
- APPLICATION FEE: $100
- ACCREDITATIONS CAIS/NAIS/WASC
- MEMBERSHIPS: ABC/CASE/ERB/ISAMA/ NACAC/SCEE/WALAC

- TUITION:
  - K-6: $22,580
  - 7-12: $26,800
- FINANCIAL AID IS AVAILABLE

OAKWOOD ELEMENTARY is located in North Hollywood on Moorpark Street alongside the Hollywood Freeway (170). The campus property adjoins tree-lined Woodbridge Park, which lends a feeling of open space and greenery to the grounds.

As of 2008, they have a new play space at the elementary campus, along with a performance space and community room. There is a new science and technology center at the elementary campus. Oakwood also is expanding the classroom technology center. The school has expanded the arts program in both academic and performance opportunities, including the addition of four jazz bands.

The facility is not sophisticated and the buildings have a rustic feeling about them much like a summer camp. The tour begins with a question and answer session supervised by principal Margo Long, with questions directed to eight bright sixth-grade students holding microphones. One parent asked the question, "Which part of the program do you like the most and which the least?" Math was a popular "like-most" answer, as was art.

Dislikes included wanting bigger classrooms, dirty bathrooms and a unanimous thumbs down to doing so many 'laps' in physical education. The students all said that there was a lot of work and homework that was sometimes overwhelming. This was in direct contrast to the impression that I had had from the school brochure, which described Oakwood as developmental. I'm sure that it starts out that way in Kindergarten, but by sixth grade, it has an academic, college preparatory curriculum with one to two hours of homework per night.

During the tour through the classrooms, the first graders told us about an experiment they were doing to teach each other what discrimination felt like. The class was divided into 'greens' and 'blues' and each child wore a color tag. For the whole day, the 'greens' would be treated special, have the best seats, use the 'green' designated bathroom, get called on first, have a longer recess, etc. Meantime, the 'blue' group would be frowned upon, have to sit on the floor, use the 'blue' bathroom, let all the 'greens' go first to lunch, recess, and so on. The 'green' children were also discouraged from talking to the 'blue' children.

By the time our parent tour rolled through the classroom I could tell by the long faces on some of the 'blue' children that they had learned quite a bit about how it felt to be discriminated against. However, I was surprised to hear that the experiment was ending that day without giving the 'green' children a chance to experience the 'blue' side of the experiment.

The kindergarten uses a whole-language approach to integrate reading, writing, and listening skills, and children learn at their own level and pace. The math program uses manipulative learning tools such as cuisinaire rods, pattern blocks, base ten blocks, chip trading, and collections.

In social studies, (K-6) topics include: the evolution of life, the pioneers, native peoples of North America and Mexico, ancient Egyptian civilization, medieval Europe, early American History, classical Greek cultures, and current world events.

All teachers have bachelors degrees, and many have completed masters and doctorate degrees. There are specialist teachers for physical education computer, music, and library. There is now a full time director for Diversity and Outreach, and a full-time Director of Community Service.

In addition to Oakwood's academic, art, and athletics programs, upper-elementary students may select mini-courses taught by teachers, parents, alumni, or outside community leaders. Past courses include: textile design, jazz dance, law, jewelry, teaching, futurism, theatrical make-up, drama and African-American history.

The Secondary Campus is located on Magnolia right off the 170 freeway. There are approximately 460 students in grades 7 to 12. The average class size is twenty students. The secondary school includes a specialized math and science building of ten classrooms, five labs, a lecture hall, and a meeting atrium. Humanities, languages, and the arts are offered in an additional 15 classrooms, plus an auditorium. The theatre is charming. When I visited students were building sets, and one was left with the impression that it is a very productive space. Across the street is the Music, Dance and Athletic center. This is an impressive building that houses the professional-looking music and dance rooms, and a 500-seat regulation gym with a separate weight training facility. There are plans to build a bridge to connect the gym to the other facilities. At the present time the children have to cross Magnolia. However, there is a full-time crossing guard.

The student who was giving me the tour said if a child is heavily into sports this might not be the right school. When you ask the high school students what they like most about the school they unanimously said, "our teachers." They told us that they could call them at home if they had homework problems, and that the teachers were more concerned with their understanding their work, not just doing well on tests. Mr. Astman said, "Teaching can be enthralling, unsettling, hysterically funny, or profoundly serious (or all four), but it is never impersonal."

A parent on the tour said he wished that he had gone to a high school like Oakwood because it felt as if he would have had the freedom to express himself. All students and staff of the secondary school meet twice weekly in town meetings on the basketball court. Here the students can talk about what is on their minds, read poems, or make announcements. Many schools talk about community, but here you are left believing that this is the heart of Oakwood.

If you are interested in Oakwood's Secondary school (7-12), call and ask for their curriculum handbook which gives a detailed, comprehensive description of the academic program. Listed below are the minimal graduation requirements for the high school, grades 9-12.

Course of Study and Graduation Requirements

The course of study offered at the Oakwood Secondary School covers six years (grades 7 to 12). The year is organized into two semesters (September-January and February-June). Students are expected to carry six subjects a semester in addition to physical education. Students are required to complete 20 periods of school service, ten in grades 7 and 8, and ten in grades 9 and 10. Students in grades 7 to 12 are required to complete 45 hours of community service, a special studies class each semester, and a senior project.

In most years 100 percent of all Oakwood graduates enroll immediately in four-year colleges and universities across the country. Oakwood provides an athletic program which includes: cross country, volleyball, equestrian, basketball, soccer, softball, and track and field. Boys' sports include the aforementioned with the addition of baseball.

Here's a word on the school philosophy taken from the brochure:

> "Although our program is college preparatory, we are equally concerned with the quality of children's experiences in the present.

We intend an Oakwood education:
1. To develop students' intellectual, artistic, physical, and social competence, and seek to develop intellectual curiosity, imagination, and independent thought.
2. To spark passion.
3. To foster morality and develop self-knowledge.
4. To help students learn about their strengths and weaknesses within a supportive environment.
5. To foster a learning community in which students experience respect for the integrity of their efforts, whether those efforts result in success or failure."

The word on the school from several Oakwood parents that I spoke with is that it is a great school with a challenging curriculum and wonderful teachers, but a disappointing campus facility, although this may be altered with the current construction. One parent said that it wasn't as arts-oriented as its reputation portrays it to be.

HISTORY

The Oakwood School is a co-educational K-12 college preparatory school. It was founded in 1950 by a group of parents who wanted to provide their children with an educational experience balanced among the arts, sciences, and humanities. It was to be challenging to creative and intellectual capacities. They wanted a learning community, which fostered independence of thought, intellectual integrity, and personal and social morality. The Secondary School was founded in 1964. In 1979, James Astman was appointed Headmaster.

AT A GLANCE

APPLICATION DEADLINE	January 9
OPEN HOUSES	October 28 and November 15
UNIFORMS	No
AFTER SCHOOL CARE	3 p.m. - 6 p.m.
SEE MAP	A on page 285

PACIFIC HILLS SCHOOL

Tel: (310) 276-3068 • Fax: (310) 657-3831
8628 Holloway Drive • West Hollywood, CA 90069
www.phschool.org

HEAD OF SCHOOL	RICHARD S. MAKOFF
ADMISSIONS ASSISTANT	SHIRLEY CHACON
TYPE OF SCHOOL	CO-EDUCATIONAL COLLEGE PREP
GRADES	6 - 12

- ENROLLMENT: 300
- ACCREDITATION: CAIS/WASC
- APPLICATION FEE: $100

- TUITION: $19,500-$20,950
- NEW FAMILY FEE: $500
- FINANCIAL AID IS AVAILABLE

PACIFIC HILLS SCHOOL is located on Holloway Drive just below Sunset Boulevard and a stone's throw from Book Soup. It's a small urban campus without playing fields, swimming pool or cafeteria. A catering truck does come into the campus every day offering the students hot or cold choices for lunch. There are approximately 15 classrooms, administrative offices, an auditorium, a computer lab with 15 computers and a library.

The school believes that a thorough education must provide for the physical, social and recreational needs of the students so, as there are no school playing fields, they bus the students to local parks and often rent out the gym at other schools. Daily P.E. is required from grades 6-11 but is optional for seniors. In the middle school, students participate in team and lifetime sports such as flag football, volleyball, soccer, floor hockey, softball, track and golf. The brochure says that "While these classes emphasize participation, skill development and fitness, they are also just plain fun!" If your child is serious about sports, there is a championship athletic program that guarantees that the more competitive students are looked after. The school has won recent C.I.F. championships in both basketball and softball.

There is a strong parent involvement at the school. In fact, in the letter to the parents it clearly states that volunteer activity and support for their annual fund-raiser are important considerations during the admissions process. It also goes on to say that "admission to the school is contingent upon an evaluation of the student's ability to succeed in the academic program, and upon an indication that acceptance would benefit both the student and the school."

Its parent body is an ethnically and socially diverse group who all seem to share a commitment to their children's school. Almost 50 percent of the student body receives some form of aid and boasts 65 percent diversity. Parents can often be seen participating in classroom activities, going on overnight field trips and attending the various sports events.

The entire school curriculum fits on one page and offers the core classes in all the major subjects with the opportunity to move from standard to honors courses or (and I quote) "from honor to standard courses," based on the students' achievement in each subject. Pacific Hills leans toward being a traditional school, however, there are more progressive educational practices being incorporated into the curriculum. A variety of clubs also pop up depending on interest, including forensics, chess, robotics, etc.

The school is able to provide students with much individualized attention since the student/teacher ratio is approximately 10:1. As students enter the upper school there is more course work, and students are expected to work independently. Teachers are available for extra help, and the school will suggest a tutor if a child falls behind. Which makes sense if you leave some children to work independently and leave them to their own devices.

Upper school students are required to complete four years of English, social science and P.E., and three years each of math, science and a foreign language. In addition, students must complete classes in human development, the fine arts, speech and various electives. Electives offered in the middle and upper schools include: art, advanced art, ceramics, photography, advanced photography, computers, theater arts, music, journalism, newspaper, yearbook, law and filmmaking. A required Outdoor Education Program sends every class, every year, off campus for a week to locations such as Big Bear, Santa Barbara, Catalina, Malibu and San Diego for kayaking, rope-courses, hiking etc. The eighth grade takes an additional trip to the State Capitol and other destinations in northern California.

From the Mission Statement

> "Pacific Hills School is dedicated to providing its students with a challenging college preparatory program in a warm and supportive environment. The school is committed to establishing a racially diverse, multi-cultural community, and to develop each student's full human potential through a comprehensive educational program."

If you are looking for a school that offers a family atmosphere and helps your child to foster self-awareness and self-esteem, as well as to read well, write clearly and coherently, to study effectively, to reason soundly, and to question thoughtfully, then you might wish to consider applying to this school. Many parents from the neighborhood are looking at Pacific Hills as an alternative to some of the Westside schools.

HISTORY

Pacific Hills School was founded in 1983 as the Bel Air Preparatory School. In 1993, Richard Makoff, the school's current headmaster, turned the school into a nonprofit organization and the school's name was changed. The school's Board is composed of a president and nine other officers. Five of these officers form the school's executive committee. The headmaster, the assistant headmaster, a faculty representative and an administrative assistant sit on the Board and are instrumental in working with other Board members to incorporate the school's policies and programs.

AT A GLANCE

APPLICATION DEADLINE	Year-round
	Grades 6, 7, & 9 have the most openings
OPEN HOUSES	11/1, 1/2, 4/9 and 3/4
ISEE OR EQUIVALENT	Yes
UNIFORMS	No
SUMMER SCHOOL	Yes
%AGE OF GRADUATES TO 4-YEAR COLLEGES	97%
SEE MAP	C on page 285

PAGE PRIVATE SCHOOLS

Hancock Park site:
565 N. Larchmont Blvd. • Los Angeles, CA 90004
Tel: (323) 463-5119 • Fax: (323) 465-9964

Beverly Hills site:
419 S. Robertson Blvd. • Beverly Hills, CA 90210
Tel: (323) 272-3429 • Fax: (310) 273-0497
www.pageschool.com

SCHOOL DIRECTOR	CONNIE RIVERA
TYPE OF SCHOOL	CO-EDUCATIONAL DAY SCHOOL
GRADES	PRESCHOOL - 8

- ENROLLMENT: 225
- ACCREDITATION/MEMBERSHIP: NCPSA
- REGISTRATION FEE: $600
- YEARLY RE-ENROLLMENT FEE: $300
- A NON-PROFIT CORPORATION
- FINANCIAL AID IS AVAILABLE

- TUITION:
    PRE: $985 MONTHLY.
    K-5: $1,360 MONTHLY
- BOOK FEES: $350-$500
- ADMINISTRATION FEE: $280

PAGE SCHOOL is conveniently located on Larchmont Boulevard in Hancock Park, just above Larchmont Village. It is a very pleasant looking school with a gated courtyard in the front. Inside there are air-conditioned, spacious classrooms and administrative offices. There is a library, computer and science labs, as well as art and music rooms.

A year ago the kindergarten classrooms were enlarged giving the children a lot more space for learning and playing. In fact, the overall look of the campus has greatly improved within the last couple of years, and the school is in the process of being remodeled. Classrooms have been painted, new computers installed. On my recent visit, the teachers were informative, friendly, and willing to answer all my questions.

Page School provides a nurturing environment for the individual child so that educational and social growth skills may be developed. The school prides itself on providing incentives for scholarship, character, and personality through individual attention.

Page is a traditional and structured school. According to the school, "There is an emphasis on the three R's." Students are required to follow a core curriculum of subjects in math, phonics and reading, spelling, English composition, penmanship, science and social studies, geography, history, computers, library science, foreign language, physical education, art, music, drama, and dance.

Here is the school Philosophy:

"To a small degree, a child may be compelled to learn. But unless he learns because he truly wants to, he will quit at first opportunity. Page strives to give students a desire to learn and thirst for knowledge, so they seek education on their own. We try to lead students into right choices, not because they will be punished if they do not make those choices, but because they want to excel. The only discipline is self-discipline.

Each subject is taught separately. Study is departmentalized at Page to those specialties. Our system has proved superior. Again and again, students tell us they like a change of pace and a change of surroundings during the school day.

Textbooks and other classroom materials are the finest. All meet our high expectations in the classroom.

At Page we also teach etiquette – the mannerly way of life. Page takes the time required to mold young ladies and gentlemen."

There are specialists in Spanish, art, music, dance, drama, computer and physical education. A strong partnership with the Music Center has been established for this academic year. Afternoon programs offer etiquette classes (possibly a vestige from its days as a girls' boarding school), music, dance, arts, and crafts. A new Art History class will be offered this year. Page has its own soccer team.

Beginning as early as pre-kindergarten, the children not only learn to operate computers but to use them in the practical aspects of schooling. Every student is required to complete classes in technology and computers. All elementary and middle school students have supervised study halls available from 3:30 to 4:30 p.m. and 8 to 8:45 a.m. daily. Attendance is on a voluntary basis unless a teacher places the student in mandatory study hall.

Behind the school, there are several sport courts which provide children with a variety of activities including tennis, racquet ball, volleyball, basketball, and badminton. The physical education teachers work hard to instill the importance of good sportsmanship, teamwork, and character. I was surprised at how much land the school has. From the front you would never believe there was room for a swimming pool, but, there is, and it is used year-round by the students. Part of the curriculum for every student is the mastery of swimming and the understanding of water safety.

The children attend daily assemblies. There's Back-to-School Night, a Halloween Carnival, Spring Program and Barbecue, Field Trips and Graduation ceremonies.

If you are looking for a traditional, academic school that concentrates on basic education and old-fashioned fundamentals, you might want to visit this campus and take a look for yourself.

HISTORY

The Los Angeles campus of the Page school was founded in 1908 by the Vaughan family and has been continuously operated by succeeding generations. Originally a girls' boarding school, Page became a military academy and day school in the 1950s. Today there are additional campuses in Beverly Hills, Garden Grove, and Costa Mesa. There are also three Florida campuses.

AT A GLANCE

APPLICATION DEADLINE	Open enrollment, as space is available
UNIFORMS	Yes
BEFORE AND AFTER SCHOOL CARE	Yes
SUMMER SCHOOL	Yes
SEE MAP	C on page 285

PASADENA WALDORF SCHOOL

Tel: (626) 794-9564 • Fax: (626) 794-4704
209 E. Mariposa St. • Altadena, CA 91001
www.pasadenawaldorf.org

COLLEGE CHAIR	KAREN LIVINGSTON
ADMISSIONS COORDINATOR	DIANE LASALLE
TYPE OF SCHOOL	CO-EDUCATIONAL DAY SCHOOL
GRADES	PRESCHOOL - 8

- ENROLLMENT: 250
- ACCREDITATION: NONE
- MEMBERSHIPS: ERB/AWSNA
- APPLICATION FEE: $100
- LIMITED FINANCIAL AID IS AVAILABLE

- TUITION:
  K: $10,050
  1-8: $12,900
- NEW FAMILY FEE: $500
- PEGASUS CAPITAL FEE: $400

The PASADENA WALDORF SCHOOL is located in Altadena on a five-acre property complete with sprawling green lawns and huge old pine, oak and eucalyptus trees. The most impressive structure is a historic California craftsman house built at the turn of the century where most of the classes are held.

The other buildings are of a more temporary nature – permanent trailer structures that can be set up quickly and cheaply to provide instant space. These are commonly seen on many campuses as an affordable way to keep up with a rapidly growing enrollment.

A parent interested in a Waldorf education for his/her child is given every opportunity to learn about the school philosophy and to observe the students in action. The orientation is very thorough. The teaching staff is passionate and enthusiastic about the Waldorf approach, and eager to educate visiting parents. Pasadena Waldorf School follows the curriculum and educational philosophy of Rudolf Steiner, integrating academics and the arts in a developmentally appropriate manner.

The school store has many books available for purchase that describe the Waldorf philosophy and method.

In 2007, the school initiated their preschool program to keep up with the demand. Children are accepted from age four and are kept in the nursery-kindergarten class until they are ready for first grade at six plus. The adults in charge are known by name and not yet thought of or referred to as teachers. There is also a resource teacher on staff.

The atmosphere is warm and un-pressured. Children play, socialize with one another, have story time, and are made comfortable by the repetition of their daily routine. This important development time and care is taken so that students are not onvolved in intellectual pursuits before they are ready.

Activities include painting, modeling, cooking, sewing, building, making things, learning nursery rhymes and songs in English, French and German. The children also learn eurythmy (an art of movement by Waldorf founder Rudolf Steiner), simple fairy tales, and participate in little plays and seasonal festivals.

The elementary school covers the ages six to fourteen. Each new class (first grade) receives a class teacher who stays with them for the whole eight years.

The curriculum includes reading, writing, composition and grammar, math, zoology, California history, mythology and local American geography. Studies include botany, geometry, chemistry, physics, American geography, economics, and histories, acient and modern. The annual eighth grade field trip travels to such places as the Yucatan, Hawaii, Costa Rica and England!

There are specialist teachers in music, art, physical education, Spanish, gardening, crafts, and woodworking. Each year the school hosts an Elves Faire Winter Celebration.

Each morning begins with a main lesson which lasts about two hours. The main lesson is devoted to the main cultural subjects, includeing mathematics, English, history, geography, science, etc. These are taught in block periods of three or four weeks each. After that the children work with the specialist teachers for the better part of the day.

The children do not use books but create their own books by copying written material from the blackboard. In first grade, they illustrate the books using lots of color. All the illustrations are taken from a rough sketch that the teacher draws on the blackboard. As the years go on, the material is dictated by the teacher after a thorough discussion of the subject matter with the class. Often the main lesson books are beautifully bound, and the covers are designed and decorated by the students.

Art is also taught by dictation with the teacher showing an example of the drawing or watercolor painting and the children then copying it. The children's art was everywhere, which gave a great feeling of cheerfulness and color. But, since all the children painted exactly the same subject, in a rather similar way, no individual drawing stood out in any particular way. The art hanging together in this fashion looks more like a mural than the work of different children.

Here is an excerpt on Waldorf philosophy as taken from the brochure:

> "Waldorf teachers utilize a variety of approaches and methods. Central among them is the integration of the arts into all subjects using movement, music, storytelling and rhythm, even in the sciences. Self-expression, self-discipline, and the wholeness of life are among the themes teachers weave into every lesson. Academic excellence is thus pursued in a balanced, supportive, nurturing, non-competitive environment. The result is a well-grounded, culturally literate creative student, curious about the world and eager to explore it."

The Waldorf schools have a unique approach to education that is best experienced through a visit to the campus. Tours are scheduled throughout the year.

HISTORY

The Pasadena Waldorf School was first established in 1979 and is one of 20 Waldorf Schools in California. The curriculum and educational philosophy of the Waldorf Schools was formulated in Germany by Rudolf Steiner, Ph.D., in 1919.

AT A GLANCE

APPLICATION DEADLINE	Ongoing as space is available, K fills up early.
OPEN HOUSES	10/8, 11/6, 12/3, 1/30 & 3/4
UNIFORMS	No
BEFORE AND AFTER SCHOOL CARE	Yes
SEE MAP	B on page 285

PILGRIM SCHOOL

Tel: (213) 385-7351 • Fax: (213) 386-7264
540 S. Commonwealth Ave. • Los Angeles, CA 90020
www.pilgrim-school.org

HEAD OF SCHOOL	MARK BROOKS
DIRECTOR OF ADMISSIONS	PATRICIA KONG/LAURA EVERETT
TYPE OF SCHOOL	CO-EDUCATIONAL DAY SCHOOL
GRADES	PRESCHOOL - 12

- ENROLLMENT: 350
- ACCREDITATION: CAIS/WASC
- MEMBERSHIPS: CRIS/NAIS
- APPLICATION FEE: $125
- NEW STUDENT ENROLLMENT FEE: $1000
- ENROLLMENT DEPOSIT: $1000
- FINANCIAL AID IS AVAILABLE

- TUITION:
  - JK: $12,600
  - K: $12,850
  - 1-5: $12,920
  - 6-8: $16,550
  - 9-12: $18,330
  - 12: $19,330

PILGRIM SCHOOL is a (non-denominational) division of the First Congregational Church of Los Angeles. The church and school buildings are arresting, massive granite structures that blend in with the downtown urban setting. The school has an old-fashioned feel to it with sash windows, varnished oak doors and molding, and black and white checkerboard tile floors.

This is a traditional academic school with a rigorous curriculum. One hundred percent of Pilgrim School graduates go on to higher education, many finding success at Stanford, UC Berkeley, UCLA, USC, Vassar, Columbia, Yale, West Point, Georgetown and the Claremont Colleges. The educators, administrators, parents, and church officials I met during my many visits have a great deal of love, dedication, and support for the school.

Pilgrim has a wonderful ethnic and socio-economic mix of children in its classrooms reflecting the rich blend of cultures that we have in the city of Los Angeles. Pilgrim has its share of celebrity families, but they are very low key about it. You never get the feeling that they cater to celebrity status at the school.

There are 33 classrooms, two libraries with 12,000 volumes, a gym, art studio, computer lab, dance studio, dark room, auditorium/theater and science lab. The campus is very well maintained and has a functional rather than deluxe feeling to it.

There is a preschool with playgrounds that have plenty of swings and metal climbing structures with rubber padding beneath. Recently a new playground and lunch area were completed, with landscaping creating a park-like atmosphere with shade trees and tables to eat at. Planters also provide a hands-on instructional laboratory for students to learn how to grow plants, fruits and vegetables.

Recently, while taking a tour of the school I was told that the school's Board of Governors envisions a new building on adjacent land that could include a new gymnasium, an expanded fine arts and science classroom, and performance space. Currently they are using an empty lot next door for football practice.

Besides boasting 42 championships in various sports, Pilgrim School students also excel outside the classroom. Art and photography students have had unusually creative and unique exhibits both on campus and in galleries throughout Los Angeles.

The elementary curriculum includes phonics, reading, arithmetic, mathematics, bible study, English, U.S. history, social studies, and geography. There are specialist teachers in music, art, storytelling, French, Spanish, and physical education.

The upper school curriculum includes courses in fine arts (studio art, music, choir, drama, dance, and photography), English (composition, public speaking, newspaper, and yearbook), Spanish, French, math (algebra, unified math, geometry, trigonometry, calculus, statistics, and computer), religion (old and new testament, ethics, and comparative religion), science, physical education, and social studies. Specialists teach foreign languages, art, and music. Elementary school sports include soccer, volleyball and flag football. There is an optional, competitive athletic program at the upper school level in football, basketball, volleyball, and softball.

There are over 20 after-school classes offered at an additional cost, including karate, early etiquette, gymnastics, magic, young chefs and candy making, cartooning and tap dancing. Pilgrim has considered ending its 'tracking' policy whereby classes are grouped by developmental and achievement ability, and for now, this has not changed. Children are given letter grades starting in kindergarten. The school espouses the 'whole child' educational philosophy.

HISTORY

Pilgrim School, founded in 1958, is an independent, co-educational, college preparatory, K-12 day school. It offers a rigorous curriculum that begins in kindergarten and grows increasingly demanding through the twelve grades.

AT A GLANCE

APPLICATION DEADLINE	Late February
OPEN HOUSES	November
UNIFORMS	Yes
ISEE TESTING	Yes
BEFORE AND AFTER SCHOOL CARE	Yes
SECURITY	At all times
SUMMER CAMP	Yes
SEE MAP	C on page 285

POLYTECHNIC SCHOOL

Tel: (626) 792-2147 • Fax: (626) 449-5727
1030 E. California Blvd. • Pasadena, CA 91106
www.polytechnic.org

HEAD OF SCHOOL	DEBORAH E. REED
DIRECTOR OF ADMISSIONS	SALLY JEANNE MCKENNA
TYPE OF SCHOOL	CO-EDUCATIONAL DAY SCHOOL
GRADES	KINDERGARTEN - 12

- ENROLLMENT: 854
- ACCREDITATION: WASC
- BOOK FEES: (6–12): $400 - $800
- FINANCIAL AID IS AVAILABLE
- APPLICATION FEE: $100
- MEMBERSHIPS: NAPSG/CAIS/NAIS/CSEE/ERB/ABC/ISAMA

- TUITION:
  - K-5: $18,675
  - 6-8: $21,950
  - 9-12: $25,225

POLYTECHNIC is a traditional college preparatory school with an outstanding reputation. The campus takes up 15 acres of prime Pasadena real estate and includes two gymnasiums, two tennis courts, an athletic field, a performing arts center, a fine arts center, two libraries, a computer lab, science and history buildings, and a media center. The campus is extensive but has more of a lived-in than a modern feeling to it.

Polytechnic is a private school that offers a great education most notably at the upper school level, but one thing that it doesn't offer is enough spaces for the hundreds that apply each year. Even school alumni have trouble getting their children enrolled at Poly.

The best time to apply is at the kindergarten level where there are the most openings: 32. Grade 6 generally has about 20 openings, and grade 9 approximately 15 to 20. All the other grades have very limited openings somewhere in the range of zero to four4.

The school philosophy is the same today as it was years ago, as written by then-principal, Virginia Pease:

> "The individual, not the class, is the unit of the teacher's interest and the development of the child's power to think and to do, rather than the following of a certain course of instruction, is the the direct aim of every teacher and the excuse for every lesson.

The School Credo:
  I. We are committed to honesty, justice, charity, and the pursuit of truth.
  II. We respect the dignity and worth of all human beings – their thoughts, their feelings, and their individuality.
  III. We seek to celebrate the joy and love that emanate from the human spirit.
  IV. We strive to be responsible and contributing members of our families, our school community, and our world."

Under one headmaster, the school is organized into three divisions with separate administrative heads and teaching staffs.

Kindergarten and first grade classes have three sections of 15 students at each grade level with a lead teacher and assistant teacher in each classroom. There are homeroom teachers for each class, supplemented by specialist teachers. Enrollment in the lower school is approximately 300 students.

The lower school teachers provide their students with a great deal of individual attention. The daily program includes language arts, mathematics and social studies. Single-subject teachers provide instruction in science, choral and instrumental music, art, Spanish, physical education, and drama. Children regularly use the library, computer facility, and resource center.

Community service is built into the curriculum in the lower and middle schools with additional volunteer opportunities after school. In the upper school, students contribute eight hours in their freshman year and complete a 30-hour project between the sophomore and senior years.

Students can select their own projects or work with organizations and schools such as: Hillsides Home for Children, Willard School, Kidspace, Huntington Memorial Hospital, Special Olympics, and AIDS Service Center.

Middle School - Courses of Study

Grade 6: English, world history; mathematics; science; computer; French, Latin and Spanish; arts and physical education.

Grade 7: English, geography, civics, cultural understanding, math, pre-algebra, geometry, astronomy, marine science, computer keyboarding, word processing, logowriter programming; French, Latin, or Spanish, arts electives, physical education

Grade 8: English, U.S. history from 1860, algebra, geometry; French, Latin or Spanish, human biology, computer keyboarding, word processing, desktop publishing, arts electives; physical education.

Upper School Requirements: English, math, history, science, language, fine arts, P.E., outdoor education, community services.

All the students at Polytechnic are required to take physical education with an emphasis on cooperation, good sportsmanship, and the development of skills rather than winning or losing.

Seventh and eighth graders are encouraged to select one or more sports of their choice from a list that includes football, volleyball, basketball, soccer, track and field, softball, tennis and baseball. Eighty percent of upper school students earn their required physical education credits by participating in after-school team sports.

The Girls Prep League competes in cross-country, track and field, swimming, volleyball, soccer, tennis, basketball and softball. The Boys Prep League competes in eight-man football, cross-country, basketball, soccer, tennis, baseball, volleyball, swimming, golf and track and field. Water polo, wrestling, badminton and equestrian teams are co-educational.

Polytechnic's Outdoor Education Program, includes hiking, backpacking, mountain climbing, and canoeing. These field trips are structured to expand on the classroom lessons in ecology, botany, geology, and history. They also teach students to work together in the planning and navigating of the trip.

There is a great deal of parent involvement at Polytechnic. Parents drive on field trips, coordinate and promote school functions, serve on committees, and participate in fundraising.

Polytechnic is a prep school that is serious about education and proud of the list of top colleges that accept its seniors each year. There is an extensive list at the back of the school brochure. The educational background of staff and teachers, is listed in the brochure. Polytechnic clearly a fine group of teachers and educators among its ranks.

HISTORY

Polytechnic and its neighbor, Caltech, evolved from the Throop Polytechnic Institute. That school, which was established in 1891, offered an academic program that extended from the primary grades through college. In spring, 1907, the trustees decided that they wanted to place greater financial and academic emphasis on the college program and closed the grammar school.

The patrons of the grammar school wasted no time in forming a committee and arranging for the incorporation of a new elementary school. Ezra S. Gosney, a sheepherder turned philanthropist, who founded the Human Betterment Foundation, came forward with $12,500. That amount was matched by 18 other donors and the property at Poly's present site was purchased.

Polytechnic Elementary School opened its doors in 1907 with 106 students and Virginia Pease as principal. It would later become the first independent school in California to be incorporated as a non-profit institution.

Polytechnic's enrollment and its physical plant were expanded in stages over the next 50 years. Grade 9 was added in 1918 and the name of the institution changed to Polytechnic Elementary and Junior High School. Polytechnic received its current name with the addition of grades 10-12 in 1958. By the early 1960s, the student body had grown to 600.

AT A GLANCE

APPLICATION DEADLINE	February 2
OPEN HOUSE	Lower school: 9/25, 10/1, 10/28, 11/5 Upper School: 11/9, 12/14
UNIFORMS	Grades 1-5
AFTER SCHOOL CARE	Yes via Tom Sawyer
SEE MAP	B on page 285

PROVIDENCE HIGH SCHOOL

Tel: (818) 846-8141 • Fax: (818) 843-8421
511 S. Buena Vista St. • Burbank, CA 91505
www.providencehigh.org

HEAD OF SCHOOL	MICHELE SCHULTE
DIRECTOR OF ADMISSIONS	JUDY EGAN UMECK
TYPE OF SCHOOL	CATHOLIC CO-ED DAY SCHOOL
GRADES	9 - 12

- ENROLLMENT: 560
- ACCREDITATION: WASC
- MEMBERSHIP: NCEA
- FINANCIAL AID AVAILABLE
- TUITION: $9,270 INCLUDES BOOKS
- APPLICATION FEE: $60
- REGISTRATION FEE: $550

PROVIDENCE HIGH SCHOOL is a Catholic, college-preparatory school. The school is located in the San Fernando Valley. If you live in Hollywood, you take Barham over the hill and it is near the Burbank Studios and very close to the Equestrian Center. The campus is nestled between a beautiful park and the neighborhood hospital. Over the past four decades, Providence High has flourished to become a recognized outstanding school in the area. Providence attracts students from a wide diversity of economic, cultural and ethnic backgrounds, a diversity which I believe enriches the educational experience of the student body. Children come from all over to attend this blue ribbon school. Providence High School works closely with the parents who are acknowledged as the primary educators of their sons and daughters and are expected to be very involved in their kids' academic lives. This will suit those of us who miss those days of volunteering in our kid's elementary school and feel left out during those middle school years. The Parent Executive Committee at the school allows parents to be involved in the high school life of their children by supporting the school, faculty and staff, and acts as a network with other parents providing a communication link for upcoming events and activities.

In 2001, the school opened the Fritz B. Burns Student Activity Center featuring a state-of-the-art gymnasium, weight room, exercise room, boys' and girls' locker rooms and conference center. It is a very impressive piece of architecture that is quite eye-catching as one pulls up the driveway. As I parked my car and headed back toward the school building, I spoke to a couple of students who answered my questions with a tremendous amount of enthusiasm. They couldn't wait to tell me about two very unique programs the school has to offer.

The first one is the four-year Health Careers Focus Program, which is offered to about 25 students from an incoming pool of about 40 to 60 freshmen. In their freshmen and sophomore years, students attend weekly rounds at the medical center next door visiting different departments. During their sophomore year, students enroll in honors biology. The Religion Department is involved with the program's second semester of the junior year through their Peace and Justice course. An honors chemistry course is a requirement during this year and students start their hospital internships. They are required to complete 120 hours of internship rotation at a medical facility of their choice. This requirement is continued into their senior year, during which time they are required to complete a minimum of 80 hours for a combined minimum of 200 hours. In their senior year, students must enroll in either AP biology or anatomy-physiology. Graduating students are honored at the Senior Awards assembly for their participation and completed internships after four years of dedication and hard work.

The second is a Media Communications Focus Program. In the first year, the student study important aspects pertaining to the history of media. For instance, the Ethics in Media course deals with questions and dilemmas concerning the role of the media and its moral impact on society. Students learn the basic principles of drawing and filming, explore creative concepts, develop perceptual skills, and learn techniques that will culminate in a major animation project. In the Video Production class they learn first hand what it is like to collaborate on a video project followed by a production oriented course that emphasizes the skills learned in video projection. In this course they will continue to practice advanced editing using AVID and Final Cut Pro software. There's a course of advanced practice in creative writing skills, concentrating on script writing, fiction, drama, and personal essays. Professional writers in film and television are invited into the classroom for special presentations throughout the semester. By the end of the four-year program, student teams will have produced an original commercial, as well as a music video.

Upon completion of the four year media program, these students are uniquely qualified to compete for positions at the best film and media schools in the nation. Your child can then return to the neighborhood and is capable of working for one of the top movie studios in the world!

Mission Statement

> "Providence High School's goal is to develop each student to his or her full potential, as a leader, a responsible citizen of the world, who is imbued with a strong set of moral values, a sense of service and a love of learning. We work in collaboration with the parents, who are acknowledged as the primary educators of their sons and daughters. We work with the belief that each student is essentially good and infinitely lovable. Guided by our Catholic tradition, we recognize Jesus Christ as the model of the total person we are seeking to develop. In our mission of education, we strive for academic excellence and the total development of the individual."

Religious women, lay men and women comprise the 32 member full-time teaching faculty. There is a ratio of one faculty member to 19 students. Average class size is 25 students, with a maximum of 30 per class. (43% boys and 57% girls).

Campus Ministry Club
The campus Ministry Club meets to plan liturgies, organize school-wide charity projects and help lead the Days of Recollection. Through these activities, students become ministers to their peers.

Community Service Program
Freshmen are required to fulfill a minimum of ten hours of service, at home, church or school. Sophomores are required to perform 20 hours of service at church or school. Juniors must fulfill a minimum of 30 hours of service for church or community. Seniors are required to do a minimum of 40 hours with service agencies in their local communities.

Kairos Retreat

The Kairos Retreat is a three-day, overnight experience open to all seniors who wish to participate. It is a highly structured program which includes talks by both faculty and student team members, small group sharing sessions, community prayers, celebration of the Eucharist and related activities. Kairos Retreats provide soon-to-be-graduating young adults the opportunity for in-depth and honest self-examination, reflection over the deeper meaning of their relationship with family and friends, and a strengthening of their faith in God. "Kairotics" overwhelmingly affirm the retreat to have been a profound faith experience and a source of personal growth.

College Counseling

The college counselors help students set academic and personal goals to achieve a successful high school experience. Starting in their freshman year, students begin building their own portfolio that they develop through all four years at PHS, which can then be used as a tool for the college application process.

The following, taken from their website, is a very helpful way to show parents how Providence is going to prepare their child for college step by step.

Pioneer Path to College

9th Grade
Take the ACT/EXPLORE for skill assessment
Freshman Study Skills Program
Introduction to course requirements for college
Meet with freshman/sophomore Counselors
10th Grade
Take the PSAT/NMSQT to prepare for junior year
Concentrate on studies and grades
Volunteer for service commitments
Explore college information on internet
Attend college fairs
11th Grade
Take the PSAT/NMSQT
Receive College Handbook
Attend college fairs and begin campus visits
Attend College Case Study Program
Meet with Junior/Senior Counselor
Participate in College internet presentations
Take the SAT I and SAT II in the spring
Continue volunteer work
Visit colleges during spring break and summer

I was impressed with the emphasis on table manners and decorum in the cafeteria. It has always been my belief that being taught good manners early in life gives a young person a foundation that will benefit them throughout their lives.

HISTORY

Providence High School opened as an all-girls, Catholic High School in Burbank, California in September 1955. Principal Sr. Maria Theresa, Sr. Isabella, and Sr. Esther administrated at the new school which then had its first class of 81 students. By 1960, the number of students swelled to 495. Under the guidance of Sr. Maria Theresa, the staff continued to grow and formed a young, enthusiastic group who worked hard to attain the highest standards, not only in the academic field, but also in games, music and other extracurricular activities. Providence began welcoming young men, as well as women to the school in 1974. The addition of another school building was completed in 1975 to accommodate the growing student population. Sister Lucille Dean became the school's principal in 1986. Providence High School has received recognition throughout its history for its academic achievement.and was designated a Blue Ribbon School in 1997.

AT A GLANCE

APPLICATION DEADLINE	January
OPEN HOUSE	Call school for dates
UNIFORMS	Yes
HSTPT TESTING	Yes
SEE MAP	A on page 285

PS #1 ELEMENTARY SCHOOL

Tel: (310) 394-1313 • Fax: (310) 395-1093
1454 Euclid St. • Santa Monica, CA 90404-2173
www.psone.org

HEAD OF SCHOOL	JOEL M. PELCYGER
DIRECTOR OF ADMISSIONS	ANDREA ROTH
TYPE OF SCHOOL	CO-EDUCATIONAL DAY SCHOOL
GRADES	NON-GRADED K - 6

- ENROLLMENT: 180
- ACCREDITATION: CAPSO/CAIS/ISAMA
- MEMBERSHIPS: CAIS/NAIS
- ANNUAL PARENTS GUILD FEE: $125
- TUITION: $18,975
- APPLICATION FEE: $100
- ANNUAL GUILD FEE: $100
- FINANCIAL AID IS AVAILABLE

PS #1 is located in a business/residential section of Santa Monica. The campus underwent a complete transformation in 1998, turning an eclectic group of buildings into a new, state-of-the-art facility for which the school received several architectural awards. All the new structures are still grouped around a cement courtyard/basketball court, but the campus now extends to 12th Street where they have an expansive play area with grass, synthetic soccer field, outdoor stages, complete with a 100-year-old oak tree and a ball court. All the classrooms are very spacious with special consideration given to air circulation, and natural and reflected lighting. The library is now four times its original size and is run by a full time librarian.

The 'PS' stands for 'pluralistic school.' At PS #1 they believe that there is never any one set way to teach a subject. This is a progressive/developmental school where pluralism is stressed, i.e., children are able to experience different approaches to education under one roof. The word 'progressive' indicates an affiliation with the philosophy of scholar and educator John Dewey. The children work with block-building, are divided into groups, not classes, and there is an emphasis on working together to problem solve. In these ways, it is progressive. But since it is a pluralistic school and there is an openness to different teaching styles, it does not adhere as strictly to Dewey's approach as some of the other progressive schools that I have visited.

As taken from the school brochure:

"A founding value of PS#1, pluralism is the belief that a community is enriched when individual differences are respected and welcomed. At PS#1, pluralism is a commitment to diversity and inter-connectedness in both our community and our curriculum. This inclusive approach to education empowers our students to thrive in learning and in life. We have been teaching to multiple intelligences since 1971.

At PS#1 we believe there are three core values in education:

- Competence: What we know.
- Confidence: How we feel about what we know.
- Connection: What we do with what we know."

As stated earlier, the children are divided into groups, not grades, and each group has two age levels, 5 to 6 year olds and 6 to 7 year olds. There are currently seven classroom groups. Each group of two classrooms shares a retreat workspace. There is plenty of outdoor space used as additional work areas which allows students to take advantage of our wonderful southern Californian climate. Students are in each group for up to two years and graduate to the next group when they are developmentally ready (they are referred to as 'youngers,' 'middles' and 'olders'). This gives each child the opportunity to be the oldest and youngest of a group and to experience the kind of socialization that is present in a family/sibling dynamic. The teachers are called by their first names, and since I last visited the school there are now fourteen classroom teachers of which two are male. There are additional male teachers on staff in the P.E. department and aftercare.

In Kindergarten (or group one) academics and socialization skills are stressed equally. Problem solving and cooperation are taught through an emphasis on group activity, praise, positive reinforcement, and logical consequences for actions. A portfolio of the students' work is compiled throughout the year. Goals for two-years are discussed with each student at the beginning of the school year at parent/teacher/student meetings. In February they meet again to discuss the student's progress and set new goals for the remainder of the year.

The curriculum includes: math, reading, English, grammar, composition, language arts, science, and social studies. There are specialist teachers in drama, P.E., music, and art. There is no grading system. Progress is evaluated in comparison to past performance and on a grid of age-appropriate skills with an assessment of each student's growth. Parents meet with teachers twice a year for conferences. Once a year parents are scheduled individually to come to the school and observe their children in class. At the end of the school year, a detailed progress report is sent home.

The favorite tradition at PS#1 is the annual school camping trip. All the students can attend. Children experience sleeping in a tent and cooking outside. To ease any fears, younger children are paired up with an older child. Other school traditions include a holiday gift program, Adopt a Family, Grandparent Day, and Staff Appreciation Day.

The after-school clubhouse offers a variety of enrichment classes including Spanish, drama, music, art, cooking, gardening, ice-skating, dance, gymnastics, as well as indoor and outdoor play.

There are two things that stand out when touring the school. The first is that there is poetry everywhere, on the black-board, hanging on the walls, and written and recited by the children. It iss fantastic to see so many children of all ages that are more literate in poetry than many adults. The study and writing of poetry is part of every child's day starting in group 1. Unfortunately, their poet-in-residence/teacher passed away, but poetry is still emphasized and thriving! The second is the level of parent participation that goes on in the school. On any given day, parents can be seen volunteering throughout the campus both inside and outside the classrooms. In addition to the Parents Guild, PS#1 parents participate in a wide variety of committees, activities and projects. So, if you're one of those parents who loves to be involved then take a closer look at this school. At PS#1 there are endless opportunities for involvement!

PS#1 graduates have a high acceptance rate at prominent independent schools who value students that bring 'Knowledge plus more' to them. Upon graduation many students go on to attend Archer, Brentwood, Crossroads, Harvard-Westlake, Marlborough, New Roads, Wildwood or Windward, among others.

HISTORY

PS#1 was founded in 1971 by Eleanor Coben and Joel Pelcyger (the school's director) in response to concern among Westside parents about the quality of elementary education. Within three years, 30 children were enrolled in 3 non-graded classes, the equivalent of K to 4. In the 1980s, the school expanded its enrollment to include kindergarten through grade 6. 'Pluralism' at PS#1 means: the sensible use of an abundance of methods to reach a common goal.

AT A GLANCE

APPLICATION DEADLINE	January 15th, priority status to first 100 received. Applications are available in September for the following year.
ORIENTATION TOURS	Tours in the fall, call school for reservations
UNIFORMS	Yes
BEFORE AND AFTER SCHOOL	Yes
SUMMER SCHOOL	Yes
SEE MAP	D on page 285

RIBÉT ACADEMY

Tel: (323) 344-4330 • Fax: (323) 344-4339
2911 San Fernando Road • Los Angeles, CA 90065
www.ribetacademy.com

PRINCIPAL	RONALD DAUZAT, ESQ.
CO-DIR. OF ADMISSIONS	VERONICA PUENTE-SMITH
	& JOAN Q. NEWTON
TYPE OF SCHOOL	CO-EDUCATIONAL DAY SCHOOL
GRADES	PK - 12

- ENROLLMENT: 500
- ACCREDITATION: WASC
- YEARLY REGISTRATION FEE: $795
- YEARLY FAMILY FEE: $375
- TUITION: $8,400–$17,400
- APPLICATION FEE: $100
- BOOKS, TRIPS, ETC.: $375-$2,375
- FINANCIAL AID IS AVAILABLE

RIBET ACADEMY is located just off of the Glendale Freeway in the San Fernando Valley. The three-story facility, which was originally a silk factory, also once housed a Catholic school for boys. The building, which can be viewed from the freeway, has something of an insitutional appearance, but don't judge this book by its cover.

Inside, the hallways are extra-wide and the classrooms are large and bright. The school administration is constantly working hard to rid the school of the institutional feeling that the facility has had in the past. The school leases the property from the Catholic church and have been on this campus for 13 years, although the church has no responsibility for maintenance. Having a tuition based budget explains for the slow but sure changes to the campus. The walls have been painted inside and out, there is a gymnasium with bleacher seating for 500+, play areas, tennis courts, football field, and track, and the school has a lovely garden. Other recent changes include the spacious inaugural marine biology classroom, and the old conversion of the maintenance room to an art studio where students can leave out projects in progress. The chapel has also been converted into a theatre which seats 100 to 120 audience members, and children can learn dramatic arts, lighting, sound, and costume design.

Ribét is a traditional academic school. Character education is also stressed. There is a school cafeteria at the sub-basement level affectionately known as Café Ribét. Here hot lunch is served and it is also used as a meeting site for students and a dance hall. Ribét has a baseball diamond, and three outside basketball courts. In addition to students already attending Ribét, the school hosts about 30 international exchange students each year and has a very active international draw.

The tours are conducted on an individual basis, and everyone that I met at the school was friendly and helpful. Joan Newton, the petite, energetic Director of Admissions was my tour guide. Although Suzy, a sixth grader was an option to conduct the tour. Select students often conduct tours, which is one of the many ways they develop their leadership skills. The school curriculum includes history, mathematics, language arts, science, geography, computer, art, and physical education. There are two mobile labs that can go into any classroom in the elementary school. Desktop computers are in most classrooms and the school is hard-wired to allow students and teachers to use laptops with wireless cards anywhere on campus. Ribét offers computer instruction beginning in kindergarten. In elementary school, a mobile laptop travels to each classroom for lessons that are incorporated with other curricular areas. There is also an upper school computer lab which is the site for 6 to 12th grade computer classes which include introductory, advanced, web design, and AP. A 23,000 volume library is also used for research.

The school has a chorus, an orchestra, and a drama program. Students learn elementary music, theory,harmony and melody. In fifth grade, all students choose a wind instrument to learn. In sixth grade and up, it becomes more specialized, and there is a jazz ensemble etc. for those students wanting to further develop their musical skills.

Foreign language study (Spanish) is required starting in seventh grade. In the upper school the core curriculum includes English, geography, social studies, science, foreign language, and math. High school electives include psychology, drama, art, business administration, and African-American history. The junior high debate team took fourth place in the 2005 National Debate Competition, and in the LA County Science Fair. No school has ever won as many awards as Ribét in the history of the Fair. The fourth floor courtroom is the impressive home of the Legal Studies Department. This elective course includes Mock Trial in the fall semester and Student Court in the spring. The course is taught by two administrators, each with a degree in Jurisprudence. Mock Trial is a national program designed to familiarize students with the workings of the American legal system, and schools can compete at the junior high to collegiate level.

Ribét participates in interscholastic sports and has teams (grades 6 to 12) in football, basketball, and baseball for boys, and volleyball, basketball, and softball for girls. The co-ed soccer and golf teams took the league championship in 2005. Ribét athletic teams have earned other championships in California Interscholastic Federation competition at league, regional, and state levels.The cheerleading squad also took first place at state competition.

Here is an excerpt from the school brochure on the school Mission Statement:

> At Ribét, we focus on three goals: Effective communicating, practical problem solving, and enthusiastic life-long learning. We offer students engaging curriculum, superior instruction and numerous opportunities to practice and to apply learned concepts. At Ribét, students are given the challenge and the chance to excel. We expect all students to become independent, responsible role models in the community.

Accelerated reading groups and math enrichment courses are available in the elementary grades, with an accelerated program for advanced students. There is an after-school program which offers gymnastics, karate, music, computer and dance. There are twenty available advanced placement classes: English language and composition, English literature and composition, French language and composition, environmental science, psychology, statistics, world history, studio art, U.S. history, U.S. politics and government,, biology, chemistry, calculus (AB), European history, Spanish language and composition, music, physics, art history.

Ribét also has a unique program, called The Reduction in Tuition Exchange Program (RITE).

They basically feature a barter arrangement, whereby tuition is reduced in exchange for goods or services, time, or skills provided to the school by the family. One family has an awning company, and provided the awning for the outside play area. Another barter re-tiled the girls' bathrooms. Painting, flooring, day-care, computer skills, foreign language classes etc, may be preferred depending on the school's needs, and what you have to offer. Once the application process has been started, a RITE application may be obtained from the admissions office, however, students must be accepted to Ribét before a RITE meeting is scheduled.

HISTORY

Ribét Academy is a privately owned school, founded in 1982 by Jaques Ribét. Mr. Ribét brought years of experience as a high school principal as well as a strong background in traditional education based on the English system to his role as founder of the Academy. Mr. Ribet specifically employs teachers who harbor a great knowledge and respect for their subjects, who make learning seem like great fun, and who truly love teaching young, talented minds. Ribét started as a small high school in La Cañada and moved to its current site in 1991. It has grown to an enrollment of 500 students from Pre-K to grade 12.

AT A GLANCE

APPLICATION DEADLINE	February 1, then rolling as space is available
OPEN HOUSES	Call school or check website for dates
ISEE	Yes
UNIFORMS	Yes
BEFORE AND AFTER SCHOOL CARE	Yes
SEE MAP	B on page 285

Tel: (213) 382-7401 • Fax: (213) 382-8918
238 S. Manhattan Place • Los Angeles, CA 90004

HEAD OF SCHOOL	SISTER MARTA ANN COTA, C.S.J.
TYPE OF SCHOOL	CO-ED. CATHOLIC ELEMENTARY
GRADES	K - 8

- ENROLLMENT 304
- ACCREDITATION WASC
- REGISTRATION FEE $25 – $50
- YEARLY CURRICULUM FEE $350

- TUITION:
- PARISH FAMILIES W/1–4 CHILDREN:
  $3,400-$8,160
- NON-PARISH FAMILIES:
  $4,000 - $11,000

ST. BRENDAN'S SCHOOL is an excellent choice for those considering a Catholic education for their children. It is under the supervision of the Department of Catholic Schools of the Archdiocese of Los Angeles. Their philosophy is to provide an academically challenging Catholic elementary education for the multi-cultural people of the parish. An integral part of the religious program is the monthly school mass which is planned by individual classes and held in the church next door.

I visited the school during the summer break. I dropped in unannounced, which didn't seem to concern the principal in the least. She invited me to look around and was very welcoming. However, the school secretary was not that happy at my unscheduled visit, and seemed a little agitated by my questions and wanted to hurry me along. So off I went on my own to explore.

I noticed a couple of teachers there and when I asked them what they were doing they explained that they wanted to get everything ready for the upcoming semester. The kindergarten teacher proudly showed me her classroom, which was bright and airy and full of brand new computers that had been donated by some of the parents. She explained that children in the kindergarten program were expected to be reading proficiently by the time they entered first grade, and that the curriculum was close to what you would find in any of the higher grades. The students are taught math, language arts, social studies, science, and health. Also included is an art and music program, physical education, and an introduction to the computer. I sure wish I had had a computer instead of struggling with an abacus.

I was introduced to the eighth grade teacher, a delightful woman who had introduced the 'Big Buddies' program to the school some twelve years ago. At the beginning of a new year, each kindergartner is allocated a Big Buddy (someone in the eighth Grade). During the first week of school, the older kids come down and sing songs and introduce themselves. Over the course of the year, they do many things together. This tradition continues into first grade where they are given to someone in the seventh grade to keep an eye on them. This gives the little ones confidence and teaches the older kids patience and how to care for people younger than themselves.

I was told that the school had recently purchased a great deal of land adjacent to the school where they are planning to build extra facilities such as an auditorium. Currently they use the church for large events.

The two-story facility is located in Hancock Park, on the corner of 3rd and Manhattan on a well-maintained street. It is well protected from the street with high metal gates out front and fences around the perimeter. I looked into the different classrooms which were all large and well-organized, so that any child would feel comfortable there. Since there is only one classroom per grade, each classroom is furnished with ample supplies.

I was impressed by their earthquake preparedness guidelines which includes an out of the area telephone number where parents can call in case of an emergency.

There are two enclosed playgrounds. The large one is for grades 1 through 8 and includes basketball and handball courts and is divided into sections. The children are separated by grades and sex and are rotated through different areas during the year. The playground for the kindergarten is smaller , but it is well-equipped with many play structures on thick rubberized mats. Trees provide a shady area for the children to sit down and eat lunch. I noticed that the large playground also had many tables and benches, which were well protected from the sun. There is no kitchen at the school which means that children bring lunch every day, although there is a hot-lunch program which the parents organize once or twice a month.

Educational field trips are a regular part of the instruction. Classes are permitted to have one trip per semester.

Students are admitted into St. Brendan School on the basis of availability. Whether the parents support the religious instruction by regular and active participation in parish religious practice and worship is also considered. They are required to participate in St. Brendan's Parent Service Program (30 hours), and help support the school by payment of fees and tuition.

The students are required to give evidence of a Christian attitude and to conform to all school regulations. They are also required to complete the required course of study and related assignments according to their ability. They must also have been baptized.

There is a student council in the spring. Students in grades 4 to 7 elect students from next year's fifth through eighth grades as 'commissioners' to serve on a student board. The purpose of the council is to train students in leadership, to encourage a high standard of scholarship, to arouse school spirit, to demonstrate the practical application of democracy, and to advance the welfare of the school and its members. If elected, a student is expected to maintain a 'B' average. All other candidates for the various offices must have at least a 'C' average.

While reading through the Parent Handbook, I noticed a heading 'Mixed Parties' and I quote:

> "Mixed parties involving the students of the upper grades, even when they are held at home or at school are strongly discouraged. Parents are asked to cooperate with this regulation, even though, strictly speaking, the matter of parent sponsored parties is under parental control and not that of the school. The only exception to this regulation would be a school-sponsored graduation party having the approval of the pastor, the principal, and the parents."

You do not have to be a parishioner to be accepted, although I believe that being one would help in the admissions selection. While this school might not be for everyone, it is far more reasonably priced than many other private schools. If you are interested, I recommend visiting the campus.

HISTORY

St. Brendan School was founded in 1912 as a Co-Ed Catholic Elementary School.

AT A GLANCE

APPLICATION DEADLINE	First week of February
UNIFORMS	Yes
AFTER SCHOOL CARE	Yes
SEE MAP	C on page 285

ST. FRANCIS HIGH SCHOOL

Tel: (818) 790-0325 • Fax: (818) 790-5542
200 Foothill Blvd. • La Cañada, CA 91011
www.sfhs.net

PRINCIPAL	THOMAS MORAN, PRINCIPAL
PRESIDENT	FRIAR TONY MARTI
ADMISSION DIRECTOR	JOE MONARREZ
TYPE OF SCHOOL	ALL BOYS CATHOLIC DAY SCHOOL
GRADES	9 - 12

- ENROLLMENT: 640
- ACCREDITATION: WASC/WCEA
- APPLICATION FEE: $60
- TUITION: $10,324
- YEARLY REG. FEE: $650
- FINANCIAL AID IS AVAILABLE

ST. FRANCIS HIGH SCHOOL is located in La Cañada-Flintridge, off the 210-East Freeway. It has a wonderful view of the San Gabriel Mountains to the north and the Verdugo Mountain range to the south. La Cañada, La Crescenta, and Glendale have become popular places to live if you have teenage children and want them to have the same sort of freedom that most of us did growing up. Friends of ours have moved there, and I can see why. The public schools are among the best in the entire country, and they offer some of the best private school education, too.

My friend took me to see her son's school, St. Francis High. The school built a new Performing Arts Center a few years ago. Since then, they have re-done the athletic stadium, put a running track around the football field and built a new field house complete with a concession stand.

We arrived during a break, and the place was teeming with students. The younger ones were outside eating lunch in the gardens surrounding the new performing arts center. The seniors have their own garden, which was very pleasant and well-manicured.

They have no kitchen at St. Francis, but what they do have is a mobile kitchen complete with chef, thanks to S&F Catering. The owner worked out an arrangement with the school and parks his truck there all day allowing the children to order freshly prepared food at any time during the school day.

In the main office, I was greeted by a Capuchin Friar, a friar dressed in a brown robe and wearing sandals. Six friars have been assigned to the school to assure a strong religious presence. They oversee a Christian Service Program requiring 100 hours of service from the students in order to graduate.It was rather heart-warming to see him being asked for some advice by a young student wearing pressed khakis and a polo shirt. Of the present members of the faculty (laymen and laywomen and religious) 14 possess Bachelor Degrees and 22 possess Master Degrees. Two have earned Ph.D. status and 21 are credentialed.

In 1999, they renovated the Fr. Lawrence Caruso Memorial Learning Center, a beautiful library with over 7,000 volumes and mission-style furniture. I met the librarian, Sister Barbarine, a delightful woman who proudly showed me around and made me feel quite sure that my son would be well looked after if he ever needed help finding something. She had strict rules about how many students could be in there at any one time, and how they were to conduct themselves while under her watchful eye. Chairs had to be put back neatly, books returned to the shelves and absolutely no gum chewing allowed. She had never heard of schools allowing children to chew gum in exams to help them concentrate!

Next door to the library is one of two computer labs. The first lab is located on the upper campus and has 30 computers, a laser printer, an optical scanner, and a large-screen television display. The second lab, donated more recently from the Ahmanson Foundation, and the Corne and Estelle Doheny Foundation, is located next door to the library and also boasts 30 computers. Students are required to use a variety of software including PowerPoint and desktop publishing. The school's website is completely student-maintained with minimal direction from the teachers. Both labs are available to teachers who would like the students to use them for class work.

St. Francis recognized the increasingly important role technology plays in education and the work environment, and so the entire campus has been networked with internet access, and every classroom has a computer station, which is linked to the school network. Additionally, each desk in the biology and chemistry labs is equipped with the same type of computers for research assistance. All teachers have websites with grade books so parents can review progress in real time.

The classrooms, all well laid out and some with amphitheater-style seating, are cantilevered out over the hill with views of both the mountain ranges and overlooking the enormous playing field below. To get anywhere one has to use the myriad of outside stairways zigzagging down the hillside connecting all the various school rooms – not a viable proposition if you are using crutches or in a wheel chair, although after speaking to many of the students, I am sure they would happily carry someone who needed help.

Freshman Year Studies: Biblical literature, English 9 or honors English 9, geography, Latin I or Spanish I, algebra I or honors algebra or geometry; principles of science or biology; physical education and health.

Sophomore Year Studies: Moral foundation/Christian worship, English 10 or honors English 10, world history or AP, Latin II or Spanish II, geometry or honors geometry, biology or honors biology, physical education; introduction to visual and performing arts.

Junior Year Studies: History of Catholicism, comparative religions, American literature or honors American literature, Latin III or Spanish III or AP Spanish, U.S. history or AP U.S. history, algebra II or honors algebra II/trig., chemistry or AP chemistry.

Senior Year Studies: Christian life; British literature or AP English; U.S. government/economics or AP U.S. government and AP economics, trigonometry/pre-calculus or calculus or AP calculus or AP statistics, AP Latin I, Spanish III or AP Spanish, physics, chemistry and AP biology.

Junior/Senior Electives: Art, constitutional law, criminology, mass media, men's chorus, psychology, sociology, sports medicine, theatre arts.

A full 99 percent of students attend college immediately following graduation and of those, 84 percent attend a four-year college or university.

In addition to the academic requirements for graduation, each student must have:

- A record of good conduct and citizenship.
- Successfully completed a course in religious studies in each semester of his enrollment.
- Attended a retreat during each year of his attendance and completed all required service hours.

Each family is required to give 25 hours of service during the school year, or they may opt to 'buy out' their assistance at the rate of $15 per hour ($375 per year). There is also the Annual Fund Parent Pledge and POSH or Mini-POSH (their annual fundraising event) which enables the school to buy new furniture when needed. Family service hours do not cover your obligations to support these development programs.

The school believes that in order for a young man to become a well-rounded person, who is not only academically developed but graced with an appreciation of the arts, he should be exposed to the influences on the style, techniques, and contributions of master artists in the different fields of the visual and performing arts.

The school offers drawing, painting, and sculpture. There are museum trips for reports on specific artists and artistic styles. Students with vocal talents may join the Men's Chorus. The chorus performs in concerts, at choral festivals, for liturgical celebrations, and for numerous school-related functions during the school year. They often perform jointly with local girls' school choruses too. There is a drama course, and the school sponsors at least two productions during the year – a play during the first semester and a musical in the spring.

Over the last four years, the Visual and Performing Arts Department has sponsored the Festival of the Arts, a week-long celebration which includes video and drama competitions, choral concerts, drama presentations, an international food fair, a swing night, art exhibits, literary magazine launching, comedy sports, and a battle of student bands.

St. Francis High School's athletic program is steeped in tradition, and the accomplishments of its athletic teams are impressive. Last year the varsity soccer team captured the CIF championship and reached the semi-final round. In July 2001, the school replaced the grass on their football field with Field Turf, a synthetic turf with a rubber and sand base that is designed to simulate natural grass and dramatically reduce the number of sports related injuries. The drainage engineering allows the field to be used during bad weather.

At the varsity and junior varsity levels, football, cross country, basketball, soccer, track, volleyball, and baseball are available to students. Golf and tennis are the other varsity sports. Football, basketball and track are also available on the freshmen/sophomore level. In all, the Golden Knights compete in nine different sports with the Mission League, which is part of the CIF Southern Section.

St Francis school has a variety of extracurricular activities. Among the clubs offered are: Art, Debate, Fishing, Asian-American, Dive, Latin, Astronomy, Drama Guild, Magicians, Comedy, Sports, Thespian Society, Roller Hockey, Computer, Film Workshop, Swing, Cheer, Filipino-American and Tennis.

The College Guidance Center utilizes a collaborative process that includes working closely with students, family, faculty, and administration on all issues relating to the college counseling process.

HISTORY

St. Francis High School was founded in 1946 by the Capuchin Franciscans. Their tradition is expressed in the ministry of St. Francis High School in regards to the family, church, and society. The Franciscan tenet includes promoting harmony, unity, and love in every special structure, the most fundamental of which is the family. The 'family spirit' is extended from each individual family to encompass the entire 'school family,' that is, administration, faculty, staff, students, and alumni.

AT A GLANCE

APPLICATION DEADLINE	February 10
OPEN HOUSE	January 10 at noon
TESTING	Only accept HSPT Testing
DRESS CODE	Yes
SUMMER SCHOOL	Yes
SEE MAP	B on page 285

St. James' School

Tel: (213) 382-2315 • Fax: (213) 382-2436
625 S. St. Andrew's Place. • Los Angeles, CA 90005
www.stjamesschool.net

HEAD OF SCHOOL	STEPHEN L. BOWERS
TYPE OF SCHOOL	CO-ED EPISCOPAL DAY SCHOOL
GRADES	PRESCHOOL - 6

- ENROLLMENT: 309 (K-6), 44 (PRE)
- ENROLLMENT FEE: $1,000
- APPLICATION FEE: $100
- ACCREDITATION: CAIS/NAES/NAIS/WASC
- TUITION: $14,000
- NEW FAMILY FEE: $1,200
- FINANCIAL AID IS AVAILABLE

ST. JAMES EPISCOPAL SCHOOL is located on St. Andrew's Place between Wilshire Boulevard and Sixth Street. It is next door to St. James' Church. The two-story building, which once housed the entire school, has been expanded into a new structure. The church purchased a large corner, commercial plot of neighboring several years back.

The newest building, designed by Brenda Levin, who recently completed the restoration of City Hall, is a wonderful addition to the campus. It rises majestically next door to the old building and stands like an actor in a leading role behind which are the supporting actors, in this case the line of modern apartment buildings that sit behind the school. The old library is now a huge classroom, and every existing classroom and the art studio has beendoubled in size. This new building has provided space for a multi-purpose room, a science lab, which had previously been run out of the basement of the church, and much larger classroom facilities.

The children have a 15,000 square foot grassy field which is so rare in an urban school, a basketball court, and a wonderful new enclosed roof top play area, where the students can play a variety of ball games. In the shaded courtyard the children can relax and read quietly outside, and they proudly boast of being the only school in the country to have a rock climbing wall in their gym.

The Ahmanson Foundation underwrote $450,000 to build a new state-of-the-art library, which is truly outstanding and might well rival some university libraries. It is run by Librarian Judy Duwitt along with parent volunteers, who are there to help the children. The parents also contribute many new books throughout the year.

St. James' has a wonderful socio-economic and ethnic mix of students. Every culture Los Angeles has to offer seems to be represented equally. The classrooms have between 20 to 22 students, and there are two classes per grade. St. James' has merged with a pre-kindergarten program under the same name, which is run by the church on another property closeby. However, attendance at St. James preschool does not insure that a child will automatically attend St. James' School. But it will help to familiarize you with the academic expectations of the elementary school if you have decided that St. James' school is for you.

The school has a reputation for being on the cutting edge of what's happening in education rather than using teaching methods from 40 years ago. The curriculum is challenging and college preparatory. Although the approach is traditional, students are encouraged to read in kindergarten. The solid academic base that the children receive at St. James' enables them to go on to such schools as Harvard-Westlake, Campbell Hall, Flintridge Preparatory, Marlborough School (for girls), and Brentwood.

Many schools claim that all their graduates are admitted to the schools of their choice. In fact this may not always run true as admissions director will attest .However one year, 24 students from St. James' applied to Marlborough, and 22 were accepted.

St. James' is an outreach of the education ministry of St. James' Church. Their religion program is Episcopalian, but they welcome families of all religions and have an inclusive approach with a curriculum that includes recognition and respect for all faiths. Their prayer services include weekly chapel and a once a month, All School Chapel. Religion is taught as a subject in each class once a week.

I asked about the classroom prayer and the Head of School, Jan Slaby, told me, "We recognize in this school that God guides our lives, and the children are given time in the morning to reflect on this in various, appropriate ways. In some cases the teacher leads this reflection, but often in the upper grades it is led by the children."

From the school brochure:

> "St. James' School, a ministry of St. James' Episcopal Church, exists to serve intellectually able students and their families of varying economic, ethnic, racial, and social backgrounds by providing a rigorous academic program, kindergarten through grade six, within a Christian environment. St. James School affirms the basic purpose of an Episcopal day school: 'To help each child understand that the knowledge and service of God lie at the heart of wisdom, and to make faith in God the unifying force which relates each student and teacher to church, the home, and the world.' "

The school tuition includes extended care and St. James' offers several after-school classes, many of which are now taught by the faculty. Courses include sewing, cooking, science fun-type classes, arts & crafts, and homework helpers.This program is run by the Parent Support Fellowship using students from Marlborough School. They have also introduced an extensive sports program.

This school offers a great academic education for a reasonable price.

HISTORY

St. James' School was founded in 1967 by St. James' Episcopal Church. The original site of the school was on Gramercy Place between Wilshire Blvd. and Sixth Street. The school opened with five students in kindergarten. Additional grades were added as these students were promoted. The first sixth grade graduation class was in June, 1974. The school moved to its new campus on St. Andrew's Place in 1980. There are now two classes in each grade.

AT A GLANCE

APPLICATION DEADLINE	January
TOURS AND OPEN HOUSES	During the fall
UNIFORMS	Yes
BEFORE AND AFTER SCHOOL CARE	Included in the tuition price
SEE MAP	C on page 285

SAINT MARK'S EPISCOPAL SCHOOL

Tel: (626) 798-8858 • Fax: (626) 798-4180
1050 E. Altadena Drive • Altadena, CA 91001
www.saint-marks.org

HEAD OF SCHOOL	DR. DOREEN OLESON
DIRECTOR OF ADMISSIONS	JOSCELLE SHEN
TYPE OF SCHOOL	CO-ED EPISCOPAL DAY SCHOOL
GRADES	PRESCHOOL – 6

- ENROLLMENT: 350
- ACCREDITATION: CAIS/WASC
- AFFILIATION: NAIS
- MEMBERSHIPS: CEE/COS/ERB
- FINANCIAL AID IS AVAILABLE

- TUITION: $10,065-$10,290
- APPLICATION FEE: $65
- YEARLY REGISTRATION FEE: $800
- NEW FAMILY FEE: $1,500

SAINT MARK'S is a neighborhood school – big in heart and spirit. It is located on a tree-lined, residential street in Altadena. The administrative offices are housed in a quaint old craftsman house on the six-acre property. Head of school, Doreen Oleson, conducts the parent tour, complete with coffee and a parent-produced video about Saint Mark's for our viewing pleasure. This place is an undiscovered gem for those looking for a private school education at a (comparatively) low price.

The architecture is sixties style. The classrooms have been renovated and science/technology rooms have been refurbished. The art program takes place in the former garage (of the craftsman house), and aside from adding a kiln and lots of supplies, it still looks and feels like a garage. My guess is that much of the work is done on tables outside and considering our fine California climate, it probably suits everyone just fine. There are two playgrounds and several large, grassy recreational fields for the children.

Saint Mark's claims that it is not an academically-oriented school, and I found that to be true at the pre-school/kindergarten level. Children will not be sitting at desks with paper and pencil, and there is plenty of playtime scheduled for the younger students. The goal of the school is to have a happy and inviting atmosphere for a student body made up of children living in the surrounding neighborhood areas. Children are not selected academically. The school feels that testing students is inappropriate. However, by fourth grade students should expect an average of one hour of homework per night, and in sixth grade, two hours. When I asked to which schools the children matriculate I was told Polytechnic, Chandler, High Point Academy, and Westridge. The school appears to be traditionally academic, even though they seem to shun that label.

The school has a student community made up of families from many different ethnic and socio-economic backgrounds. Saint Mark's has a scholarship program that is sponsored by

United Way enabling the school to offer a private school education to many children who could otherwise not afford one.

New buildings have been added to the campus providing the much needed space for the doubling of enrollment that has now been completed. One of the buildings provides a multi-purpose area for the campus. Also added were two new fifth grade classrooms, one fifth, and a new science lab, a wonderful new building with high ceilings and great natural light. Smartboards have also been installed in classrooms. New early childhood and elementary playfields accompany the new buildings and renovations on campus.

Parents are required to volunteer 30 hours of their time per year to one or more of the school's 38 committees.

Beginning in the fall of 1997, two kindergarten classes were added and this practice continued until the school's enrollment expanded to two classes at every grade level. There is a modular unit that was added in the fall of '98 to serve as a library.

The children take field trips twice a year, and in fourth grade take a two-day boat trip to simulate a pilgrim voyage to America. Before this trip the children learn nautical terms and, while on board the boat, call each other 'Mr. So & So' because they are told "there were no women allowed on ships at that time."

Chapel takes place twice per week in the church next door, and during the service the minister goes over the week's events. The music program focuses on developing a love and appreciation for sacred and secular music.

Here is the school's mission as written in the brochure:

> "We believe that children unfold and flourish most effectively in an atmosphere which nurtures self-esteem, cooperation, and respect for original thinking.
>
> Our students are encouraged to become self-directed learners in a setting which is enjoyable, stimulating, and challenging.
>
> It is our desire to educate the whole child. We believe that the moral, social, and spiritual development of our students is of equal importance to their intellectual growth.
>
> Our programs are built around a respect for individual differences in talent, maturity, motivation, and learning capability.
>
> We strive by example and action to instill not only a joy and respect for learning but moral and ethical responsibility as well.
>
> Saint Mark's School encourages its students to become self-confident, direct in purpose, self-reliant in personality, and aware of responsibilities to self, home, school, and the world community."

The kindergarten has its own separate building and play-yard. The room, divided by a partition, is bright and cheerful, and the pitched ceiling gives it a wonderful, open-space feeling. The walls are covered with the children's artwork, and the whole atmosphere is very nurturing.

From Kindergarten to sixth grade, the curriculum includes: language arts, math, social studies, science, Spanish, physical education, and computer. Reading is taught with a blend of phonetic and whole language approaches. The school brochure gives a detailed account of the syllabus studied each grade level, including textbooks used.

HISTORY

Saint Mark's School was founded in 1960 by a group of parents interested in creating a neighborhood school teaching Christian values with a warm, home-like atmosphere and inspirational, nurturing teachers. Saint Mark's School is sponsored by Saint Mark's Church, from which it receives much support and encouragement.

AT A GLANCE

APPLICATION DEADLINE	Late January/early February
UNIFORMS	Required
BEFORE AND AFTER SCHOOL CARE	Yes
SUMMER SCHOOL	June 27 thru August 5
SEE MAP	B on page 285

ST. MATTHEW'S PARISH SCHOOL

Tel: (310) 454-1350 • Fax: (310) 573-7423
1031 Bienveneda Ave • Pacific Palisades, CA 90272
stmatthewsschool.com

HEAD OF SCHOOL	DR. LES W. FROST
DIRECTOR OF ADMISSION	A. LEE QURING
TYPE OF SCHOOL	CO-EDUCATIONAL EPISCOPAL DAY
GRADES	PRESCHOOL - 8

- ENROLLMENT: 325
- ACCREDITATION: CAIS/NAES/WASC
- MEMBERSHIPS: NAIS
- NEW STUDENT FEE: $1,500

- TUITION: $12,240-$24,800
- APPLICATION FEE: $100
- FINANCIAL AID IS AVAILABLE
- NEW STUDENT FEE: $150

ST. MATTHEW'S SCHOOL is located one mile from the Pacific Ocean in Pacific Palisades. The thirty-acre campus, formerly The Garland Ranch, has rolling lawns and athletic fields, a swimming pool, tennis court, and old growth trees throughout. The grounds are well maintained but pastoral – not manicured.

The facilities are comprised of twenty-six classrooms, which include art and music rooms. In addition to the six classroom buildings, there is an administration building, a 10,000 volume library, and the church which serves as the chapel.

The educational approach is a traditional, academic one, with many of the eighth grade graduates going on to attend area prep schools such as Harvard-Westlake, Marymount, Marlborough, Brentwood, Crossroads, Buckley and Loyola.

Saint Matthew's begins with preschool, and if you are seriously interested in enrolling your child, then this is the time to apply, rather than waiting for kindergarten when there are few (1 to 2) or sometimes no spaces available. Because there are so many applicants, this is a very difficult school to get into. Siblings are given priority if their families have demonstrated a significant level of financial support, commitment and participation in school events.

As an Episcopal parish school, the administration will take into consideration families that have joined the church, although you should plan on being members for at least two years before you apply to the school.

The preschool uses a developmental approach for its three and four-year-olds and occupies five classrooms, a library, and four spacious play-grounds at the heart of the school's rustic setting. Children improve their skills through exploration of their environment and through hands-on problem solving. The classrooms are carefully prepared to accommodate individual learning styles and levels of development.

The curriculum integrates literature, art, music, movement, cooking, science, gardening, and field trips in activities that promote reading and mathematical literacy. At the kindergarten level the curriculum includes literature-based reading, language arts, a Writers Workshop, hands-on math and science, music, art, social studies, and physical education. There is a brand new science center for Kindergarten to grade 4.

The classes are self-contained and team taught. In grades 2 through 4, there are special subject teachers in art, music, computer, and physical education. Jane Young is Principal for preschool through fourth grade.

In grades 5 to 8, all students participate in an Advisory Program where groups of 12 students meet daily with a faculty advisor to plan school-wide activities, form teams for school projects, set goals, and review individual academic progress. There is an intramural sports program, and 7th-8th graders may also join competitive teams in volleyball, basketball, soccer, softball and flag football.

Students receive letter grades beginning in the third trimester of the 5th grade. By sixth grade, the program is completely compartmentalized with classes in English, mathematics, social studies, science, physical education, art, music, and introduction to foreign language. In seventh and eighth grade, students may choose between Latin and Spanish.

Preschoolers attend chapel once a week. All other grades meet twice per week. In addition, the school minister visits classrooms at all grade levels to lead age-appropriate discussions about the Bible and moral/ethical issues within the context of the Judeo-Christian tradition.

Enrichment classes are offered after school each fall or spring, and run from 3:15-4:15 on selected afternoons. The classes offered vary, but have included instrumental music lessons, video animation, foreign language, chess and drama.

Field trips are scheduled twice per year for the sixth to eighth graders. The school puts on a Christmas program (K to 8), a spring play (5 to 8), and hosts a spring fair each May.

Mission Statement

> "St. Matthew's Parish School, an Episcopal day school, is an integral part of the Parish of St. Matthew, serving the children and families of the parish and larger community. The school provides quality education through a challenging, caring, and supportive program, developing intellectual, spiritual, and physical growth. Our purpose is to create an awareness that we are all children of God and to awaken in each student a sense of self as a significant, creative, and responsible member of society."

HISTORY

Saint Matthew's Parish school was founded on May 2, 1949, through the efforts of six women who wanted to create a mission of Saint Matthew's Parish in the Palisades. It was accomplished with the help of The Rev. Kenneth Cary and Mrs. Eleanor Leach. It began as a preschool with 24 students.

In 1950, the school had grown to include grades K to 4 with a total of 105 students. Shortly after, the school purchased The Garland Ranch, a beautiful 30-acre property which is the present site of the St. Matthew's campus. Today there are approximately 325 students attending.

AT A GLANCE

APPLICATION DEADLINE	Applications are available September 1 for the following year, with the following deadlines: Pre-K: December 1, and grades 1-8: January 30.
OPEN HOUSE DATES:	November
ISEE TESTING	Required for 5-8th grade
UNIFORMS	Yes
BEFORE/AFTER SCHOOL CARE	Yes
SEE MAP	D on page 285

CORINNE A. SEEDS UNIVERSITY ELEMENTARY SCHOOL

Tel: (310) 825-1801 • Fax: (310) 206-4452
405 Hilgard Ave. • Los Angeles, CA 90024
www.ues.gseis.ucla.edu

INTERIM HEAD OF SCHOOL	KENT LEWIS
DIRECTOR OF ADMISSIONS	NANCY CHAKRAVARTY
TYPE OF SCHOOL	CO-EDUCATIONAL RESEARCH SCHOOL
GRADES	PRE-K - 6

- ENROLLMENT: 430
- ACCREDITATION: NONE
- NEW FAMILY FEE: NONE
- APPLICATION: $60 PAPER, $45 ONLINE
- TUITION: $7,780-$11,650
- AFFILIATION: UCLA
- FINANCIAL AID IS AVAILABLE

One of the most difficult things about this school (aside from actually getting in) is deciding on its name. It is referred to as "SEEDS," "UES," "The UCLA Lab School," "CORINNE A. SEEDS" and "THE UNIVERSITY ELEMENTARY SCHOOL." If you have heard any of those titles, then know that we are talking about the same place! For our purposes, I will refer to it as UES.

The school is located on nine sylvan acres on the northern UCLA campus. The property is thick with old growth pine, oak, and eucalyptus trees. It has many grassy play areas and a redwood grove. Stone Canyon creek runs through the campus and is used by the students for both pleasure and scientific/environmental observation. The red brick buildings, built in 1957, were designed for the school by architect Richard Neutra.

There are 20 state of the art classrooms, a beautiful library, community hall, dinosaur yard, playground and research studio.

UES is a laboratory of the UCLA Graduate School of Education. The approach is developmental, although being an experimental school, it does not fall neatly into any one category of educational style. Its primary functions are research, experimentation, and inquiry into the process of education. As a center of inquiry, UES has the responsibility of exploring and evaluating promising ideas related to education, innovation, and practice.

In this setting, researchers can study all aspects of the learning process, the curriculum, interaction between teachers and students and the effect of home-school relations on education, etc. Researchers use their findings to train teachers and administrators, to develop new programs for the school, and to educate the public at large on emerging educational trends. Since 1955, some 57 research studies have been conducted at the school by UCLA faculty, and graduate students primarily from the School of Education and the Department of

Psychology.

Children are divided into four multi-age levels to allow each student to work at his/her own developmental pace. There are approximately 50 children at each level. The early childhood division is made up of 4 to 6 year olds, the lower elementary division has 6 to 8 year olds, middle elementary 8 to 10 year olds, and upper elementary 10 to 12 year olds.

UES is well known for its 'team teaching' approach to education. Teachers are organized into eight two-and-a-half person teams to encourage the transfer of skills from one teacher to another and to give children access to teachers with a variety of interests and abilities.

Each teacher team plans and delivers instruction to approximately 55 students. The teaching teams meet frequently to coordinate curricular activities and schedules for their respective levels. This team approach permits teachers to have planning time, to work with individuals in small groups of children, and explore the interests of the children in an intensive manner.

Discursive Arts: Reading, writing, listening, and speaking are taught in an interrelated way because findings show that skill acquired in one area facilitates skill development in the others. Therefore, teachers at UES attend to all four, relating each one to the others, and showing how they work together.

Math: UES teaches math first through manipulation of objects, working from concrete to semi-concrete operations and then moving to abstract thinking. Staff believe that this progression is essential to develop a deep understanding of math concepts. The school is equipped with a full computer lab for the teaching of math.

Science: Science education at UES includes the three basic fields of physical, earth and life sciences. Science instruction integrates process skills, concepts and attitudes. To accomplish this integration, activities are organized around local environmental concerns. Children explore the natural and man-made world around them, test their ideas and develop the skills and attitudes needed to think scientifically. For instance, students may learn about computers by taking them apart and then putting them back together again.

Social Studies: Social education is viewed as an essential part of the overall education program. Students are provided with the opportunity to acquire the knowledge, abilities, and skills, as well as the beliefs and values that are needed to participate in the social, political, and economic life of their nation and the world. Students become familiar with the meaning and practice of democratic government, its institutions, historic values and requirements.

Visual Arts: Teachers stress the importance of aesthetics, studio art, art history, and art criticism. There is a spacious art studio and numerous field trips to museums, including those at UCLA. UES prides itself on its anti-bias curriculum and for embracing innovations in education. In choosing students for admission, the school is seeking to create a group of children representative of the nation on a number of criteria including race, sex, exceptionality, parental education, occupation, ethnicity and family income. Wishing to include some children with special needs, the school has not yet fully realised this objective.

The school has a unique extended day program which takes into account the needs of each child for a program coordinated with, but not duplicative of, his or her academic experiences.

Teachers and the program staff work together so that in the afternoon children have the opportunity to expand projects begun in the morning.

The intent of the Integrated Day Care Program is neither academic enrichment nor baby-sitting. The afternoon program nurtures a strong sense of community, emphasizes values of caring and respect for one another, and encourages appreciation of each child's culture, language and ethnicity. For each group of 20 to 25 children, there are at least three adults, one of whom is the lead teacher. All the adults are highly qualified in terms of training and experience. The Program is entirely funded by parents.

Parental involvement is encouraged through the Family School Alliance (FSA), and all parents are automatically members. The school sponsors many fundraising events with the help of the FSA, such as selling grocery scrip, the magazine drive, book fair, Spring silent and live auction, and Spring fair. FSA dues which can be anywhere from $20 to 500, or whatever a family wishes to contribute.

There are many celebrity families at UES As you may have guessed, it is really difficult to get in if you are from a white, middle to upper middle class family. This group is over-represented in the applicant pool and is flooding the admissions office with "please"and "why not?" It's a gorgeous school with excellent teachers and a comparatively low price tag for a private school education. The application fee is only $45 rather than the $75-100 fee charged at most west-side private schools. Go for it!

HISTORY

UES was founded in 1882 as a training school for teachers at the location of the LA Central Library. In 1919, the school became part of the University of California, Southern Branch (the forerunner of UCLA). Throughout the 1930s until the mid 1940s, UES occupied classrooms on Warner Avenue through a lease with the LA School Board. In 1947, UES moved to its current site at UCLA.

AT A GLANCE

APPLICATION DEADLINE	December
UNIFORMS	Yes
DAY CARE/AFTER SCHOOL CARE PROGRAM	Available
SEE MAP	D on page 285

SEQUOYAH SCHOOL

Tel: (626) 795-4351 • Fax: (626) 795-8773
535 S. Pasadena Ave. • Pasadena, CA 91105
www.sequoyahschool.org

HEAD OF SCHOOL	JOSH BRODY
DIRECTOR OF ADMISSIONS	AZIZI GIBBS
TYPE OF SCHOOL	CO-EDUCATIONAL DAY SCHOOL
GRADES	K - 8

- ENROLLMENT: 185
- ACCREDITATION: WASC
- MEMBERSHIPS: LACES/NPE
- ANNUAL 'GIVING' IS SUGGESTED
- TUITION: $15,200
  (AMOUNT BASED ON INDEX)
- FINANCIAL AID IS AVAILABLE
- APPLICATION FEE: $100

SEQUOYAH is located in Pasadena at the corner of Pasadena Ave. and California Blvd. with the 710 Freeway running behind the property. The campus has amost three acres of land with beautiful old pine, oak, and eucalyptus trees throughout.

There are four buildings and a science lab. The main building houses the four lower elementary classrooms, the library, and the administrative offices. Two additional buildings house the upper elementary and junior high classes. The Daycare House is a classic California bungalow, which was formerly a minister's house when the school facility belonged to a church.

The school has an outstanding 21,000 volume library with a vaulted ceiling, huge windows and lots of cozy reading areas (pillows and bean-bag seats) throughout.

The school teaching approach is developmental, based on the philosophies of Jean Piaget and Maria Montessori. Children are guided through their learning years as they are developmentally ready and not before. Emphasis is placed on social skills and working together as a group. When I toured the lower school, I noticed that the children sat on the floor rather than at desks while the teacher taught them. One child was lying in an old-fashioned bath tub filled with pillows-reading a book while the lesson went on in the background.

The classrooms are generally on the small side, cluttered with toys, gadgets, manipulative learning tools, and artwork. The students are clustered into age groupings, which reflect a three year age span. Whenever possible, students remain in the same classroom for two years, which allows older students to aid and encourage the education of younger children, while demystifying the role of older children for younger students.

There are no tests or grades at Sequoyah. This baffled one mother on the tour who kept asking: "You mean my son won't be bringing any papers home?" She was concerned that there would be no way for her to know what and how he was doing in class. This mother was told she would have to put her trust in the system and ask the teacher those questions during the parent-teacher conferences scheduled during the year. This mother didn't look very happy about that – possibly she was not a candidate for developmental education.

Here is a description of the curriculum from the school brochure:

> "Sequoyah School is based on an emergent curriculum from which academic skills are utilized by integrating programs and activities that evolve from a child's own interest, from his or her environment, from experiences in the family, and/or from the community at large. Learning is organic and is obtained through the integration of a variety of subjects."

Classes have between 22 and 24 students. The younger students have a full-time teacher and a full-time associate teacher. Sequoyah uses an open-education, whole language reading, integrated arts, writing approach. All students participate in the Camping Program, which is designed to let children explore the environment and work on their social skills.

The older groups have specialist teachers in science, math, and language arts, and part time teachers for Spanish, art, and music instruction. Every student gets daily exercise as part of the program and computer instruction is introduced starting in the 8 to 10 year old classes.

Parent participation is required at Sequoyah. When you enroll your child you automatically become members of the Sequoyah Educational Center, the legal name of the school. The school is a parent-owned, non-profit organization run by an advisory committee of executive officers, elected committee heads, the school staff, and the director. All members of the school community have a vote and are encouraged to participate.

Parents are required to donate 40 hours per year to fundraising and maintenance of the school. Each family is also required to participate in the annual giving fund where tax-deductible contributions are based on yearly income. The standing committees are: Admissions, Finance, Fundraising/Grants, Fundraising/Events, Publicity, Parent Resources, Parent Education, Advance Plans and Maintenance.

Each family must contribute eight hours school maintenance, eight hours fundraising and 24 hours on one of the standing committees. Parents who are unable or unwilling to fulfill their work hours are billed $25 for each hour missed.

HISTORY

The Sequoyah School is an un-graded, co-educational, humanistic school. Founded in 1958, the implementation of education at the school begins with a profound appreciation of children as unique individuals and a broad trust in their capacity for growth and learning through their own explorations. A model school for open education, The Sequoyah School provides a non-competitive environment where students can learn at their own pace while still meeting solid academic objectives.

AT A GLANCE

APPLICATION DEADLINE	January 31
OPEN HOUSES	October through January
SCHOOL TOURS	Weekly October through January. Call school or check website for specific dates.
UNIFORMS	Yes
BEFORE AND AFTER SCHOOL CARE	Yes
SEE MAP	B on page 285

SEVEN ARROWS
ELEMENTARY SCHOOL

Tel:(310) 230-0257 Fax: (310) 230-8859
15249 La Cruz • Pacific Palisades • CA • 90272
www.sevenarrows.com

EXECUTIVE DIRECTOR	MARGARITA PAGLIAI
DIRECTOR OF ADMISSIONS	OMID KHEILTASH
TYPE OF SCHOOL	INDEPENDENT DAY SCHOOL
GRADES	K-6

- ENROLLMENT: 108
- REGISTRATION FEE: NONE
- APPLICATION FEE: $100
- MEMBERSHIPS: CAIS
- ADDITIONAL DONATIONS ARE REQUESTED
- TUITION: $19,500-$21,500
- NEW STUDENT FEE: $1,500
- MISC EXPENSES: $200-$300, $200
- FINANCIAL AID IS AVAILABLE

As you enter the gates of SEVEN ARROWS SCHOOL in Pacific Palisades, one enters into another world: a world of color, shapes, foliage, and laughter. There is an air of excitement about discovering this school. Seven Arrows is an independent K-6th grade elementary school that offers an engaging curriculum. Their program motivates students, speaks to their broad –ranging curiosities, and encourages creative and critical thinking, as well as collaboration and initiative.

I was treated to a grand tour by several of the administration staff, including the executive director, Margarita Pagliai, and a passionate fifth grade teacher. I fell in love with this school, the staff and the students, the reason being the Seven Arrows Philosophy:

"The basic premise of a Seven Arrows Elementary School Education lies in the belief that the most powerful force in education is a love of learning. Our programs instill in each of our students a deep and lasting love of learning, the confidence to achieve one's best, and the knowledge that places one firmly on the road to a life full of purpose, meaning and endless opportunity.

Our goals go beyond helping our students reach academic excellence. Our diverse, multicultural community of students, teachers and parents values respect for self,

Others and the environment, honesty, integrity, empathy and responsibility. We share a deep commitment to promoting positive change in the world through the power of education and the power of our minds.

The curriculum at Seven Arrows is both academically challenging and developmentally appropriate. They integrate various "pedagogical" styles to best foster the intellectual emotional and social development of the total child. The programs are infused with a multicultural awareness designed to engender a global perspective on learning. The result is a curriculum that speaks to the broad-ranging curiosity of children, encourages creative thinking and promotes leadership."

I have seen integrated schools before, but Seven Arrows could be the poster child for this approach in action. For example, when learning about a culture, like ancient Egypt, mathematics, science, reading, writing and the arts are all integrated in the approach. The classrooms are set in motion. Children breathe history by creating pyramids or mummies. They live literature by reading stories and translations of ancient manuscripts or role-playing. Native foods are eaten and students create art or design a national costume. Studies in history are enriched and reinforced with field trips and presentations by classroom guests who are experts on the target subjects. This culminates in school wide presentations, where they read the most important paragraph about their person in history, and display the costumes designed and co-constructed.

Every Friday morning there is a "Kuyam", a whole school gathering. This is held in the outdoor amphitheatre type space, covered with a sail donated to the school by a competitive yacht team. Parents are welcome, and kids can perform. There are student bands. The children become very comfortable with public speaking.

One of the approaches that Seven Arrows uses to facilitate learning in the classroom is based on the theory of multiple intelligences. At the core of this theory is the recognition that each child thinks and learns differently. Therefore the approach is extremely individualized within a subject to make sure children are challenged and have assistance. Parents should ask the school to provide an in-depth explanation.

The arts program is incredible. It is fully integrated into whatever they are studying. Children choose a piece of artwork from the year to represent them in the yearbook. In fact, while studying California History, the fouth grade students were introduced to architect Frank Gehry of Disney Concert Hall fame, and created their own models of unique performance centers. The project finished with a gallery display of their work at the A&D museum, inspired by and dedicated to Gehry's Disney Hall.

A parent of a fourth grader gladly told me about her experience with Seven Arrows." We were looking for a school that would go beyond worksheets and math fact tests. The kids here do advanced academics, hands-on history projects and art that appears in gallery shows. We've watched our kid blossom into a curious, intelligent thinker thanks to the unique opportunities and enthusiastic guidance."

Sixth graders have a community involvement project every week, and I got to see the spectacular results of their photography project. Each sixth grader also makes their own web page, on PowerPoint. They also make their own graduation video, and do all their own filming and editing.

The specialty classes include karate, music, drama, and of course art. Spanish is taught through emergence five days a week,. Spanish is not taught academically because there are so many Spanish speakers. However, because of the ease of language acquisition at a young age, Spanish is intrinsic to math, communication and other studies. The specialty teachers are professionals in their fields, as well as educators.

History and Literature is the core of the curriculum. There are new components to the science curriculum, and brand new science and technology lab. There are computers, flat screens and projectors in the classrooms. The core curriculum for math is everyday math, cuisenaire which complements the spectrum math.

Seven Arrows offers choices within a structure. It is a small , nurturing , loving school. Parent volunteers assist in for all manner of projects and events. In this way, parents may join their children, not only for the fun, but aslso for the education!

HISTORY

Colombian born and internationally educated Margarita Pagliai, Founder and Executive Director of Little Dolphins by the Sea Preschool and Seven Arrows Elementary School, opened the elementary school in 1999 both for her own children and because of increasing demand from Little Dolphins parents to create a school that would offer a continuation of the rich philosophy and global curriculum to which they had become accustomed. Margarita assembled a team of educators and students, and together they researched the most innovative and successful elementary schools and curricula from across the nation and around the globe. What they found, along with the many wonderful programs, was a wealth of evidence highlighting the advantages of a small school environment.

With the small school model as its core vision, the team designed the engaging Seven Arrows curriculum focusing on individualized academics and providing a balance between challenging academics and a stimulating arts program. In the spring of 2005, Seven Arrows celebrated its fourth graduating class, ninety-five percent of whom have been accepted into their first choice of middle schools.

AT A GLANCE

APPLICATION DEADLINE	January 15
OPEN HOUSES	Call school to schedule tour
ISEE TESTING	Not required
CASUAL UNIFORM	Yes
AFTER SCHOOL CARE	Yes
SEE MAP	D on page 285

SIERRA CANYON SCHOOL

Lower Campus
Tel: (818) 882-8121 • Fax: (818) 882-8218
11052 Independence Avenue• Chatsworth, CA 91311
www.sierracanyon.pvt.k12.ca.us

Upper Campus
Tel: (818) 709-0134 • Fax: (818) 709-8184
19809 Nordoff Place • Chatsworth, CA 91311
www.sierracanyonhighschool.org

HEAD OF SCHOOL	JIM SKRUMBIS
DIRECTOR OF ADMISSIONS	NANCY POSEY
TYPE OF SCHOOL	CO-EDUCATIONAL DAY SCHOOL
GRADES	EARLY K - 11

- ENROLLMENT: 800
- ACCREDITATION: NIPSA/WASC
- APPLICATION FEE: $150
- A FOR PROFIT ORGANIZATION
- MEMBERSHIPS: ERB/CAG/NAESP /NAEYC/NAGC/NASSP

- TUITION: $12,500-$21,500
- REGISTRATION FEE. APPLIED: $1,400
- NEW FAMILY FEE: $1,200
- FINANCIAL AID IS AVAILABLE

SIERRA CANYON is a private, independent college preparatory day school located on two campuses in the town of Chatsworth. The lower campus is peppered with large pine, oak, and eucalyptus trees, and surrounded by hills and open fields. It feels like you're in the country, instead of minutes away from a bustling valley community.

Co-founder Howard Wang took me on a tour of the school, proudly pointing out all the features that made Sierra Canyon a Unites States Blue Ribbon School in 1990. The school has three science labs, library, computer labs, several play areas with climbing equipment, football and soccer fields, two swimming pools, and an outdoor crafts area. There is an outside eating area surrounded by orange trees,and a covered outdoor amphitheater, The school completed construction of a new middle school building in 1995. The new upper school, opened in the fall of 2005 with 46 students in grade 9. They will add a grade each year until twelfth grade.

Classes are small and individualized, all the teachers are credentialed, and assistant teachers are used throughout the program. The curriculum includes mastery of basic academic skills with children working in small groups at their own levels. There is also Sierra Canyon Television (SCTV), and a broadcast journalism class for grades 1 through 8. Student produced news shows are broadcast weekly via closed curciuit television.There are specialist teachers in foreign language, computers, music, science, physical education, and art. Intramural sports include volleyball, softball, flag football, basketball and track.

Themes are introduced at the beginning of the school year and integrated into the lesson plan. For example, one year it might be the Middle Ages. This time period would be explored in history class, social studies, and perhaps the art teacher would design a project that explored the costumes/clothing of that time period.

The school's directors are involved in the school at every level, and it shows. Howard Wang referred to the students working together in small groups as 'teams' and joked that, "At Sierra Canyon, we work hard and play hard." The children and teachers that I observed were highly motivated and passionately involved in their work, and there was a team feeling in the classrooms.

Each parent receives a detailed chart at the beginning of the year describing every subject and skill that the children will be taught at every grade level. The curriculum is constantly reviewed and updated to reflect educational tools and methods that are on the cutting edge of the world of education. All teachers meet regularly with the directors to report progress and to make sure that they are on track with the yearly plan.

A student's progress is charted throughout the year on academic profile sheets. Parent-teacher conferences take place twice a year, and report cards are issued three times a year in grades Early Kindergarten to 5 and twice each year in in the upper grades.

Sierra Canyon is a Blue Ribbon school and very proud of it. There are blue ribbons and United States Recognized School of Excellence seals on most of the school literature and on the walls of the administration building. The Blue Ribbon Schools Program identifies and gives national recognition to a diverse group of public and private schools that are unusually effective in meeting local, state, and national goals and in educating all of their students. Once nominated by the Council for American Private Education, a panel of educators visits the school and observes for two days, after which they compile extensive reports and make their recommendations to the U.S. Secretary of Education. The decision is based on conditions at the prospective school. These include leadership, student environment, student performance, teaching environment, curriculum and instruction, parent and community support, organizational vitality, student and teacher attendance rates, students' postgraduate goals, and school, staff and student awards.

Here is an excerpt on the school's philosophy and goals as written in the brochure:

> "The educational experience at Sierra Canyon promotes the concept that each child is an individual. We respect the uniqueness of each learner. The pace may differ from student to student, the content may be presented at different times and in different ways, but all students will be guided to develop their thinking process to their fullest abilities."

Parents are welcome to volunteer in the classroom on a regular basis but participation in a parent training program is mandatory. Students are invited to participate in a field trip each year. Ski trips for the entire family are also planned several times throughout the school year.

HISTORY

Sierra Canyon School was founded in 1977 by Howard Wang and Mick Horwitz. The school grew out of a continuing desire on the part of the founding directors to provide a program which valued the whole child and in which the children enjoyed learning in a setting of mutual respect.

The school began as a summer camp and later become a day school with an early kindergarten to grade 6 program. Sierra Canyon completed construction on a new middle school building in 1994 and currently offers a college preparatory curriculum for students from early kindergarten through high school.

AT A GLANCE

APPLICATION DEADLINE	February 1
OPEN HOUSES	Call school for schedule
UNIFORMS	Yes
BEFORE AND AFTER SCHOOL CARE	Yes
SCHOOL NURSE	On duty during regular school hours
ISEE TESTING	Required for 5-12th grade
SEE MAP	A on page 285

TEMPLE ISRAEL OF HOLLYWOOD

Tel: (323) 876-8330 x215 • Fax: (323) 876-8193
7300 Hollywood Blvd. • Los Angeles, CA 90046
www.tioh.org

HEAD OF SCHOOL	EILEEN HOROWITZ
TYPE OF SCHOOL	CO-ED REFORM JEWISH DAY SCHOOL
GRADES	K - 6

- ENROLLMENT: 200
- ACCREDITATION: BJE/WASC
- MEMBERSHIPS: ACSD/CFEC/ERB
- APPLICATION FEE: $150
- FINANCIAL AID IS AVAILABLE

- TUITION: $14,935
- TEMPLE MEMBERSHIPS:
    SINGLE FAMILY: $1,415
    COUPLE: $2,355

TEMPLE ISRAEL is located in a tree-lined section of Hollywood Bouelvard, in a neighborhood of well-maintained apartment buildings and old California bungalows. The building is a stone fortress that takes up a whole city block and, although surrounded by large, old trees, a decidedly urban school.

Inside, the spaces are airy and bright and classrooms are a colorful, creative, organized chaos of sorts. One has the impression of much activity. Children are involved and completely engrossed in the task at hand, whether it be drawing, cutting, pasting, working with manipulative learning tools, or creating a science project. The children seem to be genuinely enjoying themselves and were so engaged in their various activities that they hardly noticed they had a visitor.

In addition to the teacher and aide, there was a parent volunteer. One child had his own helper (hired by his parents) to help him sort out any disputes he might have with the other children. I took it as a very positive sign that the school did not turn away a child that was working out discipline problems, yet required that the family take responsibility to provide extra help in the classroom. The approach at Temple Israel is developmental and the school philosophy is as follows:

> "Temple Israel Community Day School was founded on the belief that children flourish intellectually in an environment which is caring and supportive. Through a holistic approach, which focuses on all aspects of growth - social, physical, emotional and intellectual - children discover and maximize their potential.

> Class size is kept small (20:1) and instruction is individualized in order to respond to each child's interest and needs. General and Judaic studies are integrated, enabling children to build strong academic skills along with an understanding of Jewish values and traditions.

> As one of a dozen Reform Jewish Day Schools across the United States, it plays an

integral role in the creation of full-time education program for children of Reform Jewish families."

Teaching methods are flexible, but the curriculum follows the guidelines outlined by the California Department of Education. The school uses the Whole Language approach where children are guided to read for meaning while they learn reading skills.

The classrooms are laid out in learning centers where children are taught math and science with manipulative learning tools, study a community based social studies program, and explore art, music, and dance for appreciation and to learn about other cultures.

Individual expression is encouraged and nurtured. Physical education is taught for enjoyment and self-confidence rather than competitive performance. A love for Judaism and commitment to the Jewish people is developed through an understanding and appreciation of the values of Tikkun Olam (repairing the world), Mitzvot (commandments), Tzedakah (justice), and K'lal Yisrael (the Jewish people). Customs, rituals, and traditions are learned through the celebration of holidays. The Hebrew language is taught as the language for the Jewish people and as a way for expressing prayers. Children learn to read, write and speak Hebrew.

School director, Eileen Horowitz, came to the school in July of 1995, with a wealth of experience and ideas. Eileen has taught public school, spent ten years teaching at the Center for Early Childhood Education and recently taught at Adat Ari El in the San Fernando Valley.

Ms. Horowitz is a passionate and spiritual educator who loves her work. She has already implemented many great ideas to improve and enrich the school and its curriculum. During her first six months as director, the school added a beautiful outdoor play structure, organized a school band and choir, begun raising funds for a new science lab, and refurbished the stage and theater facility for a new drama program.

The school is affiliated with the Bureau of Jewish Education, and approved by the Schools Commission of the Western Association of Schools and Colleges.

Artist/teacher, Larry Garf, heads an outstanding art program at the school which includes painting, cartooning, and art history and working with pastels. The school has an impressive computer lab with a specialist teaching the children every week.

There is a new general studies coordinator, Roz Seigel, and a new Judaic Studies Coordinator, Hadar Dohn. The school offers an after-school enrichment program and a summer day camp. There is also "Totally Shabbat" for K-2, a monthly family shabbat program.

Temple Israel Day School is growing fast and now has two classes at K through 1. They will eventually have two classes for each grade from second through sixth grade. The option of adding on to the existing building will be considered in the coming months. Although, I hear that the school is in the beginning phase of a building project to create an entirely new school facility. This school is going places, and now is the time to be part of this hidden gem before the secret is out and it becomes impossible to gain admission.

HISTORY

Temple Israel Day School was founded in 1989 by a group of dedicated Temple members and educators who were committed to establishing a school within the Reform Jewish Movement that would address the needs of the individual and his/her family. The child would be cared for and educated in a loving, nurturing environment where he can explore, investigate and discover the joy of learning. All this as their souls were being touched by the rabbis and teachers.

AT A GLANCE

APPLICATION DEADLINE	January 23
DAY SCHOOL TOUR DATES:	10/16, 10/30, 11/13, 12/14, 12/18 at 8:30 a.m.
DAY SCHOOL OPEN HOUSE	February 12 from 7-9 p.m.
UNIFORMS	Yes
AFTER SCHOOL CARE/ENRICHMENT CLASSES	Available for an additional fee.
SUMMER CAMP	Yes
SEE MAP	C on page 285

TURNING POINT SCHOOL

Tel: (310) 841-2505 • Fax: (310) 841-5420
8780 National Blvd. • Culver City, CA 90232
www.turningpointschool.org

HEAD OF SCHOOL	DEBORAH RICHMAN
DIRECTOR OF ADMISSIONS	MAGGI WRIGHT
TYPE OF SCHOOL	CO-EDUCATIONAL DAY SCHOOL
GRADES	PRIMARY DIVISION - 8

- ENROLLMENT: 353
- ACCREDITATION: CAIS/WASC
- MEMBERSHIPS: AMS/ERB/ISAMA/NAIS
- NEW FAMILY FEE :$1,000
- APPLICATION FEE: $100
- REGISTRATION FEE: $2,000, NON-REFUNDABLE, APPLIED TO TUITION

- TUITION:
  - PD: $19,740-$19,005
  - K-5: $21,785
  - 6-8: $23,680
- FINANCIAL AID IS AVAILABLE

TURNING POINT students and teachers enjoy a new state-of-the-art campus in Culver City. It is located off the 10 Freeway near Robertson Boulevard. The high-tech campus is a two story facility with a Library/Media/Research Center that includes a tiered storytelling room. The structure also houses Latin and Spanish classrooms, a multimedia art studio, wet and dry science laboratories, a full-size gymnasium, and an outdoor playground and lawn area. A music and performing arts center top off the new campus. This is quite a change from its very private, woodsy setting at the base of the Bel Air mountains.

At the primary division, the classrooms use traditional Montessori materials and methods. Teachers determine each child's stage of developmental growth, which tasks have been mastered, and which challenges the child is ready to try.

The elementary division expands on previous learning experiences. The school has a Kindergarten through 1 level to aid in this transition. The time spent making this transition is determined by the child's readiness to proceed to level two. At levels two to five, children are grouped in single levels appropriate to their process. Level five has the responsibility of organizing speakers for school lunches which helps them prepare and learn civic duties, as well as perform a service for the rest of the school.

At each level, the core curriculum includes reading, language arts, mathematics, and social studies. There are specialists in art, music, Spanish, and science. In all subjects, attention is paid to the teaching of skills in a sequential and interrelated manner. There are many study tours, field trips to museums, cultural centers, and regions of geographical interest, which the school believes instills in its students a sense of integrity and a joy of life-long learning.

The School Mission Statement:

"Turning Point provides a harmony between structure and freedom to guide each child through the many academic, creative, physical, social and ethical turning points the school years present. We succeed when our students become responsible, well-balanced adults who are confident, honest, knowledgeable, community-focused, joyful and well prepared to face a challenging and changing world."

The School Philosophy:

"Turning Point believes that children will change, grow, and face the many turning points of life in ways that are different from each other. Because of this, the school has created and will maintain an intimate, focused learning environment committed to individually understanding and respecting each child.

In essential partnership with our students' families, Turning Point balances the many dimensions of a student's life in an integrated curriculum that develops not only the intellectual and physical skills, but also the creative, emotional, and social skills critical to success and active involvement in society.

Classroom instruction is the foundation, rather than the totality of a Turning Point education. Students are immersed in rich learning experiences that foster their innate curiosity and reward their ingenuity. Students are encouraged to embrace challenges as an essential part of growth, leading to the discovery of their own resourcefulness and abilities."

School director Deborah Richman came to the school in the late '80s after having served as principal of a Pre through K through twelfth grade school in Puerto Rico for ten years. She earned her B.S.E. degree from Stephen F. Austin State University in 1970, an M.Ed. degree from the University of Houston in 1975, and has completed postgraduate studies at New York University and Inter-American University.

The teaching staff all hold baccalaureate degrees, and 15 members have advanced degrees. There is also an intern program for students teachers who work with the head teacher in each primary and elementary classroom. There is no school nurse, however, all faculty members have received instruction in first aid and CPR.

Maggi Wright, Director of Admissions and a fellow Englishwoman is a charming, passionate educator who really knows her stuff. If you like the sound of this school, give her a call and set up an appointment to take a tour.

Some of the schools that students are accepted to are: Archer, Brentwood, Buckley, Campbell Hall, Crossroads, Harvard-Westlake, Loyola, Marlborough, Viewpoint and Winward.

HISTORY

The school was founded in 1970 as a nonprofit institution, originally named "Montessori of West Los Angeles," by a group of educators and business professionals who strongly believed in the education philosophy of Dr. Maria Montessori. In October of 1988, the name was changed to Turning Point to represent the series of turning points that children experience as they grow and mature.

AT A GLANCE

APPLICATION DEADLINE	Primary-1: 11/15 Grades 2-5: 1/15
OPEN HOUSES	Primary-elementary: 10/11, middle school: 1/18
BEFORE/AFTER SCHOOL CARE	Yes
ENRICHMENT CLASSES	Yes
ISEE TESTING	Grades 5-8 on 12/6
SUMMER CAMP	6 week
THERE ARE STUDY TOURS	Available for all grades
UNIFORMS	Yes
SEE MAP	D on page 285

VIEWPOINT SCHOOL

Tel: (818) 340-2901 • Fax: (818) 591-0834
23620 Mulholland Highway • Calabasas, CA 91302
www.viewpoint.org

HEAD OF SCHOOL	ROBERT J. DWORKOSKI, PH.D.
DIRECTOR OF ADMISSION	MRS. LAUREL BAKER TEW
TYPE OF SCHOOL	CO-EDUCATIONAL DAY SCHOOL
GRADES	K - 12

- ENROLLMENT: 1,150
- ACCREDITATION: CAIS/WASC
- MEMBERSHIPS: ABC/CRIS/NAIS/NACAC /NASSP/CASE/ERB/NAPSG/CSEE/APC
- MINORITY ADMISSION PROGRAM AVAILABLE TO HISPANIC AND AFRICAN-AMERICAN STUDENTS INTERESTED IN ENTERING GRADES 9-12.

- TUITION: $20,200-$23,750
- NEW FAMILY FEE: $1,500
- FINANCIAL AID IS AVAILABLE
- APPLICATION FEE: $125

VIEWPOINT SCHOOL is located in the Santa Monica Mountains north of Malibu in Calabasas, and draws students from the San Fernando and Conejo Valleys and nearby coastal communities. After its recent acquisition of property (The Meadow School), Viewpoint school has grown to 25 acres.

The campus is surrounded by open mountain areas, with no town in sight for miles. The modern facilities include science and computer labs, art and music studios, a beautiful library containing 25,000 volumes, several athletic fields, two regulation-size swimming pools, play-grounds for elementary children, and a basketball pavilion. A 400-seat Performing Arts Center, along with an upper school Academic Center, was opened in the fall of 2005. The school is already a lively and dynamic Center for the Arts. However, the Performing Arts Center will significantly increase the school's ability to rehearse and to stage dramatic presentations, musicals, dance,and concerts. These new facilities offer Viewpoint the room to expand its numerous programs in theater arts, dance, musical preformance groups and classes.

It will be interesting to see how Viewpoint does expand its already award winning arts pro-gram with this new facility. Viewpoint won the coveted BRAVO award for 2005 in recognition of it's outstanding programs in fine and performing arts. The Music Center of Los Angeles sponsors this annual competition which honors a school in L.A. with outstanding programs in the arts. This award is open to all pre-collegiate schools, public and private.

Viewpoint provides a traditional, academic education under the direction of the brilliant Robert J. Dworkoski, headmaster since 1986. Mr. Dworkoski leads the school with enthusiasm and passion and speaks about the school and its goals with eloquence and humor. If you are interested in the school, I urge you to attend one of the evening informational meetings held during the fall. You will get a chance to hear the headmaster, teachers, and students talk about the school in great detail.

Viewpoint's kindergarten and primary school focuses on providing a nurturing environment with a variety of learning experiences to promote growth in all areas: social, emotional, physical, and intellectual.

The Carden method is a component of the curriculum in the lower school. This philosophy maintains that a good education teaches children to think and to develop good judgment. The acquisition of these skills relies upon a curriculum that interrelates all subject matter in a sequential manner.

The core of the Kindergarten through 4 curriculum is made up of language arts, spelling, reading, literature, arithmetic, science, penmanship, and social studies. There are enrichment specialists in French, computer, art, music and physical education. Each year the fourth grade travels to the Orange County Marine Institute and sleeps overnight at the Lazy W Ranch.

At the middle school level (grades 6 to 8), teachers and administrators are specialists in education for early adolescents. Academically, the middle school builds upon the skills and knowledge learned in the lower school. There are accelerated math courses in grades 6 to 8 to challenge gifted students and accelerated science courses at the eighth grade level.

Extra curricular and co-curricular electives include photography, ceramics, painting, drawing, creative writing, speech, current affairs, chorus, instrumental music, computer animation, keyboarding, and dance. There is cotillion for the 5th and 6th grades, and there are dances for seventh and eighth grades.

Students put on a musical each fall, and several Shakespearean plays throughout the year. Students in grades 5 to 8 compete in flag football, basketball, baseball, soccer, softball, swimming and volleyball.

The students in middle school go on different overnight trips such as: fifth grade Astrocamp (three days), sixth grade El Camino Pines Outdoor School (three days), seventh grade Catalina Island (four days), and eighth grade the Yosemite Institute (six days).

The upper school core curriculum consists of courses in English, mathematics, social studies, science, and foreign languages. Electives include poetry, oceanography, environmental science, Asian history, computer science, comparative governments, international relations, psychology, economics, and speech.

Arts electives include instrumental music, chorus, music theory, music history, photography, ceramics, film-making, video, and drama. In recent years students have won local awards for their films, videos, and artwork.

The upper school offers honors and Advanced Placement courses to able and motivated students. Admission to these courses is by permission of the instructor, department head, and Head of upper school. The school offers the following courses:

Honors: Geometry, Biology, Chemistry, Algebra II/Trigonometry, Pre-Calculus

Advanced Placement: English language, English Literature, Calculus AB, Calculus BC, French language, French literature, Spanish language, Spanish literature, studio art, music history, biology, chemistry, physics, economics, psychology, European history, U.S. history, computer science and music theory.

Seniors may participate in a concurrent program with local colleges (Cal State, Northridge, and Pierce College), and may replace a portion of their regular course work with a special senior project. Past projects have included a study of Einstein's theory of relativity, research on tide pools in Santa Monica Bay, and an apprenticeship with an architect.

Students are required to complete at least 45 hours of volunteer work outside the school as part of the Community Service Program. Activities in this program include feeding the homeless, helping children with learning disorders, and doing environmental work.

In the upper school athletic program, boys compete in football, cross-country, basketball, soccer, volleyball, baseball, tennis, swimming, and equestrian events. Girls compete in cross-country, basketball, softball, tennis, soccer, swimming, and equestrian events. There is a total of 20 interscholastic sports teams. Viewpoint's Varsity Boys Tennis and Volleyball teams both won CIF championships in 2005.

The school maintains that numerous debating numerous extracurricular activities develop the ability to work cooperatively with others and teach skills not always offered in the classroom. These activities include the yearbook, newspaper and literary journal, speech and debating competitions, foreign language presentations, and theatrical and musical productions.

Each year, the school hosts a foreign exchange program. High school students have lived for three weeks with families in Russia, Japan, China, France, and Spain.

Make no mistake, this is an academically competitive school. The scores of Viewpoint's students typically exceed the national average. Twenty-one percent of Viewpoint's class of 1999 were National Merit Scholars and the class of 1999s SAT average was 1315. Viewpoint typically achieves 100 percent placement of its graduates in four-year colleges and universities across the country. The information packet Viewpoint sends parents is remarkably comprehensive. In addition to the normal information, it also contains grade distribution for the most recent graduation class, and the names of colleges to which the graduates have been accepted.

A Little About Dr. Robert J. Dworkoski

Dr. Dworkoski attended George Washington University (B.A. 1968), New York University (A.M. 1971), and Columbia University (M.A. 1972, Ph.D. 1979, European History). Prior to his appointment, Dr. Dworkoski taught history at Brooklyn College in New York and was Department Chairman of Social Studies at Woodmere Academy in New York.

From 1980 through 1986, Dr. Dworkoski was the head of upper school at the Harvard School in Los Angeles. A Fulbright Scholar in Europe in 1983 and the recipient of a grant from the National Endowment for the Humanities in 1993, Dr. Dworkoski has been active in the California Association of Independent Schools (CAIS) and the National Association of Independent Schools (NAIS). He sits on the Boards of the Will Geer Theatrical Botanicum and the Gold Coast Performing Arts Association.

HISTORY

Founded in 1961, Viewpoint is a non-denominational, non-profit, independent day school that provides an enriched college preparatory program. Viewpoint offers a challenging academic program emphasizing excellence and achievement and providing individualized attention.

AT A GLANCE

APPLICATION DEADLINE	January 12
OPEN HOUSE	Call school for information
BEFORE AND AFTER SCHOOL CARE	Available
TESTING	K: Developmental screenings. Grade 1-4: In-house Academic Testing Grades 5-12: ISEE
SUMMER CAMP	Yes
UNIFORMS	Required
BUS TRANSPORTATION	In areas of greatest demand
SEE MAP	D on page 285

THE VILLAGE SCHOOL

Tel: (310) 459-8411 • Fax: (310) 459-3285
780 Swarthmore Avenue • Pacific Palisades, CA 90272-4355
www.village-school.com

HEAD OF SCHOOL	NORA MALONE
ASSISTANT HEAD/DIR. OF ADM.	BARBARA RUTH-WILLIAMS
TYPE OF SCHOOL	CO-EDUCATIONAL DAY SCHOOL
GRADES	TK - 6

- ENROLLMENT: 290
- ACCREDITATION: CAIS/WASC
- MEMBERSHIPS: ERB/NAIS
- FINANCIAL AID IS AVAILABLE

- TUITION: $18,500
- APPLICATION FEE: $125
- NEW FAMILY FEE: $1,250

THE VILLAGE SCHOOL is located in the heart of the Palisades Villageon two beautiful campuses. The main campus, a three-story building , houses sixteen classrooms, plus Spanish classrooms, a science lab, the library and several offices. The new Center for the Arts and Athletics, around the corner from the main campus, contains a multi-purpose gym/auditorium,music room with recording studio, visual arts room and a dance studio. The new location also provides children with more grassy areas, although P.E. also regularly uses the local public park .

The New Center for the Arts building project is responsible for the required yearly $1,000 Facilities Deposit. Each family must pay this yearly until a total deposit of $7,000 accrues or the student enters sixth grade—which ever comes first. The full amount (without interest) will be refunded to the family the September following that student's graduation from Village School or permanent withdrawal for other reasons. Voluntary gifts are also solicited.

The Village School has a strong academic curriculum taught in small classes (12:22) beginning at transitional kindergarten. In TK there is one class with 12 children in it. The approach here is progressive versus traditional, with children moving to the next stage of learning when they are developmentally ready. The children experience language, math, science, social studies, art, music, and physical education and study the relationships to one another.

A typical transitional kindergarten day provides two to three structured circle times, two snack times, lunch, and a one hour rest period. Materials include a MacMillan Early Science Kit, Weekly Reader (Pre-K), and Teacher-made units/games.

At the kindergarten level, there are three classes of 14 to 15 students. Generally about ten of these students are siblings. Language, mathematics, and social studies make up the core curriculum.

Children learn the basics of phonics and language expression through textbooks together with discussion, dictation, drawing and writing. Students are introduced to a new letter per week, practice rhyming and opposites through whole language activities, and learn to form letters correctly. Reading is taught in small groups when children are ready.

The curriculum from first through sixth grade follows the traditional path with: language arts, mathematics, spelling, social studies, and science, with specialist teachers for art, music, physical education, computer, library skills, and spanish. Field trips are organized twice a year, and grades four through six participate in one overnight trip.

From first through sixth grade there are two classes at each grade level with 18 to 20 children in each class. Language arts, social studies, and math are taught by the classroom teachers with specialist teachers for art, music, P.E., computer, library skills, science, and Spanish. Field trips are organized several times a year, and grades 3 through 6 participate in one overnight trip.

Every teacher is assisted by an assistant teacher. TK thorugh second grade have full-time assistants, and grade 3 through 6 have part-time assistants.

The Village School operates on a trimester system. Report cards are given after each trimester. TK through 2 have a check list of aquired skills and letter grades begin second trimester of third grade. Conferences between parents and teachers are scheduled at the end of the frist two trimesters.

Regularly assigned homework begins in K after the winter break with 5 to 15 minutes per day. Grades one and two have approximately 30 minutes per day; three and four have approximately 30 to 60 minutes each day, and grades five and six have between 60 to 90 minutes a day. No homework is assigned on weekends or holidays.

Student activities include: student council, spirit days, and community service projects. Each year the school hosts a Back to School Picnic, Halloween Carnival, Open House, with an Art Show, Science Fair and Sports Day.

The school offers three types after-school programs. Each trimester students may sign up for any number of after school clubs including things such as drama, dance,cooking, science, and many more. The after school sports program begins in fourth grade and the school belongs to a league of other schools, which includes competition in flag football, basketball, volleyball, and soccer. There is also supervised after-school care from 3:00 to 5:30 p.m.

HISTORY

The Village School was founded in 1977 with the express purpose of providing a nurturing and strongly academic program within the atmosphere of a neighborhood school. The logo of a little red school house, designed by a 3rd grade student, reflects the continuing commitment to a community school, which aims to support and celebrate families who place a high priority on education.

Nora Malone assumed her duties as head of school on July 1 in 1999 after two years as assistant head of school. Barbara Ruth Williams also joined the administrative team in 1999.

AT A GLANCE

APPLICATION DEADLINE	December 31
OPEN HOUSE	December 13
UNIFORMS ARE NOT REQUIRED	However, dress code is enforced
BEFORE AND AFTER SCHOOL CARE	Yes
SEE MAP	D on page 285

VISTAMAR SCHOOL

Tel: (310) 643-7377 Fax: (310) 643-7371
737 Hawaii Street • El Segundo, CA 90245
www.vistamarschool.org

HEAD OF SCHOOL	JIM BUCKHEIT
DIRECTOR OF ADMISSIONS	RYAN TILLSON
TYPE OF SCHOOL	CO-EDUCATIONAL DAY SCHOOL
GRADES	9 - 12

- ENROLLMENT: UNDER 200
- NEW STUDENT FEE: $1,200
- BOOKS AND MISC: $400-$700
- TUITION: $25,850
- DEPOSIT: $1,500
- FINANCIAL AID AVAILABLE

VISTAMAR SCHOOL, the first independent co-educational High school in the South Bay area, began as a spark of an idea discussed by a small but ambitious group of women who met in a Manhattan Beach eatery. The location they chose for the school was a good one. Taking up 7,600 square feet of the old Direct TV warehouse in El Segundo offered convenient access to surrounding communities, including Manhattan Beach, Redondo Beach, and Hawthorne, the 405 and 105 freeways and the green Line.

Before you think this is some elitist type school, let me tell you the inaugural class was small. The pioneer class of students (44 in ninth grade and ten in the tenth grade) came from 21 different middle and high schools in 13 different communities. Half are boys, and half are girls, and a third represent ethnic minorities. They are looking for students to help shape this community, and build it into something.

Vistamar School empowers students, preparing them to contribute and excel in higher education, and commit to:

A broad and balanced program that challenges and engages students, building individual skills and inspiring a passion for learning.

An intimate atmosphere that fosters initiative, responsibility, knowledge of self, and connection to others.

Diversity of thought and culture that encourages authentic exchange of perspectives, mutual respect, and a mature understanding of the world.

Jim Buckheit, the head of the school, as well as the assistant head and CFO have impressive credentials, and neither of them were looking for work, or considered leaving their current schools. However when offered a totally blank slate, and the opportunity to combine the best models and approaches they had found to work over the years, and combine them into one school, it was simply too exciting to pass up!

Jim Buckheit believes very strongly in borrowing practices from the other side of the world, "My travels" he says, have afforded me numerous examples of exceptional schooling that

I've been able to adapt to my own schools; applied math from England, cultural history from Holland, philosophy from France, sciences from Japan... ultimately, the culture of the school community will shape the attitudes and habits our students carry into their futures. The students will be best served by a culture of continuous learning."

But what about the classes themselves? Here is the academic program overview:

You will notice there is a minimum of three years of a language, and there's language available for 'heritage speakers,' to allow students to develop academically in their 'mother tongue' and be fully bi-lingual. Mathematics is also considered a language instead of a set of procedures. Overall, there is a strong sense of dialogue. In the tenth grade, there is a special course in Forensics, and a class to learn speechwriting and public speaking. Vistamar also recognizes the important link between Math and Science. Students will study biology, physics, and chemistry for three years starting in tenth grade, having a tri-mester each. The science lab is one of the most impressive I've seen. Included in the first phase of construction, every classroom will have Internet access and multi-media presentations. There will be banks of computers for student use in common areas, and the entire school will be wireless accessible. A dedicated server will ensure parents remote access, and students will be able to log on to their teachers web pages for notes, assignments, and links, and an extensive database of journals, reference materials and text books.

Also unique to Vistamar are seminars, which students and teachers take together. For example, they may all sit in on a lecture about 'Visual Literacy', and then open a dialogue about the subject between themselves. Teachers are also available in the many 'pod' common areas, for help and informal teaching/tutoring in any given subject.

Vistamar requires every student to be physically active, and have a variety of fitness electives. Sports teams include: basketball, baseball, cross-country, golf, soccer, tennis, lacrosse, volleyball and water polo. However, if they are involved in an after school fitness activity such as martial arts or dance, this can count towards this requirement. This is an attempt by the school to address an often-overlooked issue, that schools don't really respect a student's time.

There are also high expectations of the teachers. They are expected to spend a lot of time with their students, so they must primarily really like kids! Diversity is not limited to the student body, for a faculty with global experience is preferred. Vistamar may or may not be right for you, but I highly recommend visiting this model school. You will learn a lot about education just from the visit/tour.

HISTORY

Vistamar is an independent, co-educational high school that opened its doors in September of 2005. It offers parents another option in a region where educational choices have failed to keep pace with the gradual rise in the number of families in the South Bay area.

AT A GLANCE

APPLICATION DEADLINE	February 6, with rolling admissions
OPEN HOUSES	October, tours daily
UNIFORMS	Not required
ISEE TESTING	11/10, 12/6, 1/31 & 4/18
SEE MAP	E on page 285

WALDEN SCHOOL

Tel: (626) 792-6166 • Fax: (626) 792-1335
74 S. San Gabriel Blvd. • Pasadena, CA 91107
www.waldenschool.net

HEAD OF SCHOOL	MATT ALLIO
DIRECTOR OF ADMISSIONS	CHRISTENA BARNES
TYPE OF SCHOOL	PROGRESSIVE DEVELOPMENTAL
GRADES	PRESCHOOL - 6

- ENROLLMENT: 248
- NEW FAMILY FEE: $500
- ACCREDITATION: CAIS//NAIS/WASC/ISAMA
- MEMBERSHIPS ALLIANCE FOR MINORITY AFFAIRS
- TUITION: $13,750
- APPLICATION FEE: $70
- FINANCIAL AID IS AVAILABLE

WALDEN SCHOOL is located in a self-contained, Pasadenan urban setting. The school purchased an additional building just north of the original in 1999. The enrollment has since increased to 248. They now have a library with over 9,000 volumes, a huge dedicated art studio, three new classrooms (one of which includes a science lab), and business and development offices. Walden also has renovated both the Pre through Kindergarten and north playgrounds through a collaborative two year effort with the Sense of Place Committee, comprised of parents, students, staff, and well known architect, Ronnie Siegel. Both learning environments are unique, creative, and enchanting.

The educational approach here is developmental and draws on the philosophies of Henry David Thoreau, Socrates, Jean Piaget, John Holt, Marcy Cook, Carl Rogers, Abraham Maslow, and Maria Montessori.

Children are divided into six multi-age groups in class sizes of between 13-22 students as follows:
- Preschool: 3-5 year-olds
- K-1 grade: 5-7 year-olds
- 1-2 grade: 7-8 year-olds
- 2-3 grade: 8-9 year-olds
- 4-5 grade: 9-11 year-olds
- 5-6 grade: 12-13 year-olds

In this setting, children are encouraged to learn at their own individual pace through the teacher's guidance and by a collaboration created by the teacher and student.

Walden students select learning materials and activities from a selection provided by the teacher. They then have an agreement to work with what they have chosen. By the elementary grades, Walden students and their teachers agree on the kind and amount of academic work that will be accomplished, and children are responsible for planning their time accordingly.

Walden's approach is based on the concept that even very young children are able to plan and carry out learning activities. Walden teachers support this development of the children. The teacher and students have conferences and outline the appropriate amount of work in each subject each day. When the agreed work for the day is complete the child can then pursue other interests including special projects, extra work in a favorite academic area, library time and other activities, which give the child control of his learning. Thus, the structure of the school day provides its own reward for efficient use of time.

Walden students are also asked to abide by a series of clearly stated agreements, which outline the principles of living and working in a group. From time to time children will forget or disregard the rules and are confronted with the logical consequences of their actions, which are never humiliating or demeaning.

When a Walden child breaks an agreement, he or she is expected to find a way to make restitution. A child who breaks work materials will be expected to help repair it. A child who hurts another will be asked, "What can I do to help you feel better?" A child who drops a piece of trash may be asked to pick it up and another piece as well. In this way, the child's self-esteem remains intact. He learns that when a mistake is made, he can repair the damage. Each child is responsible to the group, yet is a valuable individual.

Walden, while founded on Montessori principles, is not a Montessori school. The learning theories, materials, and strategies of the this approach allow children to select materials from those provided by the teacher and to move at his/her own pace. Specialists teach music, Spanish, art and two for physical education one for outdoor sports, and the other for dance, yoga and movement. Walden has a library manager with a resident storyteller as part of their language arts program.

HISTORY

Walden School was founded in 1970 as a non-profit, independent, co-ed elementary school, and for twenty years rented space from a Lutheran church in Pasadena. In 1990, the school purchased its current building on South San Gabriel Blvd.

AT A GLANCE

APPLICATION DEADLINE	February 1
OPEN HOUSE	September 1
SCHOOL TOURS	Wednesdays in the fall, check website
UNIFORMS	No
BEFORE AND AFTER SCHOOL CARE	Yes
SEE MAP	B on page 285

THE WAVERLY SCHOOL

Elementary School
Tel: (626) 792-5940 • Fax: (626) 683-5460
67 W. Bellevue Drive • Pasadena, CA 91105

Middle School
Tel: (626) 792-5940 • Fax: (626) 683-5460
396 S. Pasadena Ave. • Pasadena, CA 91105

Upper School
Tel: (626) 683-5464 • Fax: (626) 584-8531
108 Waverly Drive. • Pasadena, CA 91105
www.thewaverlyschool.org

HEAD OF SCHOOL	HEIDI JOHNSON
DIRECTOR OF ADMISSIONS	JENNIFER DAKAN
TYPE OF SCHOOL	CO-EDUCATIONAL DAY SCHOOL
GRADES	PRE-K - 12

- ENROLLMENT: 300
- ACCREDITATION: WASC
- YEARLY REG. FEE: $1,000
- TUITION: $9,000–$16,780
- APPLICATION FEE: $75
- FINANCIAL AID IS AVAILABLE

WAVERKY SCHOOL is located on a quiet street in an industrial/business section of Pasadena. The two-story facility looks more like an office building than a school campus, but if you let appearances fool you, you may miss out on one of the best up and coming schools.

The building has eight classrooms, a library, cooking area, community room, teachers lounge, reception area, and administrative offices. The outside play area (along the side and back of the school) has a basketball court, climbing structure, and swings, grass, a garden, and a shaded lunch area.

The most exciting news is the relocation and development of the high school campus. Waverly has purchased land on Waverly Drive and severn historical buildings to be refurbished. This also allows The Waverly school to expand it's sports program that was previosuly very limited in the old location.

What Waverly does have to offer is a staff of some of the most outstanding educators in the greater Los Angeles area. The educational approach at waverly is a blend of progressive and developmental, employing the philosophies of John Dewey and Jean Piaget. Children are divided into multi-age groups rather than grades. The focus is on working together, cooperating as a group and being members of a democratic society.

The curriculum is social-studies based and recognizes the need for all students to move and think beyond the classroom and to participate in the real world, interacting with society, exploring and experiencing nature, and learning how to become intellectual, moral, creative and political participants in the twenty-first century.

Field trips and experiential learning are an integral part of the Waverly learning experience. Geography is thoroughly explored giving students valuable information about the world and its many cultures. Students are evaluated individually to accommodate varying developmental growth patterns. Whenever appropriate, they work at a level which leads to success. Cooperative work and group learning occur at all grade levels.

Curriculum Outline

The Primary Grades
The social studies core themes begin with the two smallest units of the society—the individual and the family. Work and play enable the children to explore their personalities, likes and dislikes, and physical appearances.

This exploration expands to a study of the family, neighborhoods, and transportation systems. Mapping becomes an important part of learning. Construction of model neighborhoods and the science of structures joins an examination of the city's transportation system.

During these years, students learn to read and write at their own pace in a language-experience approach, and mathematical concepts move from the manipulative stage to the written record stage. Science begins as a process of discovery and grows into a practice of experimentation. Drama, art and music are integrated into all aspects of the social studies core theme.

Upper Elementary, Grades 1-6
The social studies curriculum expands to explore the study of the cities within our city. food, music, literature, and culture of the many ethnic groups in our area are experienced and enjoyed. Students begin exploring the history of California. Themes such as California Native Americans, the Gold Rush, Westward Expansion and the Urban Explosion, allow students to study primary sources, play simulation games, and write about other time periods.

Reading is literature based with an emphasis on discussion and analysis of quality writing. Mathematical skills continue to develop with equal emphasis on computation and higher level thinking, problem solving, and logic. The arts become more important as students' level of sophistication increase. Scientific skills of conjecture and analysis are added to observation and experimentation to develop better understanding of the scientific method.

The Middle School, Grades 7-8
The humanities is the general theme for these grades. Students explore the human experience on a national and global scale. Important world history periods, such as the Renaissance, the Roman Empire, and the Industrial Revolution are studied in depth, with constant comparisons made to life today. War, racism, injustice, and freedom are some of the issues examined through the use of literature, film, music and drama.

Writing and reading skills are developed through intensive analysis of classic literature. Mathematical skills are guided toward preparation for algebra and geometry. Waverly does work to address parent concerns and this year they were able to offer Algebra I through the generous services of a parent mathematician. As beginning scientists, students employ the scientific method to formulate hypotheses, implement experiments, and draw conclusions.

The Upper School
The upper school grades 9 through 12, began in 1994 and concentrates on two primary goals namely preparation for the demands and discipline of the college experience, and development of the necessary interpersonal skills for graduates to become active, responsible, thinking, caring members of society. In the high school, the class sizes are small with ten students per grade. With all the extra attention, students have graduated and found their way into top colleges and universities.

HISTORY

The Tiger Tots Children Center was created as a preschool by Gayle Thompson in 1984. In 1993, it became The Waverly School K-6, and in 1996 expanded to include Kindergarten through Grade 12.

AT A GLANCE

APPLICATION DEADLINE	February 1. The school is looking for families whose goals for their children are in sync with the school philosophy
TOURS	Between October through January, call for RSVP
OPEN HOUSES	Check website or call school for open house dates
UNIFORMS	No
BEFORE/AFTER SCHOOL CARE	Yes
SUMMER CAMP	June through August
SEE MAP	B on page 285

THE WESLEY SCHOOL

Tel: (818) 508-4542 • Fax: (818) 508-4570
4832 Tujunga Ave. • North Hollywood, CA 91601
www.wesleyschool.org

HEAD OF SCHOOL	RUTH HUYLER-GLASS
DIRECTOR OF ADMISSIONS	VERENA DENOVE
TYPE OF SCHOOL	CO-EDUCATIONAL DAY SCHOOL
GRADES	K - 8

- ENROLLMENT: 200
- ACCREDITATION: CAIS/NAIS/WASC
- ONE TIME BUILDING FUND FEE: $500
- REGISTRATION FEE: 10% OF TUITION
- MEMBERSHIPS: ESAD/ERB/ISAMA/LACSS/NAIS

- TUITION: $16,660-$18,260
- APPLICATION FEE: $100
- NEW FAMILY FEE: $1,000
- FINANCIAL AID IS AVAILABLE

THE WESLEY SCHOOL was founded in 1999 and is located on four acres at the First United Methodist Church of North Hollywood. The school was formerly St. Michael's. I have met some Wesley parents who take a lot of pride in their involvement with teachers and administrators in helping the school get up and running. They have created a warm, wholesome environment, and the admissions process is not intimidating. The classrooms are a good size, there is a computer lab, and my favorite, a cedar library. The library reminds one of a woodsy cabin, a place where you would like to sit with a book.

The school is divided into a lower school of grades K through 5 and a middle school of grades 6 to 8. Each grade participates in science and health, math, reading and literature, mechanics, writing, art, music, social studies, foreign languages, computer, library, and physical education. Speech and drama are also offered as middle school electives. There is an ethics class available for eigthth grade. The Language Program is unique; French K through 2, Spanish for grades 3 to 8. A character development program with monthly themes is interwoven throughout the curriculum.

The middle school is completely departmentalized for seventh and eight grades. To allow for this transition, the sixth grade has two teachers for their academic core subjects with additional teachers for their enrichment classes. In eighth grade, students may elect to participate in a mock trial competition sponsored by the Constitutional Rights Foundation. I had the pleasure of witnessing one of these at an open house and could not have been more impressed.

Students can participate in the after-school athletic program beginning in the fourth grade. The students compete in basketball, soccer, volleyball, cross-country, flag football, and golf. Wesley belongs to both the San Fernando Valley league and the Delphic league.

The Chapel program is anchored in the Judeo-Christian tradition and students are encouraged to respect all religions. All students participate in chapel together three days a week. The Chapel program includes non-religious ceremonies and celebrations such as birthdays and academic and athletic accomplishments.

The Parent Association is very active. It is responsible for supporting the faculty and administration in many extra curricular activities including helping in the library, serving hot lunch, putting on both Halloween and winter holiday events, middle school dances and countless other wonderful extras. Every parent is a member, and the school expects every family to participate in the school community. Head of school, Ruth Glass, elaborates about the importance of parent involvement," Our children watch us-the adults in their lives-very closely. Parents and educators must work together to ensure that we conduct ourselves in ways that provide children with consistent messages and values. The Wesley School prides itself itself justifiably on parent involvement and communication. Given new technology, our opportunities to increase communication and involvement are immense, but so are the risks of creating distance. We do not take our relationships lightly or for granted, and I see a future in which that bond remains strong and mutually supportive."

I have such warm feelings for this school because when I'm out with my children at sporting events or other activities we always seem to run into students from Wesley, and without fail I find them to be friendly, honest and unaffected.

History

The Wesley School was established in 1999 as a successor to St. Michael and All Angels' Parish Day School, which had discontinued operation after nearly 40 years of service to the community. A dedicated group of parents, faculty, and administartors obtained funding and zoning and reunited as The Wesley School.

At A Glance

APPLICATION DEADLINE	Last Friday in January
OPEN HOUSES	Lower school: 10/22, 11/19 & 1/15
	Middle school: 11/11 and 1/20
UNIFORMS	Yes
BEFORE AND AFTER SCHOOL CARE	Yes
SEE MAP	B on page 285

WESTLAND SCHOOL

Tel: (310) 472-5544 • Fax: (310) 472-5807
16200 Mulholland Drive • Los Angeles, CA 90049
www.westlandschool.org

HEAD OF SCHOOL	JANIE LOU HIRSCH
DIRECTOR OF ADMISSIONS	MARGERY SEID
TYPE OF SCHOOL	INDEPENDENT DAY SCHOOL
GRADES	K - 6

- ENROLLMENT: 130
- ACCREDITATION: CAIS
- MEMBERSHIPS: CAIS
- NEW FAMILY FEE: $1,000

- TUITION: $13,980
- APPLICATION FEE: $100
- YEARLY REGISTRATION FEE: $275
- FINANCIAL AID IS AVAILABLE

WESTLAND is a Progressive school located on Mulholland Drive's 'private school row,' which includes Mirman, Curtis, Berkeley Hall and Steven S. Wise.

The modern, one-story facility sits on one and a half acres and includes large, bright classrooms, a library, conference rooms, a kitchen, and an auditorium all grouped around a central patio, which serves as a protected work area and a place for informational exchange such as school bulletin boards.

Westland has a spectacular gymnasium/auditorium, which has huge windows at the far end that overlook a grove of pine and eucalyptus trees. This grove formerly housed the play and climbing structures for the younger children, and what was once a bit of a wild, un-manicured area is now nicely landscaped. This created some controversy for a group of Westland parents who liked having a wild 'adventure' area for their kids to explore. There is now a new library, science and art labs, and three play yards.

The upper yard has a basketball court and a large, grassy field for sports. There is also a sandbox, outdoor stage, and a worm farm...yes, a worm farm, with a few pet chickens thrown in for good measure. There is also a science pond in front of the school.

The school philosophy follows the teachings of John Dewey, who believed that we should make learning more experiential, active rather than passive, educating children for a democratic society. Activities at the school are designed to be 'hands-on' and include block building, drawing, gardening, and tending animals.

Every effort is made to provide a warm, caring, and supportive environment to allow the children to develop and grow at their own pace. The sharing of ideas and group problem solving are an integral part of the system. For example, in a recent lesson on the history of dinosaurs, children were given a wide selection of dinosaur models to place in an outdoor habitat. This took hours as the children agreed on the placement of certain plant eaters near a valuable food source and argued that "you can't put those two near each other because the Rex is a 'meat eater' and will fight with the other one."

Children discover that they have an influence on and a responsibility to others and to the world outside. Music, art, drama and dance contribute to aesthetic development.

Each class has 22 students with one full-time group teacher and an assistant. All group teachers are highly qualified and experienced in progressive teaching methods. There are seven years of school and six classrooms or groups. In any group, you will find children of several ages. For example, Group I has 5, 6 and 7-year-olds, Group II has 7, 8 and 9-year-olds. Cross-age play is encouraged. As children move through the school to different levels, they are re-grouped so that the peer group does not remain constant.

Curriculum
The kindergarten at Westland is not academic. There is lots of reading readiness and language experience, but no readers or phonics workbooks. The reading program begins in earnest in group three at second grade.

Social studies forms the core of the curriculum. The school integrates reading, language arts, science, math and art into the social studies-based curriculum. By connecting all areas of study with social studies, each subject is placed in a real-world context and learning becomes relevant.

The approach to learning is one of questioning, problem solving, and learning by doing. Children may take a field trip to a restaurant and then come back and build a facsimile of it with blocks. They will discuss how the business should be run, assign jobs such as waitress, cashier, manager, and customer, and then take turns solving the daily problems that might arise in that particular setting. This way they learn by using their organizational skills, math and problem solving skills, and learn to work together. This gives them a strong connection to the community in which they live.

There is a music specialist who works with each group and who leads a community 'Sing' on Friday mornings. Visual arts are stressed at all age levels. Drama, poetry, and creative writing experiences are also important aspects of the Westland curriculum.

There is a sense of community at Westland. Every child has a commitment to his/her group, and each group has a responsibility to the school. for example, one group publishes a school newspaper and another assists in the library. Students actively participate in community service projects.

Parents participate by giving docent tours, working in the Hot Lunch Program, fund raising, driving on field trips, working in the library, taking part in weekend work groups, and donating time and materials that contribute to the school programs.

Westland is a family corporation. Each parent and staff member is entitled to one vote at business meetings. The Board of Trustees, composed of elected and appointed members, is the official governing body of the corporation.

HISTORY

Westland School was opened in 1949, during a time of intense political upheaval in the United States – the McCarthy era. The politically active founders of Westland were eager to educate children in an atmosphere of free inquiry. They were inspired by the progressive ideas of John Dewey and the work done by Jean Piaget on the developmental stages of children's learning.

AT A GLANCE

APPLICATION DEADLINE	Applications are available between September and December 1, and only the first 100 are accepted
UNIFORMS	No
BEFORE/AFTER SCHOOL CARE	Yes
SEE MAP	D on page 285

WESTMARK SCHOOL

Tel: (818) 986-5045 • Fax: Fax: (818) 380-1378
5461 Louise Ave. • Encino, CA 91316
www.westmarkschool.org

HEAD OF SCHOOL	MUIR MEREDITH
DIRECTOR OF ADMISSIONS	BETSY BREESE
TYPE OF SCHOOL	CO-EDUCATIONAL DAY SCHOOL
GRADES	4 - 12

- ENROLLMENT: 167
- ACCREDITATION: WASC
- YEARLY REGISTRATION FEE: $1,500
- FINANCIAL AID IS AVAILABLE
- TUITION: $25,500-$27,000
- APPLICATION FEE: $125
- MEMBERSHIPS: CASE

Westmark School is located on almost 5 acres in Encino, California. The school is situated in a quiet neighborhood not far from Ventura Boulevard, where there are an array of restaurants and stores. The school values safety and functions as a closed campus, with one entry and exit point. They have a security guard on duty throughout the school day and once inside you are greeted by Jenny, a fellow English woman whose jolly personality can't help but put you in a good mood.

I had met Keri Borzello, the new Director of Marketing and Community Relations at an open house for another school. I was instantly won over by her great personality, enthusiasm and knowledge about education. She invited me to visit Westmark. The tour she gave me along with some other families was fantastic. I always gauge a tour by how a prospective family behaves. If it's too long, they get irritable (and so do I) and if it's too short, they feel like they haven't been told and shown everything they need to see/hear before making a decision. At the end of it we were all happy and relaxed as could be!

Betsy Breese, the Director of Admissions, a lovely woman who you can tell really cares about her kids explained to me that Westmark is a unique school in that it serves children in elementary through high school who have average to above average academic potential, have been diagnosed with learning differences and have not been fully served in other school settings. In order to be considered for a place at this school, each family must provide a complete psycho-educational diagnostic evaluation which will help the school in determining the student's current abilities and designing a curriculum to fit the child. Not expecting the child to fit the curriculum.

School Mission Statement

"Westmark School provides a caring environment where motivated students with learning differences discover their unique paths to personal and academic excellence in preparation for a successful college experience."

Westmark helps the families of their students who might have felt a little helpless in the past by asking them to commit to open and full communication with the school. Parents may, for the first time, feel like they are really being heard and that all their concerns are being squarely met. Westmark believes that parents who are actively involved in the school-life of their child will have a profound impact on their child's success. Now I don't think that they expect the parents to know how to do a 11th grade math problem...but perhaps the parent might learn how to do it from their child!

Westmark has 34 classrooms, a Library, a tutorial room, a multi-purpose room/auditorium (with a stage for drama productions), art room, sewing room, kitchen and weight room. The library includes a computer lab with brand new Mac computers. Books are arranged by reading level. Special lighting is used in the library to enhance reading/learning.

The campus has a swimming pool that is used during the warmer months for physical education classes. They have just finished building a brand new state-of-the-art athletic field for football and soccer games. Their woodshop is under construction but will open next year.

Cooking is a very popular elective option for students. Classes utilize a new state-of-the-art kitchen, which was donated by a generous family. Additionally, the kitchen is used for campus events. Other popular electives include sewing, American Sign Language and art.

I love this one: The Westmark News Network (WNN) is a student produced television network and News Show. The program airs daily, produced by the high school students. Lower school students may participate by being featured and/or to make announcements.

The new academic building offers:

- A state-of-the-art science lab
- The WNN/digital media room
- 2 English classrooms and a math/science room
- Along with the rest of the campus, each classroom has a flat screen TV for curriculum related purposes, as well as to watch the WNN.
- Along with the rest of the campus, each classroom has an LCD projector.
- All English classes on campus, including those in the new building, can act as computer labs, housing computers for each student.
- Windows that are double-paned to block out sound.
- Chairs that are adjustable and flexible to cater to students who move about in their seats.
- The science/math room has a smart board, as do other classrooms on campus.
- The College Counseling Center

The school offers comprehensive lower, middle and secondary school programs. Middle and high school students participate in programs tailor made for each student to help them matriculate from Westmark to college or many wonderful career programs. I met Luren Leavitt the college counselor, a wonderfully articulate and energetic woman who told me how she will not only guide students towards a traditional college experience but will offer guidance and information about a variety of career options, technical schools and vocational courses of study that will lead to jobs in media arts, culinary arts, film and TV production and computer technologies. (By the way...all 29 of their seniors are off to college!)

Their whole-child approach to education in a nurturing and traditional environment is definitely working. The kids are brilliant! They genuinely seem happy to be there. As I entered each classroom I was met by happy smiling faces and impromptu offers to look over their work and to hear about what they were studying that day. These kids are not being coached in advance of a school tour, they are left alone and it is in their most relaxed state that you can see how successful this school's approach to learning can be.

HISTORY

In 1983 Landmark School of Massachusetts opened Landmark West, in Culver City as a west coast extension of their school. The Landmark Foundation purchased the Encino campus in 1991. In the fall of 1997 Landmark School was purchased by a non-profit corporation, Learning with a Difference, to provide local control over the development and implementation of the program. These leaders renamed the school Westmark. The basic educational philosophy has remained the same. Use of a multi-sensory approach continues to be effective with students with learning differences. Program changes and modifications continue to occur based on student needs and current research.

AT A GLANCE

APPLICATION DEADLINE	March 15 for the fall term
OPEN HOUSES	Call the Admissions Office to schedule a visit
ISEE TEST	No
SEE MAP	B on page 285

WESTRIDGE SCHOOL FOR GIRLS

Tel: (626) 799-1153 • Fax: (626) 799-7068
324 Madeline Drive • Pasadena, CA 91105
www.westridge.org

HEAD OF SCHOOL	FRAN NORRIS SCOBLE
DIRECTOR OF ADMISSIONS	HELEN HOPPER
TYPE OF SCHOOL	ALL GIRLS DAY SCHOOL
GRADES	4 - 12

- ENROLLMENT: 510
- ACCREDITATION: CAIS/NAIS
- MEMBERSHIPS: CAIS/NAIS/NCGS
- YEARLY REGISTRATION FEE: $500
- TUITION: $10,500-$18,000
- NEW STUDENT FEE: $1,000
- APPLICATION FEE: $60
- FINANCIAL AID IS AVAILABLE

THE WESTRIDGE campus is on a tree-lined residential area off Orange Grove Boulevard in Pasadena. You might even think you were in the country as you survey the surroundings. The school occupies an eclectic collection of buildings, some of which date as far back as 1902. Construction is currently under way on a new Performing Arts Center and an upgraded athletic field. The City of Pasadena is also re-zoning the area and eliminating the cul-de-sac that divides the campus, making it more pedestrian-friendly.

I arrived for one of the open houses, and after walking through some beautifully manicured gardens, was ushered into the auditorium. There we heard the headmistress speak, along with a number of girls who gave very well rehearsed speeches, letting us know why this school worked for them. These were the same girls that took small groups of us on a tour of the school. They were bright and articulate, and happy to answer all our questions. We visited the Joan Irvine Library, which has over 18,000 books, approximately 90 magazines and four newspaper subscriptions as well as numerous online magazines and research databases. Networked computers are also available. I asked one girl what was the worst thing about this school, and she said, "No boys." Then I asked her what was the best thing about the school, and she said, "No boys!"

Westridge is keenly aware that in order to become a top-tier school in all areas, it must reflect that in its endowment per student. A lot of careful planning has gone into its capital improvement plan, and they are highly aware of changes that need to be made not only to the school curriculum, but also to the facilities themselves, as competition stiffens and places in universities and colleges become more coveted. Unlike Marlborough, who never divulge any decisions, at Westridge they are posting information about this on their website. They say it as it is:

> "Westridge is poised to provide important additions to the facilities. Still, facilities age and grow obsolete. Because the campus is essential to support the program, and because it is a distinctive asset, the care and preservation of the campus will be one

of the highest priorities for the future. The school is committed to the completion of the North Madeline development. In addition, priorities must be set for the renewal or replacement of aging buildings."

As parents well know, every goal and aspiration articulated in a school's plan has a price, and one may be sure that an ambitious fund-raising campaign for capital gifts will be implemented.

From the school brochure:

> "The fundamental purpose of Westridge School is to develop in girls their intellectual and creative powers and their unique qualities as individuals. Essential to the school's purpose is the commitment to be a community that reflects and values diversity, respects individual differences, and responds to a changing, dynamic world.

> An intellectually engaging and challenging curriculum prepares students to continue their education in college and beyond as discerning, motivated learners who are committed to excellence and goodness in everything they do. The program offers balance among humanities, mathematics and sciences, fine and performing arts, technology and athletics.

> Westridge strives to develop young women whose joy in learning, personal ideals, commitment to ethical actions, social and environmental responsibility, courage and compassion will lead them to meaningful lives as contributing citizens of the larger world."

Westridge has traditionally provided solid preparation for college through its academic curriculum, but as more is expected of students and teachers, the school is considering extending the calendar and reorganizing the daily schedules to better serve the students' needs.

The school encourages its faculty to be guided by research about how girls learn and incorporate new strategies into their traditional teaching methods. It is hoped that over the next decade, the student experience will become an integrated combination of traditional and experiential settings. They are also committed to developing environmental awareness and to instilling in its students a sense of personal stewardship. Programs that provide hands-on experiences, field learning, and outside experts will all be incorporated into existing programs. They believe that internships and hands-on experiences should be part of every student's life at Westridge. The school firmly believes that sports, student government and community service projects provide many opportunities for leadership training. This sense of service goes past graduation. A strong alumnae association keeps everyone informed. Girls can go anywhere in the country or the world and find a 'sister' who will put them up.

In the lower school an integrated language art program focuses on a variety of literary forms. There is significant emphasis on the development of expository and creative writing, in addition to instruction in spelling, grammar and vocabulary. Mathematics involves a variety of learning experiences designed to balance the acquisition of basic concepts, reasoning and thinking skills, and problem-solving strategies with computational skills, calculator usage and estimation. In science they study physical, life and earth science. In social studies, girls study California history in grade 4, the Western Hemisphere in grade 5, and ancient civilizations in grade 6.

Grade 4 students begin using computers on a weekly basis and this continues in grades 5 and 6. There is a wonderful performing arts program, and beginning in grade 5, the students study Spanish. They take classes in drawing, painting and mixed media and a semester of ceramics is added in the sixth grade. The lower school enjoys many of its own traditions: the Pet Show, Cirque de Madeline and the Science Fair. Lower school girls also participate with middle and upper school students in big-little sister events and their annual Greek and Roman activities. In seventh grade the girls are assigned as Greeks or Romans, all upper schoolers are in friendly competition with each other throughout the year.

The middle school program blends a combination of experiential education and community service into the child's academic program. With a student/teacher ratio of 9:1 and an average class size of 15 to 20 there is plenty of individualized attention. Students learn how to do research to weigh evidence, to analyze cause and effect relationships, to synthesize information, solve problems and make concrete applications in an interdisciplinary curriculum which prepares them for the work ahead of them in the Upper School.

In the upper school, Westridge offers a 'curriculum planning' course to help each student, in consultation with her advisor and her teachers, create her own program. Requirements for graduation will determine much of the program, but there are many options for consideration which the catalogue helps each student and parents to discover. As your child plans for her freshman year, she should ask herself: are graduation requirements being met? Are special curricular interests and strengths being pursued wherever possible, and do these choices promise both pleasure and genuine interest? Before the final decisions are made, your child should ask herself, how will the days feel? How will my time be spent? The more genuine her choices are, the greater the chances are for success.

Admission and alumnae records show that Westridge students are well-prepared for college and typically 100 percent of graduating seniors are admitted each year to four-year colleges. Many returning alumnae have said, "Westridge helped me get into a college that was really right for me." Only one alum did not go to college, as she became a soap opera actress!

The school holds two open houses each year and schedules classroom visits for prospective students. If you like the idea of an all girls' school education for your daughter, then I recommend you take a look, especially if you live in the greater San Gabriel Valley.

HISTORY

In 1913, a group of parents in southwest Pasadena established Westridge School as a place where girls could pursue a demanding academic program that would prepare them for college. The original mission statement stated educating the whole girl, thus the emphasis on the arts. The idea that girls have a right to the best possible education was radical at the time and still is central to the school's mission and purpose. Within the next decade, Westridge will complete its first century of educating girls and young women. Westridge School's vision for the beginning of its second century is both a blueprint for preserving the best of an illustrious past and an incentive for the innovation and flexibility that this new century will require.

AT A GLANCE

APPLICATION DEADLINE	February 1
OPEN HOUSES	Call for school dates
ISEE TEST	Required
UNIFORMS	Yes
BEFORE AND AFTER SCHOOL CARE	Yes
SUMMER SCHOOL	Yes
SEE MAP	B on page 285

WESTSIDE NEIGHBORHOOD SCHOOL

Tel: (310) 574-8650
5401 Beethoven Street • Los Angeles, CA 90066
www.wnsk8.com

HEAD OF SCHOOL	BRAD ZACUTO
DIRECTOR OF ADMISSION	ROBIN SILLS
TYPE OF SCHOOL	PRIVATE INDEPENDENT DAY SCHOOL
GRADES	TWO YEAR K - 8

- ENROLLMENT: 340
- ACCREDITATIONS: CAIS, WASC
- MEMBERSHIPS: NAIS, ISAMA
- FINANCIAL AID IS AVAILABLE

- TUITION: $15,800–$16,600
- APPLICATION FEE: $125
- NEW STUDENT FEE: $1,100

WESTSIDE NEIGHBORHOOD SCHOOL is located near Jefferson Boulevard and Playa Vista. It is a 50,000 foot facility that is an architectural wonder—attractive, delightful and functional. There is good planning, excellent financial resources and more importantly you feel the warmth of the 60 teachers and staff. There are cheerful classrooms, a huge play yard, a multi-purpose gym, two theaters, two libraries, two technology labs, two art labs, two science labs and a visual arts lab staffed by three teachers!! They also have a performing arts curriculum that is partnered with the Music Center. One of many activities last year was West African drumming. They received a grant from the American Dermatological Academy for playground shade structures.

WNS's developmental philosophy is like Rousseau's "Hold childhood in reverence and do not be in a hurry." New students are observed by the Gesell screening to see their level of developmental maturity. This school is looking for the child's welfare in emotional, intellectual and physical growth at all grade levels. Their "Kindergarten Readiness" booklet is superb reading reminding us that each child has her or her own time line that will lead to academic success. In keeping with this philosophy, WNS has a two year transitional kindergarten for children who have outgrown their preschools but need time before starting first grade. This class admits children who turn five by January of the following year.

Bradley Zacuto, an educator with nearly 30 years' experience teaching at and managing private independent schools in Southern California, is the new head of Westside Neighborhood School. He succeeds outgoing Head of School Brenda A. Parker, whose leadership over the past 13 years shepherded the school through a key period of expansion. For the past 13 years, Zacuto has worked at St. Matthew's Parish School, a PS-8 school in the Pacific Palisades, where he oversaw the operation of the middle school as its principal. A lifelong educator, Zacuto has been a classroom teacher in fifth- through eighth grades as well as having spent 10 years at Westlake School for Girls and as a science teacher and science coordinator at John Thomas Dye School. He is also a past WNS parent and trustee

With twenty board members and seven parent committees this school is a model of community involvement. Parents are vital members of the WNS community. They serve as room parents, readers in the library, tour guides during open houses, and host parents to new families. The WNS Parent Group, in liaison with the school's administration, supports the school's mission by sponsoring educational workshops, fundraising for a portion of the school's operating budget, and organizing social events such as ice skating, the annual book fair, and other community events.

I can honestly say that this is just about a perfect school, with high educational standards, high style and bear hugs!

HISTORY

Entering its twenty-seventh year, WNS is still committed to community, quality education, and a strong sense of collaboration. As the school sets its sights on the road ahead, WNS continues to measure its progress by its ability to help students successfully meet the challenges of a rapidly changing world while maintaining the founding vision of an ideal place to learn.

AT A GLANCE

APPLICATION DEADLINE	January 31. Child must be 5 years-old no later than Jan. 31 of year of entry.
SECURITY	Yes
EMERGENCY PLAN	Yes
POTTY TRAINED	Yes
AFTER SCHOOL PROGRAMS	After class enrichment available until 6pm
FIELD TRIPS	Yes
SEE MAP	D on page 285

WILDWOOD SCHOOL

Elementary (K-5)
Tel: (310) 397-3134 • Fax: (310) 397-5134
12201 Washington Place • Los Angeles, CA 90066

Secondary (6-12)
Tel: (310) 478-7189 • Fax: (310) 478-6875
11811 W. Olympic Blvd. • Los Angeles, CA 90064

www.wildwood.org

HEAD OF SCHOOL	HOPE BOYD
ASSISTANT HEAD	MARCIA CAPPARELA
DIRECTOR OF ADMISSION	LISA GLASSMAN
TYPE OF SCHOOL	CO-EDUCATIONAL DAY SCHOOL
GRADES	K - 12

- ENROLLMENT: K-5: 300, 6-12: 400
- ACCREDITATION: CAIS/WASC
- MEMBERSHIPS: NAIS
- FINANCIAL AID IS AVAILABLE

- TUITION: $19,350-$24,425
- APPLICATION FEE $125
- NEW FAMILY FEE: $1,000

Elementary

WILDWOOD ELEMENTARY is a developmental Westside school that has wonderful teachers and a state-of-the-art facility. On the first of four visits, I was dazzled by the new buildings. These beautiful, modern, two-story structures with clean lines and bright, open spaces were designed by a Wildwood parent/architect. Facilities include a soccer field, running track, tether ball area, science lab, art room, outdoor art yard, auditorium, music room, reading room, and library. The buildings share a common courtyard that is handsomely landscaped with flowers, palm trees, and winding pathways. All the classrooms have connecting doors, a feature that helps facilitate Wildwood's 'team teaching' approach.

There are six primary 'pod' classrooms at the kindergarten through 2nd grade level. This system allows children of different ages to help and encourage each other. Each child stays in the same class for three years and has the opportunity to learn from the older children and to grow with the group. Over the years he will also be able to guide and teach the younger students.

In these six mixed-age group classes called pods, each age group is represented in equal number with a balance of gender. Each pod has a total of 24 children with a head teacher and a full-time teaching assistant. The mixed-age grouping allows for children's development at different rates.

At the third grade level, children are grouped in single grade classes there being three classes per grade level, with a maximum of 18 to 19 students per class. These classes are staffed by a head teacher and a half-time teaching assistant. Specialists work in conjunction with classroom teachers in the areas of science, music, visual arts, Spanish, physical education, performing arts and dance. A reading resource specialist and a psychological consultant are available when needed.

The educational philosophy at Wildwood is based on the teachings of cognitive theorist, Jean Piaget, who believed that children construct knowledge from their experiences in a unique, often non-linear, way and that children should be allowed to work and grow at their own developmental pace. To a lesser degree the progressive approach of John Dewey is also used at the school. It has a social studies core curriculum, encourages block building, and employs cooperative, democratic learning methods.

Each classroom is set up in centers, which house materials for children to use. Children know where to find math and writing materials, blocks, books, art, wood-working, and cleaning supplies, and are encouraged to use all of them as well as take projects from one center to another.

Elementary Curriculum
In the primary grades mathematics is taught through the use of concrete (manipulative) materials such as pattern blocks, unifix cubes, geoboards, mirrors, collections of buttons, rocks, etc., as well as a variety of measuring devices for comparing weight, length, and volume.

Over the school year, children work extensively with patterning and problem solving. Estimation, sorting and classifying, graphing, measuring, adding and subtracting, multiplying, dividing, and geometry are other areas which provide a solid basic understanding of our place value numerical system. Children who are developmentally ready are exposed to symbolic work.

In third to fifth grades children move from concrete math to a program that requires the use of abstract reasoning, problem solving, and computation.

Science activities are incorporated within the social studies program and involve exploration, discovery, experimentation, and observation. Children are encouraged to explore aspects of their world which are of particular interest to them.

The school's large auditorium is equipped with stage lighting and sound used for music, dance, movement, and performing arts which are integrated into all aspects of the curriculum.

Physical education develops coordination, balance, flexibility, responsibility, cooperation, and teamwork. There is a soccer field for team games and sports.

When homework is assigned at different points throughout the year, it is done in a purposeful and developmentally appropriate way. Pod children do not have traditional homework but are encouraged to play and engage in activities with their families that support their learning. Homework for grades 3 to 5 is assigned for further practice of skills taught in class, to help develop independent learning habits and responsibility, for review, and for research.

Language arts are taught using a variety of methods including 'whole language' as opposed to the point of view of 'skill building,' phonics work, and oral language.

Other components of the program are as follows:

Oral Language and Vocabulary: Vocabulary and oral language skills are developed through plays, story telling, sharing in class, and small group discussions.

Sight Word Approach: Words are learned through visual memorization.

Story time: Books are read to the children daily. Various types of literature and different authors are introduced. Follow-up discussions and projects help to develop comprehension skills.

Silent Sustained Reading: A time is set aside each day when the entire class spends time reading and appreciating books silently.

Reading is seen as a way to convey meaning and not merely the finished product of learning decoding skills. Writing is taught as part of everything children do at the school. Formal writing instruction is taught during the lesson time. Writer's workshop is led by the child's 'inner scribe.' During this time, students write, draw, and dictate.

The visual arts and the performing arts are a vital part of Wildwood's education. Teachers in the visual arts program meet with students regularly in the art studio where they learn painting, drawing, and three-dimensional expression. The performing arts program, which includes music, movement, and drama encourages students to express their unique voices and talents.

The admission process involves:

1. A group tour of the school (by appointment).
2. Applying and submitting an application (by October 15 for Kindergarten).
3. Parent interview (by appointment).
4. A Saturday visit day where one's child and other potential kindergarten applicants have group and individual activities so that they can be observed by the Wildwood staff.

Secondary

In September 2000, Wildwood opened its doors to a new middle and high school. The secondary campus is located two miles away from the elementary school in a converted TV production studio. It is striking piece of architecture. The spacious loft-like interior of the 50,000 square-foot space features classrooms, an open conference room, gallery, science lab, theater, library, and visual and performing arts studios. The building's high ceilings allow for a soaring mezzanine, used for activities and meetings. A state-of-the-art wireless system and many Mac laptops allow the students access to technology anywhere on the campus. On the roof of the parking structure there's a large deck that provides an outdoor area for lunch and other activities. Lacking their own playing fields, the school uses several local parks for their athletic programs. Sports teams compete in Westside leagues.

The Wildwood Secondary program is the result of five years of research by parents at the Wildwood Elementary School. They wanted a small middle and high school that would prepare their children for college without subjecting them to the stresses of standardized testing, grading, and hours and hours of homework each night. Parents turned to Theodore R.

Sizer, a veteran education reformer who has helped create hundreds of schools where the emphasis is on developing essential life skills rather than memorizing facts.

Wildwood's secondary program has four divisions rather than single grades. Division One is a single year for sixth graders, allowing for a smooth transition from elementary to secondary school. With a student/teacher ratio of 12:1 and 90-minute classes, the students gain a lot of individualized attention. Division Two (grades 7 and 8) encompasses the middle school. Division Three (grades 9 and 10) and The Senior Institute (grades 11 and 12) span the high school years.

Wildwood's program is built around a series of 'habits,' known as "Habits of Mind and Heart:"

Convention: Meeting accepted standards in any subject in order to be understood and to understand others.

Connection: Looking for patterns and for ways things fit together in order to bring together diverse material into new solutions.

Evidence: Bringing together relevant information, judging the credibility of sources, finding out for oneself.

Perspective: Addressing questions from multiple viewpoints, using a variety of ways to solve problems.

Collaboration: Making the appropriate provisions for accepting and giving assistance.

Ethical behavior: An awareness of how personal habits influence behavior and a set of principles by which to guide one's life.

Service to the common good: Demonstrating awareness of the effects of one's actions and the desire to make the community a better place for all.

These 'habits' are used by the student in every subject to set a standard that they can apply to every class, helping them to create their portfolios. The academic curriculum is structured around a series of questions and generative themes that pull together content from the core subject areas of humanities, science, math, foreign language, and visual and performing arts. Therefore in math and science, students might use physics and geometry to design and build a model of a bridge structure. To progress from one division to the next, students must fulfill a set of portfolio requirements in these areas, as well as community involvement, personal reflections, and goals for the future.

Wildwood believes that detailed narrative assessments give students and their families a clearer idea of the student's progress. Therefore this school uses narrative assessments instead of grades to inform students and their parents of how students are progressing. This also helps the school assess whether students are mastering the work given to them. These assessments are part of each student's permanent file and provide the basis for college transcripts. However, if a college or university requires a grade point average, Wildwood will convert their narrative assessments to grades, which pleased those parents who were worried about the 'no grading' approach. It should also be noted that Wildwood courses meet the criteria for the University of California system, as well as public and private colleges and universities around the country.

While founded on the idea that massive nightly homework can be counterproductive, the school believes in homework for the reinforcement of current work, review of skills, research projects, reading and reflection. While the amount of homework will vary with the particular assignments and interests of each student, homework is a significant component of the program.

Although Wildwood does have its own playing fields, it should be pointed out that they believe that properly guided athletics and competition makes students well-rounded individuals. There is a no-cut policy for the middle school sports program. Once in Division three and the Senior Institute, students can earn team positions based on athletic skill, desire and commitment.

Boys' Team Sports	Girls' Team Sports
Cross Country	Cross Country
Flag Football	Flag Football
Basketball	Basketball
Soccer	Soccer
Baseball	Softball
Golf	Volleyball
Track and Field	Track and Field
Tennis	Tennis

Wildwood's Advisory Program allows small groups of students to meet with their advisors on a daily basis to help guide their academic programs and social-emotional development. Advisors also act as mentors, monitoring each student's growth and meeting with the student's family during the year to review narrative assessments that provide parents with an in-depth look at each student's progress.

Once in the Senior Institute in eleventh and twelfth grades, Wildwood's internship program gives students the opportunity to connect what they learn at school with real-life practical experiences. Students may experience several different professions, expanding their interests by 'trying out' various career paths. Internships enrich students' educational experiences by connecting what they learn in the classroom with the professional skills they will need.

The secondary admission process involves:

1. Saturday Open Houses for parents and students(call for dates and reservations)
2. Parent campus tours-optional.
3. Application in by early December
4. Parent and student interviews(by appointment).

HISTORY

Wildwood was founded in 1971 as a co-educational elementary school for grades kinder-garten through six. It was originally located in Santa Monica and moved in September of 1993, when work was completed on the current school building at 12201 Washington Place in Culver City. It now houses the elementary school, grades K-5. Since then they have added a secondary school with founding director Dr. George H. Wood. The school serves grades 6-12, and is located at 11811 Olympic Boulevard, Los Angeles.

AT A GLANCE

APPLICATION DEADLINE	Grades 6-12 on December 8
UNIFORMS	No
BEFORE/AFTER SCHOOL CARE	Yes
PARENT INVOLVEMENT IS EXPECTED	
SEE MAP	D on page 285

THE WILLOWS COMMUNITY SCHOOL

Tel: (310) 815-0411 • Fax: (310) 815-0425
8509 Higuera Street • Culver City, CA 90232
www.thewillows.org

HEAD OF SCHOOL	LISA ROSENSTEIN
DIRECTOR OF ADMISSIONS	KIM FELDMAN
TYPE OF SCHOOL	CO-EDUCATIONAL PROGRESSIVE DAY SCHOOL
GRADES	DK - 8

- ENROLLMENT: 400
- ACCREDITATION: CAIS/WASC
- MEMBERSHIPS: ERB/ISAMA/NAEYC/NAIS
- NEW STUDENT FEE: $1,500
- YEARLY PTA REGISTRATION FEE: $75
- FINANCIAL AID IS AVAILABLE

- TUITION:
  DK: $16,010
  K–5: $17,800
  6-8: $19,900
- APPLICATION FEE: $100

Take a determined group of wealthy parents, a number of teachers that have achieved 'star' status among the educational community, a swarm of architects, planners, and facilitators, an empty warehouse in a now-defunct industrial section of Culver City, give them all a seven month deadline, and...voila! A private school is born.

The school's '94/'95 brochure was the size of a small newspaper and featured a two-page story of the struggle to open the doors in seven-month's time. The founders had to convince parents to enroll their children in a school that did not have an actual address and to schedule visits for them to the present site before the lease was signed. The glue on the floor installation was barely dry when the founding parents, new parents, and grandparents converged on the school to organize the classrooms, library, and art room.

That this feat is 'beyond amazing' is self-evident. One must admire the spirit and determination of THE WILLOWS COMMUNITY SCHOOL. The work that they have done in these first few years has been sensational. It is an organization with a tremendous amount of love and goodwill behind it.

In three months time, builders transformed this once-dilapidated 11,000 square foot warehouse into an air-conditioned, hip, modern school house with exposed wood beams, skylights and large bright classrooms. The huge, open hallway/common areas have white walls covered with some of the most wonderful children's artwork, all done large scale with splashes of bright watercolors and pastels. In the common area are homey wicker couches, and sitting on one was a well-known actress nursing her newborn baby – having just dropped her two older children off at the school.

The atmosphere at The Willows is very informal, with first names on office doors, and casually dressed children scooting to and from their classroom activities. The day I visited, the tour group was besieged by a group of children running by in stocking feet and faces painted blue preparing to shoot a video tape.

The school now has a library that has tripled in size, a large outdoor playground with climbing equipment, and a cement play area for basketball. The children take buses to a nearby park for additional recreation. In recent years the school has purchased two more buildings, one behind and one to the side, to provide room for the seventh and eighth grades. One building includes a roof-top P.E. facility, complete with basketball courts. A new full-size gym and a 200-seat theater have recently been added.

When I asked director Lisa Rosenstein how these buildings were to be financed, she smiled and said, "VERRRY well . . . next question?" Ms. Rosenstein was the Principal at Temple Isaiah Day School for many years and brought with her a following of teachers whom she had worked with over the years.

The grades start at developmental kindergarten in which there is a group of four to five-year-olds who are preparing for kindergarten but are not quite developmentally ready. Last year in DK, the curriculum included exploring the five senses, the study of seeds and the cycle of food from seed to table, the study of penguins and their young, exploring the properties of ice, and a unit on transportation.

The curriculum at the school is integrated and focuses on children learning to work together as a group. Integration, means that each subject relates to another whenever possible. For example, if children are studying tsunami waves, they might integrate that science unit with a field trip to the Los Angeles County Museum of Art to view Hokusai's woodblock print, "The Great Wave." Field trips, block building, and experiential learning are all important aspects of the program.

This is definitely a school for the art-oriented family. The program is outstanding. Art is integrated into 'units' with mathematics, language, science, and history, not as a tool to teach or illustrate these subjects, but as a partner with these disciplines and a discipline in itself. When the third grade studied caterpillars, along with research of the scientific facts, they made technical illustrations and scale drawings. In studying the artistic tradition of scientific drawing, these students learned that even the most technical drawing contains expressive and evocative elements in addition to functional and scientific ones.

This integration of art into units ensures that art is valued not just as an adjunct skill but also because it helps develop young observation skills and provides a vehicle for abstract thought and expression.

A partial list of the schools founding principles from the brochure:

> "The willows community school is committed to a strong, progressive education, rooted in academic excellence and social values. Its developmentally structured curriculum is founded on the principles of experiential learning and thematic instruction.

> The students learn to think, to have mutual respect and tolerance, and to understand the value of cooperation.

The school strives to provide an environment where children, like the trees for which The Willows is named, bend gracefully in the wind but do not break."

There is a maximum of 23 students per class with two credentialed teachers in each class. There are two classes at each grade level from DK to grade seven and one eighth grade class. The admissions staff will visit your child at his present school for an evaluation, but they do not require testing for applicants.

The curriculum includes language arts, math, science, social studies, technology, library, art, physical education, music and dramatic arts. It is referred to as 'invented curriculum' so one may be sure that subjects will probably be taught in a new and unconventional way.

AT A GLANCE

The Willows Community School was opened in September of 1994 by a group of parents with the common belief that education should be an exciting, hands-on experience that allows the curious mind freedom of expression and enjoyment of learning.

HISTORY

APPLICATION DEADLINE	December
OPEN HOUSES	Call school for the date/times
SCHOOL TOURS	Morning tours through January
UNIFORMS	Yes, although Friday is free dress
ISEE TESTING	Required Grades 6-8
BEFORE AND AFTER SCHOOL CARE	Yes
SEE MAP	D on page 285

WILSHIRE SCHOOL

Phone (323) 939-3800 • FAX (323) 937-0013
4900 Wilshire Boulevard • Los Angeles • CA 90010
www.wilshireschool.org

HEAD OF SCHOOL	MARLIN MILLER
DIRECTOR OF ADMISSIONS	RAQUEL KISLINGER
TYPE OF SCHOOL	CO-ED DAY SCHOOL
GRADES	K - 6

- ENROLLMENT: 100
- REGISTRATION FEE: (ONE TIME): $150
- ACCREDITATION: WASC
- FINANCIAL AID IS AVAILABLE

- TUITION: $7,000-$8,200
- ACTIVITIES: $110 PER YEAR
- APPLICATION FEE: $100

I recently discovered an interesting smaller private school in my very own neighborhood, a small K through 6 oasis at Wilshire and Highland. The school sits right across the street from our local public middle school, John Burroughs, and occupies a healthy piece of real estate in this Hancock Park neighborhood. The school sign outside is a little misleading since it has the words "Korean Institute of Southern California" in large letters right beside the name of the school. Because of this, I never gave the school a second glance but then I remembered that a friend of mine, a Canadian mum - had sent her son to a small private school on Wilshire Boulevard in our neighborhood and had been very happy with it, so I decided to take a closer look.

WILSHIRE SCHOOL'S philosophy as taken from their brochure:

> "Wilshire School welcomes students of all cultures in grades K through 6. Our unique learning community flourishes in an atmosphere of safety, nurturing and academic challenge. Small class size and individualized attention are the hallmarks of a Wilshire education. Students, faculty, and staff come together to model respect, tolerance, and the democratic process. The core curriculum is infused with opportunities to grow in the areas of music, technology, foreign language acquisition and service learning. To round out the program, teachers incorporate art, drama, dance and field experiences into their activities."

I arrived unannounced one morning and made my way to the main office. There I met the old head of school, Raquel Kislinger who also happened to be arriving. She was very enthusiastic and couldn't wait to show me around. As we toured the school she told me that her own experience of the school system was at Polytechnic, where for almost 16 years her two daughters enjoyed their PK through 12 years. She was both a teacher and lower school Head at the school during that time. She told me that she had read my book and resonated with my comments about the importance of finding the right school for an individual child.

The school opened 20 years ago under the umbrella organization of The Korean Institute of Southern California. While the majority of students are Korean-American, the school is open to the entire community and they are definitely wishing to attract a more diverse student population. I suggested to her that part of the problem of not being able to attract a more diverse student population might be partly due to the wording on the sign outside the school. Raquel nodded in agreement and then continued: "Here at Wilshire School, community-building is an ongoing theme. As we spell out the word "community", the letters "U-N-I" are particularly striking. How better to express the idea of collaboration, alliance, camaraderie and cooperation? "You and I" is the heart of community. School communities must embrace, empower, challenge and protect the children and adults within them. There is no magic wand to encourage connectedness, foster responsibility or create universal safety. But the "Yous" and "Is" of the world, working together, can make a difference."

We continued on the tour. The School is well laid out and the classrooms are generously stocked and clean. This is a small school with no big grassy fields or inside gymnasium, but there is a nice sized outside playground with plenty of climbing equipment for the kids. They cook for the kids every day and the cafeteria is pleasant and welcoming. I asked about the ciriculum and here is an overview of the classes offered.

Language Arts
From the earliest grades, a love of reading is fostered. Students are encouraged to read widely, learning that literature bridges the richness of all cultures and ways of thinking. As early readers become more proficient, they begin to develop writing skills. They quickly regard themselves as young authors and their writing grows in sophistication each year. By the upper grades, writing is clear and confident.

Mathematics
Students use hands-on activities to explore different areas of mathematical study, beginning with basic operations and progressing to logic, geometry and pre-algebra. Gradually, that learning is translated to the abstract symbols we use with paper, pencils and calculators. Games, software, and homework solidify new problem solving processes.

Science
Students combine in-class learning with hands-on laboratory activities. Through observing, investigating, measuring, predicting, and comparing/contrasting data, students gain firsthand information about the natural world. They are encouraged to think independently, while gaining a respect for nature.

Social Studies
Beginning in kindergarten, children learn about societal relationships through the study of their own communities. In time, they see the interrelatedness of subjects such as art, music, math, science, and literature as they explore a wide range of ancient to modern cultures. The social studies curriculum encourages an appreciation of and respect for similarities and differences among the worlds' peoples. Students learn to ask analytical questions, read maps, use a globe, take notes, do basic research, write reports, create and read tables and graphs, and give effective oral presentations.

Foreign Languages
All students in grades K through 6 have the choice of studying either Korean or Spanish. Both programs meet five days a week, offering language instruction, as well as cultural enrichment. Academic classes are taught in English, but for students needing English language

support, an ESL teacher provides assistance.

Tools and Technology
Students progress from keyboarding to word processing, researching, illustrating, and using presentation tools. A well-equipped computer lab offers internet access, with possibilities for extending and exploring a wealth of curricular topics.

Music and Art
An outstanding music program provides opportunities to join a chorus, play hand chimes, study an instrument, be part of an orchestra and participate in musical theater. Classroom teachers use a variety of tools, techniques, and materials to explore the visual arts and dance/movement.

Community, Leadership and Service
The entire school community joins together weekly to sing, brainstorm ideas, celebrate successes, discover ways to mediate conflicts, and enjoy mutual support and encouragement. The Student Council is composed of representatives from each grade level. Meetings provide an arena for the exchange of ideas, the development of leadership skills and an understanding of representative government. Service learning is a way for students to experience the joy and necessity of giving back to their communities. Whether it is through organizing a canned food drive, marching in the Korean Community Parade, or pooling resources to help those less fortunate, Wilshire students regularly participate to benefit others.

Physical Education
Students of all ages work on coordination, ball handling and agility, through the use of obstacle courses, tumbling exercises, relays and scrimmages. Gymnastics, hockey, volleyball and basketball form the core of sports instruction, with an emphasis on the value and importance of teamwork.

Parents are encouraged to participate in the school's Parent/Teacher Association(PTA). As is well known, the PTA can be a powerful tool to help the school grow and prosper. Because tuition often does not cover the cost of educating your child, the school relies on families to help raise additional operating funds. This is a great way for you as a parent to test the waters and find out if you have a future in professional fund-raising!

If you are looking for a school where you can be involved, look no further! The school welcomes parent participation at many levels. Helping out in the classroom, being a room parent, chaperoning field trips, joining the school at Community Meetings and volunteering for schoolwide events are all ways that families can show their support for this unique learning community. If this sounds as if The Wishire School might be a good fit for you and your child, do go to one of the morning "Wednesday's at Wilshire" community meetings where they will happily give you an impromptu tour of the school.

HISTORY

In 1985, Wilshire School was established as a private K through 6 community school, sharing a Board of Trustees with its parent organization, The Korean Institute of Southern California. Wilshire's history distinguishes it from any other independent school in the country. Preserving Korean language and culture while creating a school that welcomes ALL languages and cultures, is unique.

AT A GLANCE

APPLICATION DEADLINE	Rolling admissions
OPEN HOUSES	Wednesday's at Wilshire @ 8.30 a.m. 2/11 at 6:30 p.m.
UNIFORMS	Yes
SUMMER SCHOOL	Yes
AFTER SCHOOL PRGRAM	Yes
SEE MAP	C on page 285

WINDWARD SCHOOL

Tel: (310) 391-7127 • Fax: (310) 397-5655
11350 Palms Blvd. • Los Angeles, CA 90066
www.windwardschool.org

HEAD OF SCHOOL	THOMAS W. GILDER
DIRECTOR OF ADMISSION	SHARON PEARLINE
TYPE OF SCHOOL	CO-EDUCATIONAL DAY SCHOOL
GRADES	7 - 12

- ENROLLMENT: 475
- ACCREDITATION: CAIS/NAIS
- MEMBERSHIPS: WASC
- FINANCIAL AID IS AVAILABLE

- TUITION: $25,364
- NEW STUDENT FEE: $1,200
- APPLICATION FEE: $100

WINDWARD SCHOOL is located in West Los Angeles across the street from the Mar Vista Park, close to the freeway on a nine-acre spread. A man-made river runs through the entire length of the school grounds and divides the tree-lined campus. The Leichtman-Levine Bridge takes you to the heart of the campus - a group of modern classroom buildings that reminded me of the MOCA complex downtown with its sleek roof lines, pathways and striking colorful umbrellas dotted outside the school restaurant.

While I was visiting the school, I joined a group of students who were being given a tour of the school by a very enthusiastic member of staff. As he passed by the school store, which resembled a mini-Gap, he told the students, "All you have to do is sign your name for things you want because your parents automatically get an account here when you join the school." That brought smiles to their faces, so be warned, your young students could be adding to your already high tuition costs!

A new Science/Math Center and Center for Teaching and Learning is under construction. There is also a green-screen studio for production and a Mac Lab.

Mission Statement

1. Creating a balanced college-preparatory program within a caring environment.
2. Complementing strong academic preparation with the development of ethics, character and well-developed people skills.
3. Maintaining small classes and an accessible faculty, creating a positive atmosphere for learning.
4. Communicating effectively with parents, students, faculty, alumni and friends to promote a strong sense of community.
5. Developing innovative programs, challenging course work, and dynamic co-curricular activities that meet the needs of students.
6. Having faculty and staff well trained, supervised, highly motivated, and committed to Windward's vision.

7. Creating a welcoming community that embraces diversity and encourages students to develop a sophisticated understanding of the world they will inherit.
8. Providing facilities and resources to create the strongest educational setting for optimal student learning.

The Berrie Library contains more than 8,000 volumes with fully automated circulation. Additional resources include periodical and reference materials available via direct online services, a substantial CD-ROM collection and other audiovisual materials. In 2001, Windward received The Library of Congress Fellowship to participate in the American Memory Fellows Program, an outreach program of the National Digital Library Program.

The 13,000-square-foot Lewis Jackson Memorial Sports Center contains two indoor basketball courts, training facilities, and an exercise and fitness center. In the fall of 2000, there was a complete, professional renovation of the athletic fields, which seem to stretch out as far as the eye can see. The fields are home to the Winward baseball, softball, soccer, football and lacrosse teams. Physical Education is required of all students through grade 10 and students may participate in football, volleyball, basketball, soccer, lacrosse, baseball, softball and dance

Completed in the fall of 2002, the new Littlefield Plaza and Student Pavilion, gives students and faculty a place to get together and eat lunch, and a dedicated conference center to host club meetings and community projects. The Pavilion provides a venue for a natural unforced interaction between students, faculty, coaches, counselors and advisors. Also completed recently is the new Arts Center, a spacious environment containing studios for classes in computer graphics, drawing, painting, printmaking, sculpture, photography and ceramics. Their arts program offers students a truly multi-media experience.

The Irene Kleinberg Theater offers a very sophisticated and intimate environment for performing arts and a spectacular venue for choral and dance performances. Separate dance and rehearsal halls are next door. There is a wide variety of disciplines, ranging from beginning instrumental instruction to studies in film and television, and from photography to Advanced-Placement Studio Art.

The dance and theater programs begin in middle school and form the foundation for the fall play and the spring musical. Students may audition for these productions and may also participate behind the scenes as stage manager, house manager, set crew member, artist or publicity manager. In recent years, the Madrigal Singers and Chamber Orchestra have received gold medals at the prestigious Heritage Festival.

Already underway are plans constructing for an entirely new Science Center, which will have four state-of-the-art laboratories allowing for students to engage in even more hands-on laboratory experiences and scientific research.

Graduation Requirements

Upper School students must take a minimum of:
- Four years of English.
- Three years of: social studies, including U.S. history, world history and European history, mathematics, including algebra II/trigonometry, science, including one year of lab science, three years of the same foreign language or two years each of two foreign languages.
- Two years of the fine arts and physical education.

The Service Learning/Community Service Program is a big part of the Windward experience. The school believes that learning through being involved in the community and caring for the environment is every bit as important as preparation and success in academic subjects. Students are encouraged to engage in hands-on service projects through which they learn they can make a difference in their community.

There is also the opportunity to participate in a variety of extracurricular activities, such as The International Thespian Society, The Madrigal Singers, Jazz Ensemble, Chamber Players, the yearbook, the student newspaper, Robotics, and speech and debate.

Entry to this school is very competitive and openings occur traditionally at the seventh- and ninth-grade levels, although students may apply for eighth and tenth grades with permission of the admissions office. As part of the application, each student is required to submit a two-to-three-page autobiography. The interview, at which one or both parents must be present, cannot be scheduled until the school receives the application and autobiography.

HISTORY

Windward School is a not-for-profit, co-educational, college-preparatory day school founded in 1971 through the determined efforts of Shirley Windward, a well-known educator and writer.

AT A GLANCE

APPLICATION DEADLINE	December
OPEN HOUSES	October, December, February
STUDENT OPEN HOUSES	November & December
ISEE TESTING	Required for applicants
UNIFORMS	No
SEE MAP	D on page 285

STEPHEN S. WISE TEMPLE ELEMENTARY SCHOOL

Tel: (310) 889-2300 • Fax (310) 476-2353
15500 Stephen S. Wise Dr. • Los Angeles, CA 90077-1598
www.wisela.org

DIRECTOR OF EDUCATION	METUKA BENJAMIN
PRINCIPAL	ROCHELLE GINSBURG
TYPE OF SCHOOL	CO-ED REFORM JEWISH DAY SCHOOL
GRADES	K - 6

- ENROLLMENT: 520
- ACCREDITATION: WASC
- AFFILIATION: LARJE
- NEW STUDENT FEE: $1,250
- TUITION: $15,325
- APPLICATION FEE: $150
- TEMPLE MEMBERSHIP: $3,310
- FINANCIAL AID IS AVAILABLE

STEPHEN S. WISE TEMPLE ELEMENTARY SCHOOL is located in the Bel Air hills near Mulholland and the 405 freeway. The facilities are modern and beautifully laid out on the 10-acre property. The classrooms are well-stocked, clean, and bright, with flowers planted along all the walkways so that the entire campus exudes a deluxe, top-of-the-line feeling.,

There are two large playgrounds for physical education and recreational play. These areas have basketball, handball, and tetherball courts, along with special areas for kickball, softball and soccer. A rooftop play area is available for the kindergarten and first grade children.

The kindergarten also has special equipment including climbing bars, tumbling mats, and a gymnastic apparatus. The outdoor swimming pool is also available to the Milken Community High School students as part of their physical education program. There are two fully equipped technology labs, a library, art studio, two science labs, a music room and Project Studio. This is a program unique to Stephen S. Wise Temple Elementary School incorporating technology, art and science integrated into the social studies curriculum.

Stephen S. Wise offers a challenging, traditional academic program;with each class having a credentialed general studies teacher and a Judaica teacher. There are four classes at each grade level with between 18 and 22 students in each class. Subjects are taught thematically. For example, if children are studying the environment, they might build a mini-jungle to study the effects of the sun and the ozone layer on plants, animals, and organisms dependent upon them for survival. By the time they have completed the project, students will have:

- Used the library and technology to research the topic
- Incorporated math to build their jungle
- Applied biology, and science concepts
- May even have incorporated Hebrew into their work
- Used their artistic abilities

A typical kindergarten day begins at 8:00 a.m., with the children socializing and working in various 'centers' such as housekeeping, blocks, books, technology, science, a listening center and art. At 8:30 a.m., they have a group meeting to locate the date on the room calendar, record the weather conditions, and review the days' activities. Next comes language arts, reading (whole language approach), mathematics, and Judaic studies when the children begin building a Hebrew vocabulary. In the afternoon, there is instruction in social studies and science. There are specialist teachers in art, music, technology, library, and physical education.

As a synagogue school, the rabbis and cantors are actively involved in the children's lives through classroom visits, Shabbat services, and creative bible programs. Students learn about their Jewish heritage as it is used thematically throughout the program in art, writing, history, and social studies.

The school hosts a Hesed Program to give children the opportunity to become involved in the community. Each grade adopts a community group to care about and to assist. For over ten years, as an example, fifth graders have dedicated their efforts to the St. Joseph Center for the Homeless. The children serve food, stock groceries, and help in the child care center at St. Joseph.

The school philosophy:

> "Stephen S. Wise Temple Day Schools are Reform Jewish day schools dedicated to the continuity of the Jewish people and to the intellectual, emotional, social, creative, physical and spiritual growth of each child. As part of a Reform Temple, the schools are committed to individual autonomy in Jewish life, responsibility to the covenant between God and the Jewish people, and tikkun olam (the betterment of the world)."

Students applying to the school do not need to be Temple members. however, it is necessary to join before the child is enrolled.

Parents are required to volunteer a fixed number of hours during the school year to support the school. The Temple Parent Association (TPA) is the official school-parent organization, and all parents are encouraged to become members. TPA members organize, supervise, and help at school activities and fund-raisers such as the Book Fair, Junior Olympics, traditional Friday yogurt days, uniform sales and field trips.

Students at Wise Temple Elementary School continue middle and highschool at the Milken Community High School which offers a disciplined academic curriculum in an individualized program. Students in the middle school continue to develop good study habits, critical thinking skills, and cooperative learning. Electives offered are computer science, the arts, and physical education.

At the high school level, courses become more challenging, and the students may participate in advanced placement and honors classes. Academics are supplemented with athletics, Judaism, and the arts. Stephen S. Wise Community High School is a member of the California Interscholastic Federation (CIF), and sports teams compete in a variety of (CIF) competitions.

HISTORY

Stephen S. Wise Temple Elementary School is a synagogue school offering an academic/Judaic education to students in grades kindergarten through sixth grade.

AT A GLANCE

APPLICATION DEADLINE	January
OPEN HOUSES	Call school for dates
UNIFORMS	Yes
BEFORE AND AFTER SCHOOL CARE	Yes
SUMMER CAMP	Yes
SEE MAP	D on page 285

PUBLIC SCHOOL: ALTERNATIVE PROGRAMS

Families who want to use the Los Angeles Public School System but want a higher quality education, i.e. schools with smaller classes, special teaching approaches, and subject-specific programs often choose one of the following.

CHARTER SCHOOLS

Charter Schools represent the opportunity to examine practices and develop structures that can help solve the many challenges facing schools in the Los Angeles Unified School District and the greater educational community.

Mission Statement from Los Angeles Unified School District:

"The Los Angeles Unified School District views charter schools as part of the District's family and as an asset from which we can learn. Therefore, the Los Angeles Unified School District will encourage and nurture the development and continuation of charter schools that are accountable for improved student learning and that can:

Provide possible solutions to urban school challenges through practices that can:

- Ease the shortage of school facilities and seat space.
- Narrow the achievement gap among students of various backgrounds.
- Increase responsible parent and student involvement in learning.
- Improve teacher quality and performance evaluation systems.
- Provide data to help identify and evaluate issues that affect quality educational programs and student learning and achievement.
- Serve as laboratories to test, demonstrate and disseminate ideas that can promote better educational practices.
- Provide an additional educational option for parents."

Charter Schools are public schools that have received charters from local Boards of Education. In our case, The Los Angeles School District (LAUSD) Board of Education. The school district guides each charter, but the school is free from the rules and regulations that govern standard public schools. In plain English, Charter schools can be started by anyone – outsiders with a vision, parents, teachers, anyone who can win approval from the local school board, and given the demographic trends, the LAUSD will feel pressured to approve lots of new charter proposals. If some of you parents banded together and decided to open one, I bet you could!

That was the case with one of the first charter schools in California, The Los Angeles Open Charter School. It was opened in 1993 by a group of parents and teachers who wanted an alternative to the 'back to basics' approach that dominated the district at that time. They wanted to model their school on the principals of Jerome Bruner and the practices of the English elementary schools. By applying these principals, the school has become the premier charter school in the Los Angeles area. Getting in is tough, there are far more applications than spaces.

Charter schools are still very much in their infancy. The first charter school opened 16 years ago in St. Paul, Minn. There are now more than 400 charter schools in California and nearly 2,700 nationwide. They are required to participate in the statewide assessment test, called the STAR (Standardized Testing and Reporting) program. The law also requires that a public charter school be nonsectarian in its programs, admissions policies, employment practices, and all other operations. Each of these schools has a special focus like the arts, multiculturalism, military discipline or just good old rigid academics.

Social Justice is the focus of the most recently opened charter school in the mid-Wilshire district – The Leadership Academy. The school rents space at the Immanuel Presbyterian Church near the old Ambassador Hotel on Wilshire Boulevard. This year-old school is the vision of the school's founders, Roger Lowenstein, a 60-year old former attorney-turned TV writer, and Susanne Coie, a 33-year old teacher. Lowenstein built an impressive network of backers. Among them are Steve Tish and his wife who have pledged $250,000 over five years and Lowenstein, who put $200,000 of his own money in.

The mid-Wilshire district is a very densely populated area where the public middle schools bulge with as many as 3,400 students. The high school has about 5,500 students, which is among the nations largest. Because of over-crowding, 900 high school students and 1,500 middle school students are bused from the area to the western San Fernando Valley. The good news is that the LAUSD plans to build 79 new schools and expand 80 others during the next six years. In addition to these regular public schools, the district expects to add at least 100, possibly 200, more charter schools to the 51 already operating. If you have a newborn or are just thinking about starting a family, this is the time to get involved – hell, even if you're single and still in school! It's never too early to begin laying the foundations for your child's education.

We were there at the outset, one of the first families to show our support by turning up at every meeting. Because of that, I got my name down near the top of the list and was as good as guaranteed a place. If you're interested in a charter school for your child, I recommend that you participate early on. Show your enthusiasm, put your hand up, and ask questions. They want parents like that involved. But I also caution you to do your homework and find out what your teachers' credentials are. Several teachers at The Leadership Academy were teaching subjects they had never taught before. I don't know about you, but I don't want my child being used as a guinea pig while they iron out those sort of problems!

However, what a charter school does offer is educational niche marketing, in the form of a specialty that might appeal to you and your child. So if you're interested, you can attend one of the monthly development meetings to find out more about starting your own charter school.

The Charter Schools Office will continue to hold monthly orientation meetings for potential Charter School Developers. The meetings are held at:

333 South Beaudry Avenue, 25th Floor, Room 102, Los Angeles, California 90017

For more Information call (213) 241-4625 or visit their website at: www.LAUSD.net/charterschools.

NEWS FLASH!

All it takes is a determined group of parents and educators to open a Charter School, and that's what happened with the Larchmont Charter. The school opened a couple of years ago with 100 children in grades Kindergarten through 2.

Larchmont Charter School is now operating on two campuses. Their 2/3 multi-aged, and 4-5 year olds are on the Holly Grove Campus and their un-graded primary is at St. Ambrose Church.

The new school, Larchmont Charter, West Hollywood, is on the St. Ambrose campus as well with two Kindergarten classes and one first grade class. They have two offices, one for Larchmont Charter, and one headed by Kristin Elson, the Larchmont Charter West Hollywood principal. They share the campus, although their finances are separate. They are hoping that Larchmont Charter West Hollywood will eventually have their own site.

Both schools have modeled themselves after the Open Charter School, one of the most acclaimed public elementary schools in California. So grab your 'Choices' catalog and look for these schools. You can visit both schools through the www.LAUSD.net/charterschools website.

Here are some Charter Schools I would recommend taking a closer look at. You can find out more by visiting:

www.edreform.com/charter_schools/websites/california

Camino Nuevo Charter Academy
Burlington site, Los Angeles• Opened August 2000 • Grades K-5 • Enrollment 280

Camino Nuevo Charter Academy
Town House site, Los Angeles • Opened August 2000 • Grades K-5 • Enrollment 130

Camino Nuevo Charter Middle Academy
Harvard site, Los Angeles • Opened August 2001

CHIME Charter School
Woodland Hills • Opened 2001 • Grades K-5 • Enrollment 110

Kenter Canyon LEARN/Charter School
Los Angeles • Opened 1993 • Grades K-5 • Enrollment 435

Los Angeles Leadership Academy
Los Angeles • Opened 2002 • Grades 6-7 • Enrollment 130

Marquez Charter School
Pacific Palisades • Opened 1993 • Grades K-5 • Enrollment 663

The Open Charter Magnet School
Los Angeles • Opened 1993 • Grades K-5 • Enrollment 364

Paul Revere Charter Middle School
Los Angeles • Opened 1995 • Grades 6-8 • Enrollment 1982

Tom Bradley Environmental Science & Humanities Magnet: Crenshaw/Dorsey
Los Angeles • Opened 1999 • Grades K-5 • Enrollment 694

<u>Westwood Charter School</u>
Los Angeles • Opened 1993 • Grades K-5 • Enrollment 750
<u>Westwood Charter School</u>
Westwood • Opened 2001 • Grades K-12 • Enrollment 400
<u>Santa Monica Boulevard Community Charter School</u>
Hollywood • Opened 2002 • Grades K-5 • Enrollment 1,299

MAGNET SCHOOLS

You can pick up a Magnet School Directory (known as the 'Choices' catalogue) at any public school office, they are usually available by October. Here is a brief description of how the program works.

Magnet schools are set up for integration purposes and are governed by the Los Angeles Unified School District (LAUSD). These programs are special learning centers for students living within LAUSD. There are two types of magnets. One type centers on a particular subject specialty such as math, science, performing arts, or business. The other type uses a special teaching approach such as alternative, gifted or fundamental.

Some magnets involve the entire school, so everyone attending is part of the magnet program. In others, the magnet program is a school within a school, and exists separately within a normal Los Angeles Public school.

There are magnet programs for gifted/high ability children, and these require special testing before a child may apply. There are also Highly Gifted Magnets which require students to meet the criteria of 95 percent on an intellectual assessment administered by the LAUSD Psychological Services branch.

Magnets have smaller classes, and they receive additional funds for special activities, facilities, and labs. Many magnet programs work hand-in-hand with local universities and businesses.

There are 155 magnet programs located all over Los Angeles. You apply by submitting an application, but this is not to say that magnets are easy to get in to. A computer picks from the applicant pool looking for a balanced ethnic mix, equally represented socio-economic backgrounds and geographic locations so you can put your letters of recommendation away.

Here is how the computer processes the application. Once all the information on the application is verified, the computer automatically assigns each applicant a priority, according to the following criteria:

a) (12 points) Students who are eligible to matriculate (graduate) from one magnet program to another.
b) (4 points) Students whose resident LAUSD schools are designated as overcrowded schools.
c) (4 points) Students whose resident LAUSD schools are designated predominantly Hispanic, Black, Asian or Other Non-Anglo.
d) (4 points each year) Students on magnet waiting lists for the current and/or the last two years. Priority credit is given for each of these three years a student has been on

an official magnet waiting list.
e) (3 points) Students with a brother or sister continuing in the same magnet.

Applications are selected at random; yours will receive priority depending on how many points you have, the number of openings at your school of choice, and the number of applicants for that grade and race/ethnicity category.

Here's a trick – if you currently have a child in a private school but want to look at a magnet for the future, you can begin 'earning' points by applying every year. Choose a school where you are unlikely to get in (i.e., loads of applicants and not nearly enough spaces). This way, in a couple of years when you're ready to move your child, you will have:

a) Enough points, and
b) Carefully chosen a school that you have a good chance to get into.

For more information about magnet programs, call the Office of Student Integration Services in Los Angeles at: (213) 625-4177 or (213) 625-6572.

For information on Gifted And Talented Education program (G.A.T.E) call:

Los Angeles: (213) 625-6500
San Fernando Valley: (818) 782-2306

ACCREDITATION/MEMBERSHIP CODES*

AEGUS	Association for Educating Gifted Underachieving Students
AMS	American Montessori Society
AWSNA	American Waldorf Schools of North America
BJE	Bureau of Jewish Education
CAGC	The California Association of Gifted Children
CAIS	The California Association of Independent Schools
CASE	The Council for the Advancement of Support in Education
CHADD	Children & Adults with Attention Deficit/Hyperactivity Disorder
CEEB	College Entrance Examination Board
CIF	California Interscholastic Federation
CLS	Cum Laude Society
CRIS	The Council for Religion in Independent Schools
CSF	California Scholarship Federation
ERB	Educational Records Bureau
FCE	Friends Council on Education
ISAMA	Independent School Alliance for Schools Minority Affairs
ISM	Independent School Management
LABJE	The L.A. Bureau of Jewish Education
LACS	Los Angeles Commission on Schools
LACSS	Los Angeles Consortium of Secondary Schools
LAD	Learning Disabilities Association
NACAC	The National Association of College Admissions Counselors
NAES	The National Association of Episcopal Schools
NAEYC	The National Association for the Education of Young Children
NAGC	The National Association of Gifted Children
NAIS	The National Association of Independent Schools
NAPSG	The National Association of Principles of Schools for Girls
NCGS	The National Coalition of Girl's Schools
NIPSA	The National Independent Private School Association
SCCC	Studio City Chamber of Commerce
SKWLD	Smart Kids With Learning Disabilities
SSDSA	Solomon Schechter Day School Association
WASC	The Western Association of Schools and Colleges

*Please note:
The author has made every effort to list the acronyms used by the schools in this guide;
on occasion, for the sake of space, we have made up acronyms for organizations.

TABLE OF SCHOOLS BY PHILOSOPHY

TRADITIONAL

Archer School for Girls
Berkeley Hall
Brawerman
Brentwood
Buckley
Campbell Hall
Carlthorp
Cavalry Christian
Chadwick
Chandler
Chaminade
Christ the King
Clairbourn
Crespi

Crestview
Crossroads
Curtis
JT Dye
Flintridge Prep
Flintridge Sacred Heart Academy
Fountain Day
Gooden
Harvard/Westlake
Immaculate Heart
Laurence School
LILA (French School)
Loyola High School
Marlborough

Marymount
Mayfield
Mirman
Notre Dame
Notre Dame H.S.
Oakwood
Pacific Hills
Page School
Pilgrim
Polytechnic
Providence
Calvary Christian
Ribét Academy
Sierra Canyon
St. Brendan

St. Francis
St. James
St. Mark's Episcopal
St. Matthew's Parish
Steven S. Wise
Turning Point
Viewpoint
Village School
Westridge
Wildwood
Wilshire
Winward

DEVELOPMENTAL

Adat Ari El
Brentwood
Calmont
Center for Early Education
Country School
Crossroads

Echo Horizon
Friends Western
Hollywood Schoolhouse
The Oaks
Oakwood
Pacific Oaks

Sequoyah
Seven Arrows
Temple Israel
UES (Seeds)
Vistamar
Walden
Waverly

Westmark
Westside Neighborhood School
Wildwood

PROGRESSIVE

Bridges
Children's Community School

PS #1 Elementary
New Heights
New Roads

Westland

Willows Community School

WALDORF

Pasadena Waldorf

CARDEN

Highpoint Academy

MONTESSORI

Gendale Montessori

Glendale Montessori Elementary

Turning Point

MAP OF LOS ANGELES COUNTY

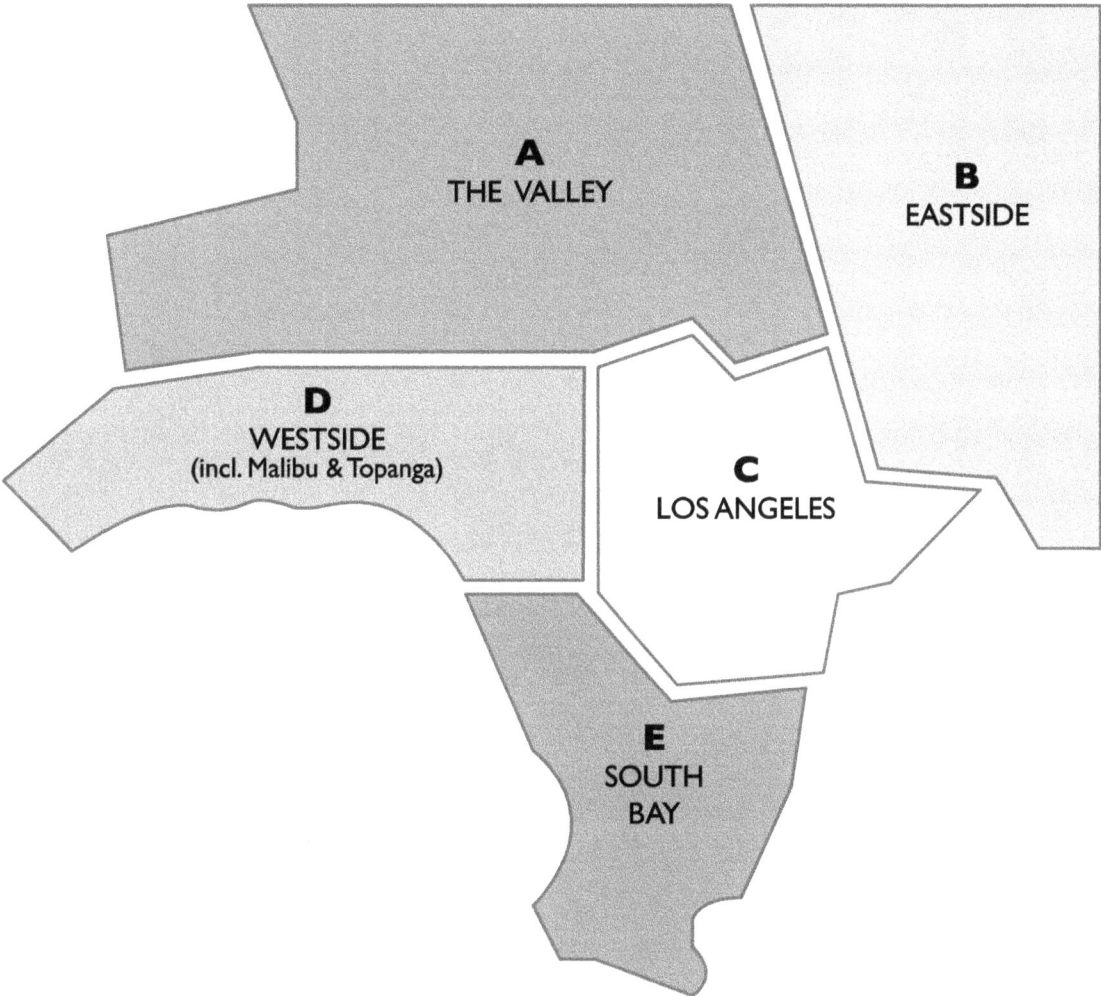

A
THE VALLEY

B
EASTSIDE

D
WESTSIDE
(incl. Malibu & Topanga)

C
LOS ANGELES

E
SOUTH
BAY